D1681186

D. G. ROSSETTI'S POEMS.

D G Rossetti

From a Photograph, Cheyne Walk. 1864.

THE POETICAL WORKS

OF

DANTE GABRIEL ROSSETTI

EDITED WITH PREFACE BY
WILLIAM M. ROSSETTI

A NEW EDITION IN ONE VOLUME

ELLIS AND ELVEY
LONDON
1900

All rights reserved

PRINTED BY
HAZELL, WATSON, AND VINEY, LD.,
LONDON AND AYLESBURY.

CONTENTS.

	PAGE
PREFACE BY WILLIAM M. ROSSETTI	XV

POEMS.

I.—PRINCIPAL POEMS:—

Dante at Verona	1
A Last Confession	18
The Bride's Prelude	35
Sister Helen	66
The Staff and Scrip	75
Jenny	83
The Stream's Secret	95
Rose Mary	103
The White Ship	137
The King's Tragedy	148

The House of Life, A Sonnet-Sequence—

Introductory Sonnet	176

Part I.—Youth and Change:—

1. Love Enthroned	177
2. Bridal Birth	177
3. Love's Testament	178
4. Lovesight	178
5. Heart's Hope	179
6. The Kiss	179
7. Supreme Surrender	180
8. Love's Lovers	180

CONTENTS.

		PAGE
9. Passion and Worship		181
10. The Portrait		181
11. The Love-letter		182
12. The Lovers' Walk		182
13. Youth's Antiphony		183
14. Youth's Spring-tribute		183
15. The Birth-bond		184
16. A Day of Love		184
17. Beauty's Pageant		185
18. Genius in Beauty		185
19. Silent Noon		186
20. Gracious Moonlight		186
21. Love-sweetness		187
22. Heart's Haven		187
23. Love's Baubles		188
24. Pride of Youth		188
25. Winged Hours		189
26. Mid-rapture		189
27. Heart's Compass		190
28. Soul-light		190
29. The Moonstar		191
30. Last Fire		191
31. Her Gifts		192
32. Equal Troth		192
33. Venus Victrix		193
34. The Dark Glass		193
35. The Lamp's Shrine		194
36. Life-in-love		194
37. The Love-moon		195
38. The Morrow's Message		195
39. Sleepless Dreams		196
40. Severed Selves		196
41. Through Death to Love		197
42. Hope Overtaken		197
43. Love and Hope		198
44. Cloud and Wind		198
45. Secret Parting		199
46. Parted Love		199
47. Broken Music		200

CONTENTS.

		PAGE
48. Death-in-love		200
49, 50, 51, 52. Willow-wood		201
53. Without Her		203
54. Love's Fatality		203
55. Stillborn Love		204
56, 57, 58. True Woman (Herself—Her Love—Her Heaven)		204
59. Love's Last Gift		206

Part II.—Change and Fate:—

60. Transfigured Life		207
61. The Song-Throe		207
62. The Soul's Sphere		208
63. Inclusiveness		208
64. Ardour and Memory		209
65. Known in Vain		209
66. The Heart of the Night		210
67. The Landmark		210
68. A Dark Day		211
69. Autumn Idleness		211
70. The Hill Summit		212
71, 72, 73. The Choice		212
74, 75, 76. Old and New Art (St. Luke the Painter—Not as These—The Husbandmen)		214
77. Soul's Beauty		215
78. Body's Beauty		216
79. The Monochord		216
80. From Dawn to Noon		217
81. Memorial Thresholds		217
82. Hoarded Joy		218
83. Barren Spring		218
84. Farewell to the Glen		219
85. Vain Virtues		219
86. Lost Days		220
87. Death's Songsters		220
88. Hero's Lamp		221
89. The Trees of the Garden		221
90. Retro me, Sathana		222
91. Lost on Both Sides		222

92, 93. The Sun's Shame	223
94. Michelangelo's Kiss	224
95. The Vase of Life	224
96. Life the Beloved	225
97. A Superscription	225
98. He and I	226
99, 100. Newborn Death	226
101. The One Hope	227

II.—MISCELLANEOUS POEMS:—

My Sister's Sleep	229
The Blessed Damozel	232
At the Sun-rise in 1848	237
Autumn Song	237
The Lady's Lament	238
The Portrait	240
Ave	244
The Card-Dealer	248
World's Worth	250
On Refusal of Aid between Nations	252
On the Vita Nuova of Dante	252
Song and Music	253
The Sea-Limits	254
A Trip to Paris and Belgium (London to Folkestone—Boulogne to Amiens and Paris—The Paris Railway-station—Reaching Brussels—Antwerp to Ghent)	255
The Staircase of Notre Dame, Paris	261
Place de la Bastille, Paris	261
Near Brussels—A Halfway Pause	262
Antwerp and Bruges	263
On Leaving Bruges	264
Vox Ecclesiæ, Vox Christi	265
The Burden of Nineveh	266
The Church-Porch	272
The Mirror	272
A Young Fir-Wood	273
During Music	273
Stratton Water	274
Wellington's Funeral	280

CONTENTS.

	PAGE
Penumbra	283
On the Site of a Mulberry-Tree, planted by William Shakspeare, etc.	285
On certain Elizabethan Revivals	285
English May	286
Beauty and the Bird	286
A Match with the Moon	287
Love's Nocturn	288
First Love Remembered	293
Plighted Promise	294
Sudden Light	295
A New Year's Burden	296
Even so	297
The Woodspurge	298
The Honeysuckle	298
Dantis Tenebræ	299
Words on the Window-pane	299
An Old Song Ended	300
The Song of the Bower	301
Dawn on the Night Journey	303
A Little While	304
Troy Town	305
Eden Bower	308
Love-lily	315
Sunset Wings	316
The Cloud Confines	317
Down Stream	319
Three Shadows	321
A Death-parting	322
Spring	323
Untimely Lost—Oliver Madox Brown	323
Parted Presence	324
Spheral Change	326
Alas, So Long!	327
Insomnia	328
Possession	329
Chimes	330
Adieu	333
Soothsay	334

CONTENTS.

PAGE

Five English Poets:—
    1. Thomas Chatterton 337
    2. William Blake 338
    3. Samuel Taylor Coleridge 338
    4. John Keats 339
    5. Percy Bysshe Shelley 339
To Philip Bourke Marston 340
Tiber, Nile, and Thames 340
Raleigh's Cell in the Tower 341
Winter 341
The Last Three from Trafalgar 342
Czar Alexander the Second 342

III.—Sonnets on Pictures:—

For an Annunciation, Early German 343
For our Lady of the Rocks, by Leonardo da Vinci . . 344
For a Venetian Pastoral, by Giorgione . . . 345
For an Allegorical Dance of Women, by Andrea Mantegna 346
For Ruggiero and Angelica, by Ingres . . . 347
For a Virgin and Child, by Hans Memmelinck . . 348
For a Marriage of St. Catherine, by the same . . 349
For the Wine of Circe, by Edward Burne Jones . . 350
For the Holy Family, by Michelangelo . . . 351
For Spring, by Sandro Botticelli 352

IV.—Sonnets and Verses for Rossetti's own Works of Art:—

Mary's Girlhood 353
The Passover in the Holy Family 355
Mary Magdalene at the Door of Simon the Pharisee . 356
Michael Scott's Wooing 357
Aspecta Medusa 357
Cassandra 358
Venus Verticordia 360
Pandora 360
A Sea-spell 361
Astarte Syriaca 361
Mnemosyne 362

	PAGE
Fiammetta	362
Found	363
The Day-dream	364

V.—POEMS IN ITALIAN (OR ITALIAN AND ENGLISH), FRENCH, AND LATIN :—

Gioventù e Signorìa	366
Youth and Lordship	367
Proserpina	370
La Ricordanza	370
Proserpina	371
Memory	371
La Bella Mano	372
Con Manto d'Oro, etc.	372
Robe d'Or, etc.	372
La Bella Mano	373
With Golden Mantle, etc.	373
A Golden Robe, etc.	373
Barcarola	374
Barcarola	375
Bambino Fasciato	375
Thomæ Fides	376

VI.—VERSICLES AND FRAGMENTS :—

The Orchard-pit	377
To Art	378
On Burns	378
Fin di Maggio	378
I saw the Sibyl at Cumæ	378
As balmy as the breath, etc.	378
Was it a friend, etc.	379
At her step, etc.	379
Would God I knew, etc.	379
I shut myself in with my soul	379
If I could die, etc.	379
She bound her green sleeve, etc.	379
Where is the man, etc.	380
As much as in a hundred years she's dead	380
Who shall say, etc.	380

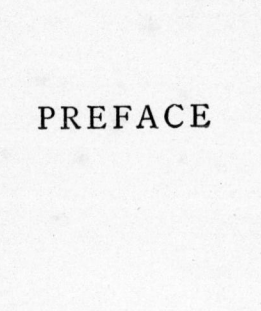

PREFACE

PREFACE.

THE Collected Works of Dante Gabriel Rossetti, poetry and prose, original and translated, were published under my editorship in two volumes at the close of 1886. The time seems now to have arrived for the issue of an edition better adapted, by limitation of contents and of price, to a wide circulation. In the present volume, therefore, I include all the original poems, but nothing else. My ensuing Preface is condensed from that which appeared in the Collected Works.

The most adequate mode of prefacing the poems of Rossetti, as of most authors, would probably be to offer a broad general view of his writings, and to analyse with some critical precision his relation to other writers, contemporary or otherwise, and the merits and defects of his performances. In this case, as in how few others, one would also have to consider in what degree his mind worked consentaneously or diversely in two several arts—the art of poetry and the art of painting. But the hand of a brother is not the fittest to undertake any work of this scope. My preface will not therefore deal with themes such as these, but will be confined to minor matters, which may nevertheless be relevant also within their limits. And first may come a very brief outline of the few events of an outwardly uneventful life.

Gabriel Charles Dante Rossetti, who, at an early stage of his professional career, modified his name into Dante Gabriel Rossetti, was born on 12th May 1828, at No. 38 Charlotte Street, Portland Place, London. In blood he was three-fourths Italian, and only one-fourth English; being on the father's side wholly Italian (Abruzzese), and on the mother's side half Italian (Tuscan) and half English. His father was Gabriele Rossetti, born in 1783 at Vasto, in the Abruzzi, Adriatic coast, in the then kingdom of Naples. Gabriele Rossetti (died 1854) was a man of letters, a custodian of ancient bronzes in the Museo Borbonico of Naples, and a poet; he distinguished himself by patriotic lays which fostered the popular movement resulting in the grant of a constitution by Ferdinand I. of Naples in 1820. The King, after the fashion of Bourbons and tyrants, revoked the constitution in 1821, and persecuted the abettors of it, and Rossetti had to escape. He settled in London towards 1824, married, and became Professor of Italian in King's College, London, publishing also various works of bold speculation in the way of Dantesque commentary and exposition. His wife was Frances Mary Lavinia Polidori (died 1886), daughter of Gaetano Polidori (died 1853), a teacher of Italian and literary man who had in early youth been secretary to the poet Alfieri, and who published various books, including a complete translation of Milton's poems. Frances Polidori was English on the side of her mother, whose maiden name was Pierce. The family of Rossetti and his wife consisted of four children, born in four successive years—Maria Francesca (died 1876), Dante Gabriel, William Michael, and Christina Georgina. Few more affectionate husbands and fathers have lived, and no better wife and mother, than

Gabriele and Frances Rossetti. The means of the family were always strictly moderate, and became scanty towards 1843, when the father's health began to fail. In that year Dante Gabriel left King's College School, where he had learned Latin, French, and a beginning of Greek; and he entered upon the study of the art of painting, to which he had from earliest childhood exhibited a very marked bent. After a while he was admitted to the school of the Royal Academy, but never proceeded beyond its antique section. In 1848 Rossetti co-operated with two of his fellow-students in painting, John Everett Millais and William Holman Hunt, and with the sculptor Thomas Woolner, in forming the so-called Præraphaelite Brotherhood. There were three other members of the Brotherhood—James Collinson (succeeded after two or three years by Walter Howell Deverell), Frederic George Stephens, and the present writer. Ford Madox Brown, the historical painter, was known to Rossetti much about the same time when the Præraphaelite scheme was started, and bore an important part both in directing his studies and in upholding the movement, but he did not think fit to join the Brotherhood in any direct or complete sense. Through Deverell, Rossetti came to know Elizabeth Eleanor Siddal, daughter of a Sheffield cutler, herself a dressmaker's assistant, gifted with some artistic and some poetic faculty; in the Spring of 1860, after a long engagement, they married. Their wedded life was of short duration, as she died in February 1862, having meanwhile given birth to a still-born child. For several years up to this date Rossetti, designing and painting many works, in oil-colour or as yet more frequently in water-colour, had resided at No. 14 Chatham Place, Blackfriars Bridge, a line of street now demolished. In the autumn of 1862 he removed to No. 16 Cheyne Walk, Chelsea. At first certain apartments in the house were occupied by Mr. George Meredith the novelist, Mr. Swinburne the poet, and myself. This arrangement did not last long, although I myself remained a partial inmate of the house up to 1873. My brother continued domiciled in Cheyne Walk until his death; but from about 1869 he was frequently away at Kelmscot Manorhouse, in Oxfordshire, not far from Lechlade, occupied jointly by himself, and by the poet Mr. William Morris with his family. From the autumn of 1872 till the summer of 1874 he was wholly settled at Kelmscot, scarcely visiting London at all. He then returned to London, and Kelmscot passed out of his ken.

In the early months of 1850 the members of the Præraphaelite Brotherhood, with the co-operation of some friends, brought out a short-lived magazine named *The Germ* (afterwards *Art and Poetry*); here appeared the first verses and the first prose published by Rossetti, including *The Blessed Damozel* and *Hand and Soul*. In 1856 he contributed a little to *The Oxford and Cambridge Magazine*, printing there *The Burden of Nineveh*. In 1861, during his married life, he published his volume of translations *The Early Italian Poets*, now entitled *Dante and his Circle*. By the time therefore of the death of his wife he had a certain restricted yet far from inconsiderable reputation as a poet, along with his recognized position as a painter—a non-exhibiting painter, it may here be observed, for, after the first two or three years of his professional course, he adhered with practical uniformity to the plan of abstaining from exhibition altogether. He had contemplated bringing out in or about 1862 a volume of original poems; but, in the grief and dismay which overwhelmed him in losing his wife, he determined to sacrifice to her memory this long-cherished project, and he buried in her coffin the manuscripts which would have furnished forth the volume. With the lapse of years he came to see that, as a final settlement of the matter, this was neither obligatory nor desirable; so in 1869 the manuscripts were disinterred, and in 1870 his volume named *Poems* was issued. For some considerable while it was hailed with general and lofty praise, chequered by only moderate stricture or demur; but late in 1871 Mr. Robert Buchanan published under a pseudonym, in the *Contemporary Review*, a very hostile article named *The Fleshly School of Poetry*, attacking the poems on literary and more especially on moral grounds. The article, in an enlarged form, was afterwards reissued as a pamphlet. The assault produced on Rossetti an effect altogether disproportionate to its intrinsic importance; indeed, it developed in his character an excess of sensitiveness and of distempered brooding which his nearest relatives and friends had never before surmised,—for hitherto he had on the whole had an ample sufficiency of high spirits, combined with a certain underlying gloominess or abrupt moodiness of nature and outlook. Unfortunately there was in him already only too much of morbid material on which this venom of detraction was to work. For some years the state of his eyesight had given very grave cause for apprehension, he himself fancying from time to time that the evil might end in absolute blindness, a fate with which our father had been formidably threatened in his closing years. From this or other causes insomnia had ensued,

PREFACE.

coped with by far too free a use of chloral, which may have begun towards the end of 1869. In the summer of 1872 he had a dangerous crisis of illness; and from that time forward, but more especially from the middle of 1874, he became secluded in his habits of life, and often depressed, fanciful, and gloomy. Not indeed that there were no intervals of serenity, even of brightness; for in fact he was often genial and pleasant, and a most agreeable companion, with as much *bonhomie* as acuteness for wiling an evening away. He continued also to prosecute his pictorial work with ardour and diligence, and at times he added to his product as a poet. The second of his original volumes, *Ballads and Sonnets*, was published in the autumn of 1881. About the same time he sought change of air and scene in the Vale of St. John, near Keswick, Cumberland; but he returned to town more shattered in health and in mental tone than he had ever been before. In December a shock of a quasi-paralytic character struck him down. He rallied sufficiently to remove to Birchington-on-Sea, near Margate. The hand of death was then upon him, and was to be relaxed no more. The last stage of his maladies was uræmia. Tended by his mother and his sister Christina, with the constant companionship at Birchington of Mr. Hall Caine, and in the presence likewise of Mr. Theodore Watts, Mr. Frederick Shields, and myself, he died on Easter Sunday, April 9th 1882. His sister-in-law, the daughter of Madox Brown, arrived immediately after his latest breath had been drawn. He lies buried in the churchyard of Birchington.

Few brothers were more constantly together, or shared one another's feelings and thoughts more intimately, in childhood, boyhood, and well on into mature manhood, than Dante Gabriel and myself. I have no idea of limning his character here at any length, but will define a few of its leading traits. He was always and essentially of a dominant turn, in intellect and in temperament a leader. He was impetuous and vehement, and necessarily therefore impatient; easily angered, easily appeased, although the embittered feelings of his later years obscured this amiable quality to some extent; constant and helpful as a friend where he perceived constancy to be reciprocated; free-handed and heedless of expenditure, whether for himself or for others; in family affection warm and equable, and (except in relation to our mother, for whom he had a fondling love) not demonstrative. Never on stilts in matters of the intellect or of aspiration, but steeped in the sense of beauty, and loving, if not always practising, the good; keenly alive also (though many people seem to discredit this now) to the laughable as well as the grave or solemn side of things; superstitious in grain, and anti-scientific to the marrow. Throughout his youth and early manhood I considered him to be markedly free from vanity, though certainly well equipped in pride; the distinction between these two tendencies was less definite in his closing years. Extremely natural and therefore totally unaffected in tone and manner, with the naturalism characteristic of Italian blood; good-natured and hearty, without being complaisant or accommodating; reserved at times, yet not haughty; desultory enough in youth, diligent and persistent in maturity; self-centred always, and brushing aside whatever traversed his purpose or his bent. He was very generally and very greatly liked by persons of extremely diverse character; indeed, I think it cannot be an exaggeration to say that no one ever disliked him. Of course I do not here confound the question of liking a man's personality with that of approving his conduct out-and-out.

Of his manner I can perhaps convey but a vague impression. I have said that it was natural; it was likewise eminently easy, and even of the free-and-easy kind. There was a certain British bluffness, streaking the finely poised Italian suppleness and facility. As he was thoroughly unconventional, caring not at all to fall in with the humours or prepossessions of any particular class of society, or to conciliate or approximate the socially distinguished, there was little in him of any veneer or varnish of elegance; none the less he was courteous and well-bred, meeting all sorts of persons upon equal terms—*i.e.*, upon his own terms; and I am satisfied that those who are most exacting in such matters found in Rossetti nothing to derogate from the standard of their requirements. In habit of body he was indolent and lounging, disinclined to any prescribed or trying exertion of any sort, and very difficult to stir out of his ordinary groove, yet not wanting in active promptitude whenever it suited his liking. He often seemed totally unoccupied, especially of an evening; no doubt the brain was busy enough.

The appearance of my brother was to my eye rather Italian than English, though I have more than once heard it said that there was nothing observable to bespeak foreign blood. He was of rather low middle stature, say five feet seven and a half, like our father; and, as the years advanced, he resembled our father not a little in a characteristic way, yet with highly obvious divergences. Meagre in youth, he was at times decidedly fat in mature age. The complexion, clear and warm, was also dark, but not dusky or sombre. The hair was dark and somewhat silky; the brow grandly spacious and solid; the full-sized eyes blueish-grey; the nose shapely, decided, and rather projecting, with an aquiline tendency and large nostrils, and perhaps no detail in the face was more noticeable at a first glance than the very strong indentation at the spring of the nose below the forehead; the mouth moderately well-shaped, but with a rather thick and unmoulded underlip; the chin unremarkable; the line of the jaw, after youth was passed, full, rounded, and sweeping; the ears well-formed and rather small than large. His hips were wide, his hands and feet small; the hands very much those of the artist or author type, white, delicate, plump, and soft as a woman's. His gait was resolute and rapid, his general aspect compact and determined, the prevailing expression of the face that of a fiery and dictatorial mind concentrated into repose. Some people regarded Rossetti as eminently handsome; few, I think, would have refused him the epithet of well-looking. It rather surprises me to find from Mr. Caine's book of *Recollections* that that gentleman, when he first saw Rossetti in 1880, considered him to look full ten years older than he really was,—namely, to look as if sixty-two years old. To my own eye nothing of the sort was apparent. He wore moustaches from early youth, shaving his cheeks; from 1870 or thereabouts he grew whiskers and beard, moderately full and auburn-tinted, as well as moustaches. His voice was deep and harmonious; in the reading of poetry, remarkably rich, with rolling swell and musical cadence.

My brother was very little of a traveller; he disliked the interruption of his ordinary habits of life, and the flurry or discomfort, involved in locomotion. In boyhood he knew Boulogne: he was in Paris three or four times, and twice visited some principal cities of Belgium. This was the whole extent of his foreign travelling. He crossed the Scottish border more than once, and knew various parts of England pretty well—Hastings, Bath, Oxford, Matlock, Stratford-on-Avon, Newcastle-on-Tyne, Bognor, Herne Bay; Kelmscot, Keswick, and Birchington-on-Sea, have been already mentioned. From 1878 or thereabouts he became, until he went to the neighbourhood of Keswick, an absolute home-keeping recluse, never even straying outside the large garden of his own house, except to visit from time to time our mother in the central part of London.

From an early period of life he had a large circle of friends, and could always have commanded any amount of intercourse with any number of ardent or kindly well-wishers, had he but felt elasticity and cheerfulness of mind enough for the purpose. I should do injustice to my own feelings if I were not to mention here some of his leading friends. First and foremost I name Mr. Madox Brown, his chief intimate throughout life, on the unexhausted resources of whose affection and converse he drew incessantly for long years; they were at last separated by the removal of Mr. Brown to Manchester, for the purpose of painting the Town Hall frescoes. The Præraphaelites—Millais, Hunt, Woolner, Stephens, Collinson, Deverell—were on terms of unbounded familiarity with him in youth; owing to death or other causes, he lost sight eventually of all of them except Mr. Stephens. Mr. William Bell Scott was, like Mr. Brown, a close friend from a very early period until the last; Scott being both poet and painter, there was a strict bond of affinity between him and Rossetti. Mr. Ruskin was extremely intimate with my brother from 1854 till about 1865, and was of material help to his professional career. Robert and Mrs. Browning were personally known to Rossetti, perhaps rather earlier than Ruskin. As he rose towards celebrity, Rossetti also knew Burne Jones, and through him Morris and Swinburne, all staunch and fervently sympathetic friends. Mr. Shields was a rather later acquaintance, who soon became an intimate, equally respected and cherished. Then Mr. Hueffer, the musical critic (editor of the Tauchnitz edition of Rossetti's works), and Dr. Hake the poet. Through the latter my brother came to know Mr. Theodore Watts, whose intellectual companionship and incessant assiduity of friendship did more than anything else towards assuaging the discomforts and depression of his closing years. In the latest period the most intimate among new acquaintances were Mr. William Sharp and Mr. Hall Caine, both of them known to Rossettian readers as his biographers. Nor should I omit to speak of the extremely friendly relation in which my brother stood to some of the principal purchasers of his pictures—Mr. Leathart, Mr. Rae, Mr. Leyland, Mr. Graham, Mr. Valpy, Mr. Turner, and his early associate Mr. Boyce. Other names crowd upon me; but I forbear.

Before proceeding to some brief account of the sequence of my brother's writings, it may be worth while to speak of the poets who were particularly influential in nurturing his mind and educing its own poetic endowment. The first poet with whom he became partially familiar was Shakespeare. Then followed the usual boyish fancies for Walter Scott and

Byron. The Bible was deeply impressive to him, perhaps above all Job, Ecclesiastes, and the Apocalypse. Byron gave place to Shelley when my brother was about sixteen years of age: the old English or Scottish ballads and Mrs. Browning rapidly ensued. It may have been towards this date, say 1845, that he first seriously applied himself to Dante, and drank deep of that inexhaustible well-head of poesy and thought; for the Florentine, though familiar to him as a name, and in some sense as a pervading penetrative influence, from earliest childhood, was not really assimilated until boyhood was practically past. Bailey's *Festus* was enormously relished about the same time—read again and yet again; also *Faust*, Victor Hugo, De Musset (and along with them a swarm of French novelists), and Keats, whom my brother for the most part, though not without some compunctious visitings now and then, truly preferred to Shelley. The only classical poet whom he took to in any degree worth speaking of was Homer, the Odyssey considerably more than the Iliad. Tennyson reigned along with Keats, and Edgar Poe and Coleridge along with Tennyson. In the long run he perhaps enjoyed and revered Coleridge beyond any other modern poet whatsoever; but Coleridge was not so distinctly or separately in the ascendant, at any particular period of youth, as several of the others. Blake likewise had his peculiar meed of homage, and Charles Wells, the influence of whose prose style, in the *Stories after Nature*, I trace to some extent in Rossetti's *Hand and Soul*. Lastly came Browning, and for a time, like the serpent-rod of Moses, swallowed up all the rest. This was still at an early stage of life: for I think the year 1847 cannot certainly have been passed before my brother was deep in Browning. One prose-work of great influence upon his mind, and upon his product as a painter, must not be left unspecified—Malory's *Mort d'Arthur*, which engrossed him towards 1856. The only poet whom I feel it needful to add to the above is Chatterton. In the last two or three years of his life my brother entertained an abnormal—I think an exaggerated—admiration of Chatterton. It appears to me that (to use a very hackneyed phrase) he " evolved this from his inner consciousness" at that late period; certainly in youth and early manhood he had no such feeling. He then read the poems of Chatterton with cursory glance and unexcited spirit, recognizing them as very singular performances for their date in English literature, and for the author's boyish years, but beyond that laying no marked stress upon them.

The reader may perhaps be surprised to find some names unmentioned in this list: I have stated the facts as I remember and know them. Chaucer, Spenser, the Elizabethan dramatists (other than Shakespeare), Milton, Dryden, Pope, Wordsworth, are unnamed. It should not be supposed that he read them not at all, or cared not for any of them; but, if we except Chaucer in a rather loose way and (at a late period of life) Marlowe in some of his non-dramatic poems, they were comparatively neglected. Thomas Hood he valued highly; also very highly Burns in mature years, but he was not a constant reader of the Scottish lyrist. Of Italian poets he earnestly loved none save Dante: Cavalcanti in his degree, and also Poliziano and Michelangelo — not Petrarca, Boccaccio, Ariosto, Tasso, or Leopardi, though in boyhood he delighted well enough in Ariosto. Of French poets, none beyond Hugo and De Musset;

except Villon, and partially Dumas, whose novels ranked among his favourite reading. In German poetry he read nothing currently in the original, although he had in earliest youth so far mastered the language as to make some translations. Calderon, in Fitzgerald's version, he admired deeply; but this was only at a late date. He had no liking for the specialities of Scandinavian, nor indeed of Teutonic, thought and work, and little or no curiosity about Oriental—such as Indian, Persian, or Arabic—poetry. Any writing about devils, spectres, or the supernatural generally, whether in poetry or in prose, had always a fascination for him; at one time, say 1844, his supreme delight was the blood-curdling romance of Maturin, *Melmoth the Wanderer*.

I now pass to a specification of my brother's own writings. Of his merely childish or boyish performances I will here say nothing.

His version of *Der Arme Heinrich*, and the beginning of his translations from the early Italians, may have been in full career in 1846. They show a keen sensitiveness to whatsoever is poetic in the originals, and a sinuous strength and ease in providing English equivalents, with the command of a rich and romantic vocabulary. In his nineteenth year, or before 12th May, 1847, he wrote *The Blessed Damozel*;* universally recognized as one of his typical or consummate productions, marking the high level of his faculty whether inventive or executive.

Dante Rossetti's published works were as follows: three volumes, chiefly of poetry.

* My brother said so, in a letter published by Mr. Caine. He must presumably have been correct; otherwise I should have thought that his twentieth year, or even his twenty-first, would be nearer the mark.

(1ª) The Early Italian Poets from Ciullo d'Alcamo to Dante Alighieri (1100—1200—1300) in the Original Metres. Together with Dante's Vita Nuova. 1861.

(1ᵇ) Dante and his Circle, with the Italian Poets preceding him (1100—1200—1300). A Collection of Lyrics, edited, and translated in the original metres. Revised and rearranged edition. 1874.

(2ª) Poems. 1870.

(2ᵇ) Poems. A new edition. 1881.

(3) Ballads and Sonnets. 1881.

The reader will understand that 1ᵇ is essentially the same book as 1ª, but altered in arrangement, chiefly by inverting the order in which the poems of Dante and of the Dantesque epoch, and those of an earlier period, are printed. The volume 2ᵇ is to a great extent the same as 2ª, yet by no means identical with it. 2ª contained a section named *Sonnets and Songs, towards a work to be called "The House of Life."* In 1881, when 2ᵇ and 3 were published simultaneously, *The House of Life* was completed, was made to consist solely of sonnets, and was transferred to 3; while the gap thus left in 2ᵇ was filled up by other poems.

The reader who inspects my table of contents will be readily able to follow the method of arrangement which is here adopted. I have divided the materials into Principal Poems, Miscellaneous Poems, and some minor headings; and have in each section arranged the compositions in some approximate order of date. The order of date is certainly not very far from correct; but I could not make it absolute, having frequently no distinct information to go by.

Dante Rossetti was a very fastidious writer, and, I might add, a very fastidious painter. He did not indeed "cudgel his brains" for the idea of a poem or the structure or diction of a stanza. He wrote out of a large fund or reserve of thought and consideration, which would culminate in a clear impulse or (as we say) an inspiration. In the execution he was always heedful and reflective from the first, and he spared no after-pains in clarifying and perfecting. He abhorred anything straggling, slipshod, profuse, or uncondensed. He often recurred to his old poems, and was reluctant to leave them merely as they were. A natural concomitant of this state of mind was a great repugnance to the notion of publishing, or of having published after his death, whatever he regarded as juvenile, petty, or inadequate. The amount of unpublished work which he left behind him was by no means large; out of the moderate bulk I have been careful to select only such examples as I suppose that he would himself have approved for the purpose, or would, at any rate, not gravely have objected to.

I have not unfrequently heard my brother say that he considered himself more essentially a poet than a painter. To vary the form of expression, he thought that he had mastered the means of embodying poetical conceptions in the verbal and rhythmical vehicle more thoroughly than in form and design, perhaps more thoroughly than in colour.

WILLIAM M. ROSSETTI.

LONDON, *November* 1890.

I add here the dedications to Rossetti's volumes 2ª, 2ᵇ, and 3.

2ª.—*Poems*, 1870:

To William Michael Rossetti, these Poems, to so many of which, so many years back, he gave the first brotherly hearing, are now at last dedicated.

2ᵇ.—*Poems*, 1881:

Same dedication, adding the dates "1870—1881."

3.—*Ballads and Sonnets:*

To Theodore Watts, the Friend whom my verse won for me, these few more pages are affectionately inscribed.

In the Poems, 1881, appeared the ensuing "Advertisement":

"'Many poems in this volume were written between 1847 and 1853. Others are of recent date, and a few belong to the intervening period. It has been thought unnecessary to specify the earlier work, as nothing is included which the author believes to be immature.'

"The above brief note was prefixed to these poems when first published in 1870. They have now been for some time out of print.

"The fifty sonnets of the *House of Life*, which first appeared here, are now embodied with the full series in the volume entitled *Ballads and Sonnets*.

"The fragment of *The Bride's Prelude*, now first printed, was written very early, and is here associated with other work of the same date; though its publication in an unfinished form needs some indulgence."

I.—PRINCIPAL POEMS.

DANTE AT VERONA.

Yea, thou shalt learn how salt his food who fares
  Upon another's bread,—how steep his path
Who treadeth up and down another's stairs.
            (*Div. Com. Parad.* xvii.)

Behold, even I, even I am Beatrice.
            (*Div. Com. Purg.* xxx.)

Of Florence and of Beatrice
  Servant and singer from of old,
  O'er Dante's heart in youth had toll'd
The knell that gave his Lady peace;
  And now in manhood flew the dart
  Wherewith his City pierced his heart.

Yet if his Lady's home above
  Was Heaven, on earth she filled his soul;
  And if his City held control
To cast the body forth to rove,
  The soul could soar from earth's vain throng,
  And Heaven and Hell fulfil the song.

Follow his feet's appointed way;—
  But little light we find that clears
  The darkness of the exiled years.
Follow his spirit's journey:—nay,
  What fires are blent, what winds are blown
  On paths his feet may tread alone?

Yet of the twofold life he led
　　In chainless thought and fettered will
　　Some glimpses reach us,—somewhat still
Of the steep stairs and bitter bread,—
　　Of the soul's quest whose stern avow
　　For years had made him haggard now.

Alas! the Sacred Song whereto
　　Both heaven and earth had set their hand
　　Not only at Fame's gate did stand
Knocking to claim the passage through,
　　But toiled to ope that heavier door
　　Which Florence shut for evermore.

Shall not his birth's baptismal Town
　　One last high presage yet fulfil,
　　And at that font in Florence still
His forehead take the laurel-crown?
　　O God! or shall dead souls deny
　　The undying soul its prophecy?

Aye, 'tis their hour.　Not yet forgot
　　The bitter words he spoke that day
　　When for some great charge far away
Her rulers his acceptance sought.
　　"And if I go, who stays?"—so rose
　　His scorn:—"and if I stay, who goes?"

"Lo! thou art gone now, and we stay"
　　(The curled lips mutter): "and no star
　　Is from thy mortal path so far
As streets where childhood knew the way.
　　To Heaven and Hell thy feet may win,
　　But thine own house they come not in."

Therefore, the loftier rose the song
　　To touch the secret things of God,
　　The deeper pierced the hate that trod

On base men's track who wrought the wrong;
   Till the soul's effluence came to be
   Its own exceeding agony.

Arriving only to depart,
   From court to court, from land to land,
   Like flame within the naked hand
His body bore his burning heart
   That still on Florence strove to bring
   God's fire for a burnt offering.

Even such was Dante's mood, when now,
   Mocked for long years with Fortune's sport
   He dwelt at yet another court,
There where Verona's knee did bow
   And her voice hailed with all acclaim
   Can Grande della Scala's name.

As that lord's kingly guest awhile
   His life we follow; through the days
   Which walked in exile's barren ways,—
The nights which still beneath one smile
   Heard through all spheres one song increase,—
   "Even I, even I am Beatrice."

At Can La Scala's court, no doubt,
   Due reverence did his steps attend;
   The ushers on his path would bend
At ingoing as at going out;
   The penmen waited on his call
   At council-board, the grooms in hall.

And pages hushed their laughter down,
   And gay squires stilled the merry stir,
   When he passed up the dais-chamber
With set brows lordlier than a frown;
   And tire-maids hidden among these
   Drew close their loosened bodices.

Perhaps the priests, (exact to span
   All God's circumference,) if at whiles
   They found him wandering in their aisles,
Grudged ghostly greeting to the man
   By whom, though not of ghostly guild,
   With Heaven and Hell men's hearts were fill'd.

And the court-poets (he, forsooth,
   A whole world's poet strayed to court!)
   Had for his scorn their hate's retort.
He'd meet them flushed with easy youth,
   Hot on their errands. Like noon-flies
   They vexed him in the ears and eyes.

But at this court, peace still must wrench
   Her chaplet from the teeth of war:
   By day they held high watch afar,
At night they cried across the trench;
   And still, in Dante's path, the fierce
   Gaunt soldiers wrangled o'er their spears.

But vain seemed all the strength to him,
   As golden convoys sunk at sea
   Whose wealth might root out penury:
Because it was not, limb with limb,
   Knit like his heart-strings round the wall
   Of Florence, that ill pride might fall.

Yet in the tiltyard, when the dust
   Cleared from the sundered press of knights
   Ere yet again it swoops and smites,
He almost deemed his longing must
   Find force to wield that multitude
   And hurl that strength the way he would.

How should he move them,—fame and gain
   On all hands calling them at strife?
   He still might find but his one life

DANTE AT VERONA.

To give, by Florence counted vain :
  One heart the false hearts made her doubt,
  One voice she heard once and cast out.

Oh! if his Florence could but come,
  A lily-sceptred damsel fair,
  As her own Giotto painted her
On many shields and gates at home,—
  A lady crowned, at a soft pace
  Riding the lists round to the dais :

Till where Can Grande rules the lists,
  As young as Truth, as calm as Force,
  She draws her rein now, while her horse
Bows at the turn of the white wrists ;
  And when each knight within his stall
  Gives ear, she speaks and tells them all :

All the foul tale,—truth sworn untrue
  And falsehood's triumph. All the tale ?
  Great God! and must she not prevail
To fire them ere they heard it through,—
  And hand achieve ere heart could rest
  That high adventure of her quest ?

How would his Florence lead them forth,
  Her bridle ringing as she went ;
  And at the last within her tent,
'Neath golden lilies worship-worth,
  How queenly would she bend the while
  And thank the victors with her smile !

Also her lips should turn his way
  And murmur : "O thou tried and true,
  With whom I wept the long years through !
What shall it profit if I say,
  Thee I remember ? Nay, through thee
  All ages shall remember me."

Peace, Dante, peace ! The task is long,
   The time wears short to compass it.
   Within thine heart such hopes may flit
And find a voice in deathless song :
   But lo ! as children of man's earth,
   Those hopes are dead before their birth.

Fame tells us that Verona's court
   Was a fair place. The feet might still
   Wander for ever at their will
In many ways of sweet resort;
   And still in many a heart around
   The Poet's name due honour found.

Watch we his steps. He comes upon
   The women at their palm-playing.
   The conduits round the gardens sing
And meet in scoops of milk-white stone,
   Where wearied damsels rest and hold
   Their hands in the wet spurt of gold.

One of whom, knowing well that he,
   By some found stern, was mild with them,
   Would run and pluck his garment's hem,
Saying, " Messer Dante, pardon me,"—
   Praying that they might hear the song
   Which first of all he made, when young

" Donne che avete " * . . . Thereunto
   Thus would he murmur, having first
   Drawn near the fountain, while she nurs'd
His hand against her side : a few
   Sweet words, and scarcely those, half said :
   Then turned, and changed, and bowed his head

---

   * Donne che avete intellettod'amore :—the first canzone of the Vita Nuova.

For then the voice said in his heart,
  "Even I, even I am Beatrice;"
  And his whole life would yearn to cease:
Till having reached his room, apart
  Beyond vast lengths of palace-floor,
  He drew the arras round his door.

At such times, Dante, thou hast set
  Thy forehead to the painted pane
  Full oft, I know; and if the rain
Smote it outside, her fingers met
  Thy brow; and if the sun fell there,
  Her breath was on thy face and hair.

Then, weeping, I think certainly
  Thou hast beheld, past sight of eyne,—
  Within another room of thine
Where now thy body may not be
  But where in thought thou still remain'st,—
  A window often wept against:

The window thou, a youth, hast sought,
  Flushed in the limpid eventime,
  Ending with daylight the day's rhyme
Of her; where oftenwhiles her thought
  Held thee—the lamp untrimmed to write—
  In joy through the blue lapse of night.

At Can La Scala's court, no doubt,
  Guests seldom wept. It was brave sport,
  No doubt, at Can La Scala's court,
Within the palace and without;
  Where music, set to madrigals,
  Loitered all day through groves and halls.

Because Can Grande of his life
  Had not had six-and-twenty years
  As yet. And when the chroniclers

Tell you of that Vicenza strife
　　And of strifes elsewhere,—you must not
　　Conceive for church-sooth he had got

Just nothing in his wits but war:
　　Though doubtless 'twas the young man's joy
　　(Grown with his growth from a mere boy,)
To mark his "Viva Cane!" scare
　　The foe's shut front, till it would reel
　　All blind with shaken points of steel.

But there were places—held too sweet
　　For eyes that had not the due veil
　　Of lashes and clear lids—as well
In favour as his saddle-seat:
　　Breath of low speech he scorned not there
　　Nor light cool fingers in his hair.

Yet if the child whom the sire's plan
　　Made free of a deep treasure-chest
　　Scoffed it with ill-conditioned jest,—
We may be sure too that the man
　　Was not mere thews, nor all content
　　With lewdness swathed in sentiment.

So you may read and marvel not
　　That such a man as Dante—one
　　Who, while Can Grande's deeds were done,
Had drawn his robe round him and thought—
　　Now at the same guest-table far'd
　　Where keen Uguccio wiped his beard.*

Through leaves and trellis-work the sun
　　Left the wine cool within the glass,—
　　They feasting where no sun could pass:

---

* Uguccione della Faggiuola, Dante's former protector, was now his fellow-guest at Verona.

And when the women, all as one,
   Rose up with brightened cheeks to go,
   It was a comely thing, we know.

But Dante recked not of the wine;
   Whether the women stayed or went,
   His visage held one stern intent:
And when the music had its sign
   To breathe upon them for more ease,
   Sometimes he turned and bade it cease.

And as he spared not to rebuke
   The mirth, so oft in council he
   To bitter truth bore testimony:
And when the crafty balance shook
   Well poised to make the wrong prevail,
   Then Dante's hand would turn the scale.

And if some envoy from afar
   Sailed to Verona's sovereign port
   For aid or peace, and all the court
Fawned on its lord, "the Mars of war,
   Sole arbiter of life and death,"—
   Be sure that Dante saved his breath.

And Can La Scala marked askance
   These things, accepting them for shame
   And scorn, till Dante's guestship came
To be a peevish sufferance:
   His host sought ways to make his days
   Hateful; and such have many ways.

There was a Jester, a foul lout
   Whom the court loved for graceless arts;
   Sworn scholiast of the bestial parts
Of speech; a ribald mouth to shout
   In Folly's horny tympanum
   Such things as make the wise man dumb.

Much loved, him Dante loathed.   And so,
   One day when Dante felt perplex'd
   If any day that could come next
Were worth the waiting for or no,
   And mute he sat amid their din,—
   Can Grande called the Jester in.

Rank words, with such, are wit's best wealth.
   Lords mouthed approval; ladies kept
   Twittering with clustered heads, except
Some few that took their trains by stealth
   And went.   Can Grande shook his hair
   And smote his thighs and laughed i' the air

Then, facing on his guest, he cried,—
   "Say, Messer Dante, how it is
   I get out of a clown like this
More than your wisdom can provide."
   And Dante: "'Tis man's ancient whim
   That still his like seems good to him."

Also a tale is told, how once,
   At clearing tables after meat,
   Piled for a jest at Dante's feet
Were found the dinner's well-picked bones;
   So laid, to please the banquet's lord,
   By one who crouched beneath the board.

Then smiled Can Grande to the rest:—
   " Our Dante's tuneful mouth indeed
   Lacks not the gift on flesh to feed!"
"Fair host of mine," replied the guest,
   "So many bones you'd not descry
   If so it chanced the *dog* were I."*

---

* "*Messere, voi non vedreste tant 'ossa se cane io fossi.*"   The point of the reproach is difficult to render, depending as it does on the literal meaning of the name *Cane*.

But wherefore should we turn the grout
   In a drained cup, or be at strife
   From the worn garment of a life
To rip the twisted ravel out?
   Good needs expounding; but of ill
   Each hath enough to guess his fill.

They named him Justicer-at-Law:
   Each month to bear the tale in mind
   Of hues a wench might wear unfin'd
And of the load an ox might draw;
   To cavil in the weight of bread
   And to see purse-thieves gibbeted.

And when his spirit wove the spell
   (From under even to over-noon
   In converse with itself alone,)
As high as Heaven, as low as Hell,—
   He would be summoned and must go:
   For had not Gian stabbed Giacomo?

Therefore the bread he had to eat
   Seemed brackish, less like corn than tares;
   And the rush-strown accustomed stairs
Each day were steeper to his feet;
   And when the night-vigil was done,
   His brows would ache to feel the sun.

Nevertheless, when from his kin
   There came the tidings how at last
   In Florence a decree was pass'd
Whereby all banished folk might win
   Free pardon, so a fine were paid
   And act of public penance made,—

This Dante writ in answer thus,
   Words such as these: "That clearly they
   In Florence must not have to say,—

The man abode aloof from us
  Nigh fifteen years, yet lastly skulk'd
  Hither to candleshrift and mulct.

"That he was one the Heavens forbid
  To traffic in God's justice sold
  By market-weight of earthly gold,
Or to bow down over the lid
  Of steaming censers, and so be
  Made clean of manhood's obloquy.

"That since no gate led, by God's will,
  To Florence, but the one whereat
  The priests and money-changers sat,
He still would wander; for that still,
  Even through the body's prison-bars,
  His soul possessed the sun and stars."

Such were his words. It is indeed
  For ever well our singers should
  Utter good words and know them good
Not through song only; with close heed
  Lest, having spent for the work's sake
  Six days, the man be left to make.

Months o'er Verona, till the feast
  Was come for Florence the Free Town:
  And at the shrine of Baptist John
The exiles, girt with many a priest
  And carrying candles as they went,
  Were held to mercy of the saint.

On the high seats in sober state,—
  Gold neck-chains range o'er range below
  Gold screen-work where the lilies grow,—
The heads of the Republic sate,
  Marking the humbled face go by
  Each one of his house-enemy.

And as each proscript rose and stood
   From kneeling in the ashen dust
   On the shrine-steps, some magnate thrust
A beard into the velvet hood
   Of his front colleague's gown, to see
   The cinders stuck in his bare knee.

Tosinghi passed, Manelli passed,
   Rinucci passed, each in his place;
   But not an Alighieri's face
Went by that day from first to last
   In the Republic's triumph; nor
   A foot came home to Dante's door.

(RESPUBLICA—a public thing:
   A shameful shameless prostitute,
   Whose lust with one lord may not suit,
So takes by turn its revelling
   A night with each, till each at morn
   Is stripped and beaten forth forlorn,

And leaves her, cursing her. If she,
   Indeed, have not some spice-draught, hid
   In scent under a silver lid,
To drench his open throat with—he
   Once hard asleep; and thrust him not
   At dawn beneath the stairs to rot.

Such *this* Republic!—not the Maid
   He yearned for; she who yet should stand
   With Heaven's accepted hand in hand,
Invulnerable and unbetray'd:
   To whom, even as to God, should be
   Obeisance one with Liberty.)

Years filled out their twelve moons, and ceased
   One in another; and alway
   There were the whole twelve hour each day

And each night as the years increased;
    And rising moon and setting sun
    Beheld that Dante's work was done.

What of his work for Florence? Well
    It was, he knew, and well must be.
    Yet evermore her hate's decree
Dwelt in his thought intolerable:—
    His body to be burned,*—his soul
    To beat its wings at hope's vain goal.

What of his work for Beatrice?
    Now well-nigh was the third song writ,—
    The stars a third time sealing it
With sudden music of pure peace:
    For echoing thrice the threefold song,
    The unnumbered stars the tone prolong.†

Each hour, as then the Vision pass'd,
    He heard the utter harmony
    Of the nine trembling spheres, till she
Bowed her eyes towards him in the last,
    So that all ended with her eyes,
    Hell, Purgatory, Paradise.

"It is my trust, as the years fall,
    To write more worthily of her
    Who now, being made God's minister,
Looks on His visage and knows all."
    Such was the hope that love dar'd blend
    With grief's slow fires, to make an end

---

* Such was the last sentence passed by Florence against Dante, as a recalcitrant exile.

† E quindi uscimmo a riveder le *stelle*.—INFERNO.
Puro e disposto a salire alle *stelle*.—PURGATORIO.
L'amor che muove il sole e l' altre *stelle*.—PARADISO.

DANTE AT VERONA.

Of the "New Life," his youth's dear book:
    Adding thereunto: "In such trust
    I labour, and believe I must
Accomplish this which my soul took
    In charge, if God, my Lord and hers,
    Leave my life with me a few years."

The trust which he had borne in youth
    Was all at length accomplished. He
    At length had written worthily—
Yea even of her; no rhymes uncouth
    'Twixt tongue and tongue; but by God's aid
    The first words Italy had said.

Ah! haply now the heavenly guide
    Was not the last form seen by him:
    But there that Beatrice stood slim
And bowed in passing at his side,
    For whom in youth his heart made moan
    Then when the city sat alone.*

Clearly herself: the same whom he
    Met, not past girlhood, in the street,
    Low-bosomed and with hidden feet;
And then as woman perfectly,
    In years that followed, many an once,—
    And now at last among the suns

In that high vision. But indeed
    It may be memory might recall
    Last to him then the first of all,—
The child his boyhood bore in heed
    Nine years. At length the voice brought peace,—
    "Even I, even I am Beatrice."

---

* *Quomodo sedet sola civitas!*—The words quoted by Dante in the Vita Nuova when he speaks of the death of Beatrice.

All this, being there, we had not seen.
  Seen only was the shadow wrought
  On the strong features bound in thought;
The vagueness gaining gait and mien;
  The white streaks gathering clear to view
  In the burnt beard the women knew.

For a tale tells that on his track,
  As through Verona's streets he went,
  This saying certain women sent:—
"Lo, he that strolls to Hell and back
  At will! Behold him, how Hell's reek
  Has crisped his beard and singed his cheek."

"Whereat" (Boccaccio's words) "he smil'd
  For pride in fame." It might be so:
  Nevertheless we cannot know
If haply he were not beguil'd
  To bitterer mirth, who scarce could tell
  If he indeed were back from Hell.

So the day came, after a space,
  When Dante felt assured that there
  The sunshine must lie sicklier
Even than in any other place,
  Save only Florence. When that day
  Had come, he rose and went his way.

He went and turned not. From his shoes
  It may be that he shook the dust,
  As every righteous dealer must
Once and again ere life can close:
  And unaccomplished destiny
  Struck cold his forehead, it may be.

No book keeps record how the Prince
  Sunned himself out of Dante's reach,
  Nor how the Jester stank in speech:

While courtiers, used to cringe and wince,
   Poets and harlots, all the throng,
   Let loose their scandal and their song.

No book keeps record if the seat
   Which Dante held at his host's board
   Were sat in next by clerk or lord,—
If leman lolled with dainty feet
   At ease, or hostage brooded there,
   Or priest lacked silence for his prayer.

Eat and wash hands, Can Grande;—scarce
   We know their deeds now: hands which fed
   Our Dante with that bitter bread;
And thou the watch-dog of those stairs
   Which, of all paths his feet knew well,
   Were steeper found than Heaven or Hell.

A LAST CONFESSION.

(Regno Lombardo-Veneto, 1848.)

⁂   *   *   *   *   *   *   ⁂   ⁂

Our Lombard country-girls along the coast
Wear daggers in their garters: for they know
That they might hate another girl to death
Or meet a German lover. Such a knife
I bought her, with a hilt of horn and pearl.

Father, you cannot know of all my thoughts
That day in going to meet her,—that last day
For the last time, she said;—of all the love
And all the hopeless hope that she might change
And go back with me. Ah! and everywhere,
At places we both knew along the road,
Some fresh shape of herself as once she was
Grew present at my side; until it seemed—
So close they gathered round me—they would all
Be with me when I reached the spot at last,
To plead my cause with her against herself
So changed. O Father, if you knew all this
You cannot know, then you would know too, Father.
And only then, if God can pardon me.
What can be told I'll tell, if you will hear.

I passed a village-fair upon my road,
And thought, being empty-handed, I would take
Some little present: such might prove, I said,
Either a pledge between us, or (God help me!)
A parting gift. And there it was I bought
The knife I spoke of, such as women wear.

A LAST CONFESSION.

That day, some three hours afterwards, I found
For certain, it must be a parting gift.
And, standing silent now at last, I looked
Into her scornful face; and heard the sea
Still trying hard to din into my ears
Some speech it knew which still might change her heart,
If only it could make me understand.
One moment thus. Another, and her face
Seemed further off than the last line of sea,
So that I thought, if now she were to speak
I could not hear her. Then again I knew
All, as we stood together on the sand
At Iglio, in the first thin shade o' the hills.

"Take it," I said, and held it out to her,
While the hilt glanced within my trembling hold;
"Take it and keep it for my sake," I said.
Her neck unbent not, neither did her eyes
Move, nor her foot left beating of the sand;
Only she put it by from her and laughed.

Father, you hear my speech and not her laugh;
But God heard that. Will God remember all?

It was another laugh than the sweet sound
Which rose from her sweet childish heart, that day
Eleven years before, when first I found her
Alone upon the hill-side; and her curls
Shook down in the warm grass as she looked up
Out of her curls in my eyes bent to hers.
She might have served a painter to pourtray
That heavenly child which in the latter days
Shall walk between the lion and the lamb.
I had been for nights in hiding, worn and sick
And hardly fed; and so her words at first
Seemed fitful like the talking of the trees
And voices in the air that knew my name.
And I remember that I sat me down
Upon the slope with her, and thought the world

Must be all over or had never been,
We seemed there so alone. And soon she told me
Her parents both were gone away from her.
I thought perhaps she meant that they had died;
But when I asked her this, she looked again
Into my face and said that yestereve
They kissed her long, and wept and made her weep,
And gave her all the bread they had with them,
And then had gone together up the hill
Where we were sitting now, and had walked on
Into the great red light; "and so," she said,
"I have come up here too; and when this evening
They step out of the light as they stepped in,
I shall be here to kiss them." And she laughed.

Then I bethought me suddenly of the famine;
And how the church-steps throughout all the town,
When last I had been there a month ago,
Swarmed with starved folk; and how the bread was weighed
By Austrians armed; and women that I knew
For wives and mothers walked the public street,
Saying aloud that if their husbands feared
To snatch the children's food, themselves would stay
Till they had earned it there. So then this child
Was piteous to me; for all told me then
Her parents must have left her to God's chance,
To man's or to the Church's charity,
Because of the great famine, rather than
To watch her growing thin between their knees.
With that, God took my mother's voice and spoke,
And sights and sounds came back and things long since,
And all my childhood found me on the hills;
And so I took her with me.
                    I was young,
Scarce man then, Father: but the cause which gave
The wounds I die of now had brought me then
Some wounds already; and I lived alone,

As any hiding hunted man must live.
It was no easy thing to keep a child
In safety ; for herself it was not safe,
And doubled my own danger : but I knew
That God would help me.
                    Yet a little while
Pardon me, Father, if I pause.   I think
I have been speaking to you of some matters
There was no need to speak of, have I not ?
You do not know how clearly those things stood
Within my mind, which I have spoken of,
Nor how they strove for utterance.   Life all past
Is like the sky when the sun sets in it,
Clearest where furthest off.
                      I told you how
She scorned my parting gift and laughed.   And yet
A woman's laugh's another thing sometimes :
I think they laugh in Heaven.   I know last night
I dreamed I saw into the garden of God,
Where women walked whose painted images
I have seen with candles round them in the church.
They bent this way and that, one to another,
Playing : and over the long golden hair
Of each there floated like a ring of fire
Which when she stooped stooped with her, and when she
    rose
Rose with her.   Then a breeze flew in among them,
As if a window had been opened in heaven
For God to give His blessing from, before
This world of ours should set ; (for in my dream
I thought our world was setting, and the sun
Flared, a spent taper ;) and beneath that gust
The rings of light quivered like forest-leaves.
Then all the blessed maidens who were there
Stood up together, as it were a voice
That called them ; and they threw their tresses back,
And smote their palms, and all laughed up at once,
For the strong heavenly joy they had in them

To hear God bless the world.   Wherewith I woke
And looking round, I saw as usual
That she was standing there with her long locks
Pressed to her side; and her laugh ended theirs.

For always when I see her now, she laughs.
And yet her childish laughter haunts me too,
The life of this dead terror; as in days
When she, a child, dwelt with me. I must tell
Something of those days yet before the end.

I brought her from the city—one such day
When she was still a merry loving child,—
The earliest gift I mind my giving her;
A little image of a flying Love
Made of our coloured glass-ware, in his hands
A dart of gilded metal and a torch.
And him she kissed and me, and fain would know
Why were his poor eyes blindfold, why the wings
And why the arrow.   What I knew I told
Of Venus and of Cupid,—strange old tales.
And when she heard that he could rule the loves
Of men and women, still she shook her head
And wondered; and, "Nay, nay," she murmured still,
"So strong, and he a younger child than I!"
And then she'd have me fix him on the wall
Fronting her little bed; and then again
She needs must fix him there herself, because
I gave him to her and she loved him so,
And he should make her love me better yet,
If women loved the more, the more they grew.
But the fit place upon the wall was high
For her, and so I held her in my arms:
And each time that the heavy pruning-hook
I gave her for a hammer slipped away
As it would often, still she laughed and laughed
And kissed and kissed me.   But amid her mirth,
Just as she hung the image on the nail,

It slipped and all its fragments strewed the ground:
And as it fell she screamed, for in her hand
The dart had entered deeply and drawn blood.
And so her laughter turned to tears: and "Oh!"
I said, the while I bandaged the small hand,—
"That I should be the first to make you bleed,
Who love and love and love you!"—kissing still
The fingers till I got her safe to bed.
And still she sobbed,—"not for the pain at all,"
She said, "but for the Love, the poor good Love
You gave me." So she cried herself to sleep.

Another later thing comes back to me.
'Twas in those hardest foulest days of all,
When still from his shut palace, sitting clean
Above the splash of blood, old Metternich
(May his soul die, and never-dying worms
Feast on its pain for ever!) used to thin
His year's doomed hundreds daintily, each month
Thirties and fifties. This time, as I think,
Was when his thrift forbad the poor to take
That evil brackish salt which the dry rocks
Keep all through winter when the sea draws in.
The first I heard of it was a chance shot
In the street here and there, and on the stones
A stumbling clatter as of horse hemmed round.
Then, when she saw me hurry out of doors,
My gun slung at my shoulder and my knife
Stuck in my girdle, she smoothed down my hair
And laughed to see me look so brave, and leaped
Up to my neck and kissed me. She was still
A child; and yet that kiss was on my lips
So hot all day where the smoke shut us in.

For now, being always with her, the first love
I had—the father's, brother's love—was changed,
I think, in somewise; like a holy thought
Which is a prayer before one knows of it.

The first time I perceived this, I remember,
Was once when after hunting I came home
Weary, and she brought food and fruit for me,
And sat down at my feet upon the floor
Leaning against my side. But when I felt
Her sweet head reach from that low seat of hers
So high as to be laid upon my heart,
I turned and looked upon my darling there
And marked for the first time how tall she was;
And my heart beat with so much violence
Under her cheek, I thought she could not choose
But wonder at it soon and ask me why;
And so I bade her rise and eat with me.
And when, remembering all and counting back
The time, I made out fourteen years for her
And told her so, she gazed at me with eyes
As of the sky and sea on a grey day,
And drew her long hands through her hair, and asked me
If she was not a woman; and then laughed:
And as she stooped in laughing, I could see
Beneath the growing throat the breasts half-globed
Like folded lilies deepset in the stream.

Yes, let me think of her as then; for so
Her image, Father, is not like the sights
Which come when you are gone. She had a mouth
Made to bring death to life,—the underlip
Sucked in, as if it strove to kiss itself.
Her face was pearly pale, as when one stoops
Over wan water; and the dark crisped hair
And the hair's shadow made it paler still:—
Deep-serried locks, the dimness of the cloud
Where the moon's gaze is set in eddying gloom.
Her body bore her neck as the tree's stem
Bears the top branch; and as the branch sustains
The flower of the year's pride, her high neck bore
That face made wonderful with night and day.

Her voice was swift, yet ever the last words
Fell lingeringly; and rounded finger-tips
She had, that clung a little where they touched
And then were gone o' the instant. Her great eyes,
That sometimes turned half dizzily beneath
The passionate lids, as faint, when she would speak,
Had also in them hidden springs of mirth,
Which under the dark lashes evermore
Shook to her laugh, as when a bird flies low
Between the water and the willow-leaves,
And the shade quivers till he wins the light.

I was a moody comrade to her then,
For all the love I bore her. Italy,
The weeping desolate mother, long has claimed
Her sons' strong arms to lean on, and their hands
To lop the poisonous thicket from her path,
Cleaving her way to light. And from her need
Had grown the fashion of my whole poor life
Which I was proud to yield her, as my father
Had yielded his. And this had come to be
A game to play, a love to clasp, a hate
To wreak, all things together that a man
Needs for his blood to ripen; till at times
All else seemed shadows, and I wondered still
To see such life pass muster and be deemed
Time's bodily substance. In those hours, no doubt,
To the young girl my eyes were like my soul,—
Dark wells of death-in-life that yearned for day.
And though she ruled me always, I remember
That once when I was thus and she still kept
Leaping about the place and laughing, I
Did almost chide her; whereupon she knelt
And putting her two hands into my breast
Sang me a song. Are these tears in my eyes?
'Tis long since I have wept for anything.
I thought that song forgotten out of mind;
And now, just as I spoke of it, it came

All back. It is but a rude thing, ill rhymed,
Such as a blind man chaunts and his dog hears
Holding the platter, when the children run
To merrier sport and leave him. Thus it goes:—

> La bella donna*
> Piangendo disse:
> " Come son fisse
> Le stelle in cielo!
> Quel fiato anelo
> Dello stanco sole,
> Quanto m' assonna!

---

* She wept, sweet lady,
And said in weeping:
"What spell is keeping
The stars so steady?
Why does the power
Of the sun's noon-hour
To sleep so move me?
And the moon in heaven,
Stained where she passes
As a worn-out glass is,—
Wearily driven,
Why walks she above me?

"Stars, moon, and sun too,
I'm tired of either
And all together!
Whom speak they unto
That I should listen?
For very surely,
Though my arms and shoulders
Dazzle beholders,
And my eyes glisten,
All's nothing purely!
What are words said for
At all about them,
If he they are made for
Can do without them?"

She laughed, sweet lady,
And said in laughing:
"His hand clings half in
My own already!
Oh! do you love me?
Oh! speak of passion
In no new fashion,
No loud inveighings,
But the old sayings
You once said of me.

"You said: 'As summer,
Through boughs grown brittle,
Comes back a little
Ere frosts benumb her,—
So bring'st thou to me
All leaves and flowers,
Though autumn's gloomy
To-day in the bowers.'

"Oh! does he love me,
When my voice teaches
The very speeches
He then spoke of me?
Alas! what flavour
Still with me lingers?"
(But she laughed as my kisses
Glowed in her fingers
With love's old blisses.)
"Oh! what one favour
Remains to woo him,
Whose whole poor savour
Belongs not to him?"

E la luna, macchiata
Come uno specchio
Logoro e vecchio,—
Faccia affannata,
Che cosa vuole?

"Chè stelle, luna, e sole,
Ciascun m' annoja
E m' annojano insieme;
Non me ne preme
Nè ci prendo gioja.
E veramente,
Che le spalle sien franche
E le braccia bianche
E il seno caldo e tondo,
Non mi fa niente.
Che cosa al mondo
Posso più far di questi
Se non piacciono a te, come dicesti?"

La donna rise
E riprese ridendo:—
" Questa mano che prendo
È dunque mia?
Tu m' ami dunque?
Dimmelo ancora,
Non in modo qualunque,
Ma le parole
Belle e precise
Che dicesti pria.

' *Siccome suole*
La state talora
(Dicesti) un qualche istante
Tornare innanzi inverno,
Così tu fai ch' io scerno
Le foglie tutte quante,
Ben ch' io certo tenessi
Per passato l' autunno.

"Eccolo il mio alunno!
Io debbo insegnargli
Quei cari detti istessi
Ch' ei mi disse una volta!

Oimè! Che cosa dargli,"
(Ma ridea piano piano
Dei baci in sulla mano,)
"Ch' ei non m'abbia da lungo tempo tolta?"

That I should sing upon this bed!—with you
To listen, and such words still left to say!
Yet was it I that sang? The voice seemed hers,
As on the very day she sang to me;
When, having done, she took out of my hand
Something that I had played with all the while
And laid it down beyond my reach; and so
Turning my face round till it fronted hers,—
"Weeping or laughing, which was best?" she said.

But these are foolish tales. How should I show
The heart that glowed then with love's heat, each day
More and more brightly?—when for long years now
The very flame that flew about the heart,
And gave it fiery wings, has come to be
The lapping blaze of hell's environment
Whose tongues all bid the molten heart despair.

Yet one more thing comes back on me to-night
Which I may tell you: for it bore my soul
Dread firstlings of the brood that rend it now.
It chanced that in our last year's wanderings
We dwelt at Monza, far away from home,
If home we had: and in the Duomo there
I sometimes entered with her when she prayed.
An image of Our Lady stands there, wrought
In marble by some great Italian hand
In the great days when she and Italy
Sat on one throne together: and to her
And to none else my loved one told her heart.
She was a woman then; and as she knelt,—
Her sweet brow in the sweet brow's shadow there,—
They seemed two kindred forms whereby our land

(Whose work still serves the world for miracle)
Made manifest herself in womanhood.
Father, the day I speak of was the first
For weeks that I had borne her company
Into the Duomo; and those weeks had been
Much troubled, for then first the glimpses came
Of some impenetrable restlessness
Growing in her to make her changed and cold.
And as we entered there that day, I bent
My eyes on the fair Image, and I said
Within my heart, "Oh turn her heart to me!"
And so I left her to her prayers, and went
To gaze upon the pride of Monza's shrine,
Where in the sacristy the light still falls
Upon the Iron Crown of Italy,
On whose crowned heads the day has closed, nor yet
The daybreak gilds another head to crown.
But coming back, I wondered when I saw
That the sweet Lady of her prayers now stood
Alone without her; until further off,
Before some new Madonna gaily decked,
Tinselled and gewgawed, a slight German toy,
I saw her kneel, still praying. At my step
She rose, and side by side we left the church.
I was much moved, and sharply questioned her
Of her transferred devotion; but she seemed
Stubborn and heedless; till she lightly laughed
And said: "The old Madonna? Aye indeed,
She had my old thoughts,—this one has my new."
Then silent to the soul I held my way:
And from the fountains of the public place
Unto the pigeon-haunted pinnacles,
Bright wings and water winnowed the bright air;
And stately with her laugh's subsiding smile
She went, with clear-swayed waist and towering neck
And hands held light before her; and the face
Which long had made a day in my life's night
Was night in day to me; as all men's eyes

Turned on her beauty, and she seemed to tread
Beyond my heart to the world made for her.

Ah, there! my wounds will snatch my sense again:
The pain comes billowing on like a full cloud
Of thunder, and the flash that breaks from it
Leaves my brain burning. That's the wound he gave
The Austrian whose white coat I still made match
With his white face, only the two grew red
As suits his trade. The devil makes them wear
White for a livery, that the blood may show
Braver that brings them to him. So he looks
Sheer o'er the field and knows his own at once.

Give me a draught of water in that cup;
My voice feels thick; perhaps you do not hear;
But you *must* hear. If you mistake my words
And so absolve me, I am sure the blessing
Will burn my soul. If you mistake my words
And so absolve me, Father, the great sin
Is yours, not mine: mark this: your soul shall burn
With mine for it. I have seen pictures where
Souls burned with Latin shriekings in their mouths:
Shall my end be as theirs? Nay, but I know
'Tis you shall shriek in Latin. Some bell rings,
Rings through my brain: it strikes the hour in hell.

You see I cannot, Father; I have tried,
But cannot, as you see. These twenty times
Beginning, I have come to the same point
And stopped. Beyond, there are but broken words
Which will not let you understand my tale.
It is that then we have her with us here,
As when she wrung her hair out in my dream
To-night, till all the darkness reeked of it.
Her hair is always wet, for she has kept
Its tresses wrapped about her side for years;
And when she wrung them round over the floor,

A LAST CONFESSION.

I heard the blood between her fingers hiss;
So that I sat up in my bed and screamed
Once and again; and once to once, she laughed.
Look that you turn not now,—she's at your back:
Gather your robe up, Father, and keep close,
Or she'll sit down on it and send you mad

At Iglio in the first thin shade o' the hills
The sand is black and red. The black was black
When what was spilt that day sank into it,
And the red scarcely darkened. There I stood
This night with her, and saw the sand the same.

* * * * * *

What would you have me tell you? Father, father,
How shall I make you know? You have not known
The dreadful soul of woman, who one day
Forgets the old and takes the new to heart,
Forgets what man remembers, and therewith
Forgets the man. Nor can I clearly tell
How the change happened between her and me.
Her eyes looked on me from an emptied heart
When most my heart was full of her; and still
In every corner of myself I sought
To find what service failed her; and no less
Than in the good time past, there all was hers.
What do you love? Your Heaven? Conceive it spread
For one first year of all eternity
All round you with all joys and gifts of God;
And then when most your soul is blent with it
And all yields song together,—then it stands
O' the sudden like a pool that once gave back
Your image, but now drowns it and is clear
Again,—or like a sun bewitched, that burns
Your shadow from you, and still shines in sight.
How could you bear it? Would you not cry out,
Among those eyes grown blind to you, those ears
That hear no more your voice you hear the same,—

"God! what is left but hell for company,
But hell, hell, hell?"—until the name so breathed
Whirled with hot wind and sucked you down in fire?
Even so I stood the day her empty heart
Left her place empty in our home, while yet
I knew not why she went nor where she went
Nor how to reach her: so I stood the day
When to my prayers at last one sight of her
Was granted, and I looked on heaven made pale
With scorn, and heard heaven mock me in that laugh.

O sweet, long sweet! Was that some ghost of you,
Even as your ghost that haunts me now,—twin shapes
Of fear and hatred? May I find you yet
Mine when death wakes? Ah! be it even in flame,
We may have sweetness yet, if you but say
As once in childish sorrow: "Not my pain,
My pain was nothing: oh your poor poor love,
Your broken love!"
      My Father, have I not
Yet told you the last things of that last day
On which I went to meet her by the sea?
O God, O God! but I must tell you all.

Midway upon my journey, when I stopped
To buy the dagger at the village fair,
I saw two cursed rats about the place
I knew for spies—blood-sellers both. That day
Was not yet over; for three hours to come
I prized my life: and so I looked around
For safety. A poor painted mountebank
Was playing tricks and shouting in a crowd.
I knew he must have heard my name, so I
Pushed past and whispered to him who I was,
And of my danger. Straight he hustled me
Into his booth, as it were in the trick,
And brought me out next minute with my face
All smeared in patches and a zany's gown;

A LAST CONFESSION.

And there I handed him his cups and balls
And swung the sand-bags round to clear the ring
For half an hour. The spies came once and looked;
And while they stopped, and made all sights and sounds
Sharp to my startled senses, I remember
A woman laughed above me. I looked up
And saw where a brown-shouldered harlot leaned
Half through a tavern window thick with vine.
Some man had come behind her in the room
And caught her by her arms, and she had turned
With that coarse empty laugh on him, as now
He munched her neck with kisses, while the vine
Crawled in her back.

     And three hours afterwards,
When she that I had run all risks to meet
Laughed as I told you, my life burned to death
Within me, for I thought it like the laugh
Heard at the fair. She had not left me long;
But all she might have changed to, or might change to,
(I know nought since—she never speaks a word—)
Seemed in that laugh. Have I not told you yet,
Not told you all this time what happened, Father,
When I had offered her the little knife,
And bade her keep it for my sake that loved her,
And she had laughed? Have I not told you yet?

"Take it," I said to her the second time,
"Take it and keep it." And then came a fire
That burnt my hand; and then the fire was blood,
And sea and sky were blood and fire, and all
The day was one red blindness; till it seemed,
Within the whirling brain's eclipse, that she
Or I or all things bled or burned to death.
And then I found her laid against my feet
And knew that I had stabbed her, and saw still
Her look in falling. For she took the knife
Deep in her heart, even as I bade her then,

And fell ; and her stiff bodice scooped the sand
Into her bosom.
                    And she keeps it, see,
Do you not see she keeps it ?—there, beneath
Wet fingers and wet tresses, in her heart.
For look you, when she stirs her hand, it shows
The little hilt of horn and pearl,—even such
A dagger as our women of the coast
Twist in their garters.
                    Father, I have done :
And from her side she now unwinds the thick
Dark hair ; all round her side it is wet through,
But, like the sand at Iglio, does not change.
Now you may see the dagger clearly.   Father,
I have told all : tell me at once what hope
Can reach me still. For now she draws it out
Slowly, and only smiles as yet : look, Father,
She scarcely smiles : but I shall hear her laugh
Soon, when she shows the crimson steel to God.

THE BRIDE'S PRELUDE.

"SISTER," said busy Amelotte
    To listless Aloÿse ;
"Along your wedding-road the wheat
Bends as to hear your horse's feet,
And the noonday stands still for heat."

Amelotte laughed into the air
    With eyes that sought the sun:
But where the walls in long brocade
Were screened, as one who is afraid
Sat Aloÿse within the shade.

And even in shade was gleam enough
    To shut out full repose
From the bride's 'tiring-chamber, which
Was like the inner altar-niche
Whose dimness worship has made rich.

Within the window's heaped recess
    The light was counterchanged
In blent reflexes manifold
From perfume-caskets of wrought gold
And gems the bride's hair could not hold

All thrust together: and with these
    A slim-curved lute, which now,
At Amelotte's sudden passing there,
Was swept in somewise unaware,
And shook to music the close air.

Against the haloed lattice-panes
    The bridesmaid sunned her breast;
Then to the glass turned tall and free,
And braced and shifted daintily
Her loin-belt through her cote-hardie.

The belt was silver, and the clasp
    Of lozenged arm-bearings;
A world of mirrored tints minute
The rippling sunshine wrought into 't,
That flushed her hand and warmed her foot.

At least an hour had Aloÿse,—
    Her jewels in her hair,—
Her white gown, as became a bride,
Quartered in silver at each side,—
Sat thus aloof, as if to hide.

Over her bosom, that lay still,
    The vest was rich in grain,
With close pearls wholly overset:
Around her throat the fastenings met
Of chevesayle and mantelet.

Her arms were laid along her lap
    With the hands open: life
Itself did seem at fault in her:
Beneath the drooping brows, the stir
Of thought made noonday heavier.

Long sat she silent; and then raised
    Her head, with such a gasp
As while she summoned breath to speak
Fanned high that furnace in the cheek
But sucked the heart-pulse cold and weak.

THE BRIDE'S PRELUDE.

(Oh gather round her now, all ye
    Past seasons of her fear,—
Sick springs, and summers deadly cold!
To flight your hovering wings unfold,
For now your secret shall be told.

Ye many sunlights, barbed with darts
    Of dread detecting flame,—
Gaunt moonlights that like sentinels
Went past with iron clank of bells,—
Draw round and render up your spells!)

"Sister," said Aloÿse, "I had
    A thing to tell thee of
Long since, and could not. But do thou
Kneel first in prayer awhile, and bow
Thine heart, and I will tell thee now."

Amelotte wondered with her eyes;
    But her heart said in her:
"Dear Aloÿse would have me pray
Because the awe she feels to-day
Must need more prayers than she can say."

So Amelotte put by the folds
    That covered up her feet,
And knelt,—beyond the arras'd gloom
And the hot window's dull perfume,—
Where day was stillest in the room.

"Queen Mary, hear," she said, "and say
    To Jesus the Lord Christ,
This bride's new joy, which He confers,
New joy to many ministers,
And many griefs are bound in hers."

The bride turned in her chair, and hid
    Her face against the back,
And took her pearl-girt elbows in
Her hands, and could not yet begin,
But shuddering, uttered, "Urscelyn!"

Most weak she was; for as she pressed
    Her hand against her throat,
Along the arras she let trail
Her face, as if all heart did fail,
And sat with shut eyes, dumb and pale.

Amelotte still was on her knees
    As she had kneeled to pray.
Deeming her sister swooned, she thought,
At first, some succour to have brought;
But Aloÿse rocked, as one distraught.

She would have pushed the lattice wide
    To gain what breeze might be;
But marking that no leaf once beat
The outside casement, it seemed meet
Not to bring in more scent and heat.

So she said only: "Aloÿse,
    Sister, when happened it
At any time that the bride came
To ill, or spoke in fear of shame
When speaking first the bridegroom's name?'

A bird had out its song and ceased
    Ere the bride spoke. At length
She said: "The name is as the thing:—
Sin hath no second christening,
And shame is all that shame can bring.

"In divers places many an while
　　I would have told thee this;
But faintness took me, or a fit
Like fever.　God would not permit
That I should change thine eyes with it.

"Yet once I spoke, hadst thou but heard:—
　　That time we wandered out
All the sun's hours, but missed our way
When evening darkened, and so lay
The whole night covered up in hay.

"At last my face was hidden: so,
　　Having God's hint, I paused
Not long; but drew myself more near
Where thou wast laid, and shook off fear,
And whispered quick into thine ear

"Something of the whole tale.　At first
　　I lay and bit my hair
For the sore silence thou didst keep:
Till, as thy breath came long and deep,
I knew that thou hadst been asleep.

"The moon was covered, but the stars
　　Lasted till morning broke.
Awake, thou told'st me that thy dream
Had been of me,—that all did seem
At jar,—but that it was a dream.

"I knew God's hand and might not speak.
　　After that night I kept
Silence and let the record swell:
Till now there is much more to tell
Which must be told out ill or well."

She paused then, weary, with dry lips
  Apart. From the outside
By fits there boomed a dull report
From where i' the hanging tennis-court
The bridegroom's retinue made sport.

The room lay still in dusty glare,
  Having no sound through it
Except the chirp of a caged bird
That came and ceased: and if she stirred,
Amelotte's raiment could be heard.

Quoth Amelotte: "The night this chanced
  Was a late summer night
Last year! What secret, for Christ's love,
Keep'st thou since then? Mary above!
What thing is this thou speakest of?

"Mary and Christ! Lest when 'tis told
  I should be prone to wrath,—
This prayer beforehand! How she errs
Soe'er, take count of grief like hers,
Whereof the days are turned to years!"

She bowed her neck, and having said,
  Kept on her knees to hear;
And then, because strained thought demands
Quiet before it understands,
Darkened her eyesight with her hands.

So when at last her sister spoke,
  She did not see the pain
O' the mouth nor the ashamèd eyes,
But marked the breath that came in sighs
And the half-pausing for replies.

THE BRIDE'S PRELUDE.

This was the bride's sad prelude-strain :—
    " I' the convent where a girl
I dwelt till near my womanhood,
I had but preachings of the rood
And Aves told in solitude

" To spend my heart on : and my hand
    Had but the weary skill
To eke out upon silken cloth
Christ's visage, or the long bright growth
Of Mary's hair, or Satan wroth.

" So when at last I went, and thou,
    A child not known before,
Didst come to take the place I left,—
My limbs, after such lifelong theft
Of life, could be but little deft

" In all that ministers delight
    To noble women : I
Had learned no word of youth's discourse,
Nor gazed on games of warriors,
Nor trained a hound, nor ruled a horse.

" Besides, the daily life i' the sun
    Made me at first hold back.
To thee this came at once; to me
It crept with pauses timidly;
I am not blithe and strong like thee.

"Yet my feet liked the dances well,
    The songs went to my voice,
The music made me shake and weep;
And often, all night long, my sleep
Gave dreams I had been fain to keep.

"But though I loved not holy things,
    To hear them scorned brought pain,—
They were my childhood; and these dames
Were merely perjured in saints' names
And fixed upon saints' days for games.

"And sometimes when my father rode
    To hunt with his loud friends,
I dared not bring him to be quaff'd,
As my wont was, his stirrup-draught,
Because they jested so and laugh'd.

"At last one day my brothers said,
    'The girl must not grow thus,—
Bring her a jennet,—she shall ride.'
They helped my mounting, and I tried
To laugh with them and keep their side.

"But brakes were rough and bents were steep
    Upon our path that day:
My palfrey threw me; and I went
Upon men's shoulders home, sore spent,
While the chase followed up the scent.

"Our shrift-father (and he alone
    Of all the household there
Had skill in leechcraft,) was away
When I reached home. I tossed, and lay
Sullen with anguish the whole day.

"For the day passed ere some one brought
    To mind that in the hunt
Rode a young lord she named, long bred
Among the priests, whose art (she said)
Might chance to stand me in much stead.

THE BRIDE'S PRELUDE.

"I bade them seek and summon him:
    But long ere this, the chase
Had scattered, and he was not found.
I lay in the same weary stound,
Therefore, until the night came round.

"It was dead night and near on twelve
    When the horse-tramp at length
Beat up the echoes of the court :
By then, my feverish breath was short
With pain the sense could scarce support.

"My fond nurse sitting near my feet
    Rose softly,—her lamp's flame
Held in her hand, lest it should make
My heated lids, in passing, ache;
And she passed softly, for my sake.

"Returning soon, she brought the youth
    They spoke of.   Meek he seemed,
But good knights held him of stout heart.
He was akin to us in part,
And bore our shield, but barred athwart.

"I now remembered to have seen
    His face, and heard him praised
For letter-lore and medicine,
Seeing his youth was nurtured in
Priests' knowledge, as mine own had been."

The bride's voice did not weaken here,
    Yet by her sudden pause
She seemed to look for questioning;
Or else (small need though) 'twas to bring
Well to her mind the bygone thing.

Her thought, long stagnant, stirred by speech,
    Gave her a sick recoil;
As, dip thy fingers through the green
That masks a pool,— where they have been
The naked depth is black between.

Amelotte kept her knees; her face
    Was shut within her hands,
As it had been throughout the tale;
Her forehead's whiteness might avail
Nothing to say if she were pale.

Although the lattice had dropped loose,
    There was no wind; the heat
Being so at rest that Amelotte
Heard far beneath the plunge and float
Of a hound swimming in the moat.

Some minutes since, two rooks had toiled
    Home to the nests that crowned
Ancestral ash-trees. Through the glare
Beating again, they seemed to tear
With that thick caw the woof o' the air.

But else, 'twas at the dead of noon
    Absolute silence; all,
From the raised bridge and guarded sconce
To green-clad places of pleasaunce
Where the long lake was white with swans.

Amelotte spoke not any word
    Nor moved she once; but felt
Between her hands in narrow space
Her own hot breath upon her face,
And kept in silence the same place.

Aloÿse did not hear at all
    The sounds without.   She heard
The inward voice (past help obey'd)
Which might not slacken nor be stay'd,
But urged her till the whole were said.

Therefore she spoke again : "That night
    But little could be done :
My foot, held in my nurse's hands,
He swathed up heedfully in bands,
And for my rest gave close commands.

" I slept till noon, but an ill sleep
    Of dreams : through all that day
My side was stiff and caught the breath ;
Next day, such pain as sickeneth
Took me, and I was nigh to death.

" Life strove, Death claimed me for his own,
    Through days and nights : but now
'Twas the good father tended me,
Having returned.   Still, I did see
The youth I spoke of constantly.

" For he would with my brothers come
    To stay beside my couch,
And fix my eyes against his own,
Noting my pulse ; or else alone,
To sit at gaze while I made moan.

" (Some nights I knew he kept the watch,
    Because my women laid
The rushes thick for his steel shoes.)
Through many days this pain did use
The life God would not let me lose.

"At length, with my good nurse to aid,
　　I could walk forth again:
And still, as one who broods or grieves,
At noons I'd meet him and at eves,
With idle feet that drove the leaves.

"The day when I first walked alone
　　Was thinned in grass and leaf,
And yet a goodly day o' the year:
The last bird's cry upon mine ear
Left my brain weak, it was so clear.

"The tears were sharp within mine eyes.
　　I sat down, being glad,
And wept; but stayed the sudden flow
Anon, for footsteps that fell slow;
'Twas that youth passed me, bowing low.

"He passed me without speech; but when,
　　At least an hour gone by,
Rethreading the same covert, he
Saw I was still beneath the tree,
He spoke and sat him down with me.

"Little we said; nor one heart heard
　　Even what was said within;
And, faltering some farewell, I soon
Rose up; but then i' the autumn noon
My feeble brain whirled like a swoon.

"He made me sit. 'Cousin, I grieve
　　Your sickness stays by you.'
'I would,' said I, 'that you did err
So grieving. I am wearier
Than death, of the sickening dying year.'

THE BRIDE'S PRELUDE.

"He answered: 'If your weariness
    Accepts a remedy,
I hold one and can give it you.'
I gazed: 'What ministers thereto,
Be sure,' I said, 'that I will do.'

"He went on quickly:—'Twas a cure
    He had not ever named
Unto our kin lest they should stint
Their favour, for some foolish hint
Of wizardry or magic in't:

"But that if he were let to come
    Within my bower that night,
(My women still attending me,
He said, while he remain'd there,) he
Could teach me the cure privily.

"I bade him come that night. He came;
    But little in his speech
Was cure or sickness spoken of,
Only a passionate fierce love
That clamoured upon God above.

"My women wondered, leaning close
    Aloof. At mine own heart
I think great wonder was not stirr'd.
I dared not listen, yet I heard
His tangled speech, word within word.

"He craved my pardon first,—all else
    Wild tumult. In the end
He remained silent at my feet
Fumbling the rushes. Strange quick heat
Made all the blood of my life meet.

"And lo! I loved him. I but said,
    If he would leave me then,
His hope some future might forecast.
His hot lips stung my hand: at last
My damsels led him forth in haste."

The bride took breath to pause; and turned
    Her gaze where Amelotte
Knelt,—the gold hair upon her back
Quite still in all its threads,—the track
Of her still shadow sharp and black.

That listening without sight had grown
    To stealthy dread; and now
That the one sound she had to mark
Left her alone too, she was stark
Afraid, as children in the dark.

Her fingers felt her temples beat;
    Then came that brain-sickness
Which thinks to scream, and murmureth;
And pent between her hands, the breath
Was damp against her face like death.

Her arms both fell at once; but when
    She gasped upon the light,
Her sense returned. She would have pray'd
To change whatever words still stay'd
Behind, but felt there was no aid.

So she rose up, and having gone
    Within the window's arch
Once more, she sat there, all intent
On torturing doubts, and once more bent
To hear, in mute bewilderment.

THE BRIDE'S PRELUDE.

But Aloÿse still paused. Thereon
    Amelotte gathered voice
In somewise from the torpid fear
Coiled round her spirit. Low but clear
She said: "Speak, sister; for I hear."

But Aloÿse threw up her neck
    And called the name of God:—
"Judge, God, 'twixt her and me to-day!
She knows how hard this is to say,
Yet will not have one word away."

Her sister was quite silent. Then
    Afresh:—"Not she, dear Lord!
Thou be my judge, on Thee I call!"
She ceased,—her forehead smote the wall:
"Is there a God," she said, "at all?"

Amelotte shuddered at the soul,
    But did not speak. The pause
Was long this time. At length the bride
Pressed her hand hard against her side,
And trembling between shame and pride

Said by fierce effort: "From that night
    Often at nights we met:
That night, his passion could but rave:
The next, what grace his lips did crave
I knew not, but I know I gave."

Where Amelotte was sitting, all
    The light and warmth of day
Were so upon her without shade
That the thing seemed by sunshine made
Most foul and wanton to be said.

She would have questioned more, and known
    The whole truth at its worst,
But held her silent, in mere shame
Of day. 'Twas only these words came:—
"Sister, thou hast not said his name."

"Sister," quoth Aloÿse, "thou know'st
    His name. I said that he
Was in a manner of our kin.
Waiting the title he might win,
They called him the Lord Urscelyn."

The bridegroom's name, to Amelotte
    Daily familiar,—heard
Thus in this dreadful history,—
Was dreadful to her; as might be
Thine own voice speaking unto thee.

The day's mid-hour was almost full;
    Upon the dial-plate
The angel's sword stood near at One.
An hour's remaining yet; the sun
Will not decrease till all be done.

Through the bride's lattice there crept in
    At whiles (from where the train
Of minstrels, till the marriage-call,
Loitered at windows of the wall,)
Stray lute-notes, sweet and musical.

They clung in the green growths and moss
    Against the outside stone;
Low like dirge-wail or requiem
They murmured, lost 'twixt leaf and stem:
There was no wind to carry them.

THE BRIDE'S PRELUDE.

Amelotte gathered herself back
    Into the wide recess
That the sun flooded : it o'erspread
Like flame the hair upon her head
And fringed her face with burning red.

All things seemed shaken and at change :
    A silent place o' the hills
She knew, into her spirit came :
Within herself she said its name
And wondered was it still the same.

The bride (whom silence goaded) now
    Said strongly,—her despair
By stubborn will kept underneath :—
"Sister, 'twere well thou didst not breathe
That curse of thine.   Give me my wreath."

"Sister," said Amelotte, "abide
    In peace.   Be God thy judge,
As thou hast said—not I.   For me,
I merely will thank God that he
Whom thou hast lovèd loveth thee."

Then Aloÿse lay back, and laughed
    With wan lips bitterly,
Saying, "Nay, thank thou God for this,—
That never any soul like his
Shall have its portion where love is."

Weary of wonder, Amelotte
    Sat silent : she would ask
No more, though all was unexplained :
She was too weak ; the ache still pained
Her eyes,—her forehead's pulse remained.

The silence lengthened. Aloÿse
    Was fain to turn her face
Apart, to where the arras told
Two Testaments, the New and Old,
In shapes and meanings manifold.

One solace that was gained, she hid.
    Her sister, from whose curse
Her heart recoiled, had blessed instead :
Yet would not her pride have it said
How much the blessing comforted.

Only, on looking round again
    After some while, the face
Which from the arras turned away
Was more at peace and less at bay
With shame than it had been that day.

She spoke right on, as if no pause
    Had come between her speech :
"That year from warmth grew bleak and pass'd,"
She said; " the days from first to last
How slow,—woe's me! the nights how fast!

" From first to last it was not known :
    My nurse, and of my train
Some four or five, alone could tell
What terror kept inscrutable :
There was good need to guard it well.

" Not the guilt only made the shame,
    But he was without land
And born amiss. He had but come
To train his youth here at our home,
And, being man, depart therefrom.

"Of the whole time each single day
    Brought fear and great unrest:
It seemed that all would not avail
Some once,—that my close watch would fail,
And some sign, somehow, tell the tale.

"The noble maidens that I knew,
    My fellows, oftentimes
Midway in talk or sport, would look
A wonder which my fears mistook,
To see how I turned faint and shook.

"They had a game of cards, where each
    By painted arms might find
What knight she should be given to.
Ever with trembling hand I threw
Lest I should learn the thing I knew.

"And once it came. And Aure d'Honvaulx
    Held up the bended shield
And laughed: 'Gramercy for our share!—
If to our bridal we but fare
To smutch the blazon that we bear!'

"But proud Denise de Villenbois
    Kissed me, and gave her wench
The card, and said: 'If in these bowers
You women play at paramours,
You must not mix your game with ours.'

"And one upcast it from her hand:
    'Lo! see how high he'll soar!'
But then their laugh was bitterest;
For the wind veered at fate's behest
And blew it back into my breast.

"Oh! if I met him in the day
  Or heard his voice,—at meals
Or at the Mass or through the hall,—
A look turned towards me would appal
My heart by seeming to know all.

"Yet I grew curious of my shame,
  And sometimes in the church,
On hearing such a sin rebuked,
Have held my girdle-glass unhooked
To see how such a woman looked.

"But if at night he did not come,
  I lay all deadly cold
To think they might have smitten sore
And slain him, and as the night wore,
His corpse be lying at my door.

"And entering or going forth,
  Our proud shield o'er the gate
Seemed to arraign my shrinking eyes.
With tremors and unspoken lies
The year went past me in this wise.

"About the spring of the next year
  An ailing fell on me;
(I had been stronger till the spring;)
'Twas mine old sickness gathering,
I thought; but 'twas another thing.

"I had such yearnings as brought tears,
  And a wan dizziness:
Motion, like feeling, grew intense;
Sight was a haunting evidence
And sound a pang that snatched the sense.

THE BRIDE'S PRELUDE.

" It now was hard on that great ill
    Which lost our wealth from us
And all our lands. Accursed be
The peevish fools of liberty
Who will not let themselves be free!

" The Prince was fled into the west:
    A price was on his blood,
But he was safe. To us his friends
He left that ruin which attends
The strife against God's secret ends.

" The league dropped all asunder,—lord,
    Gentle and serf. Our house
Was marked to fall. And a day came
When half the wealth that propped our name
Went from us in a wind of flame.

" Six hours I lay upon the wall
    And saw it burn. But when
It clogged the day in a black bed
Of louring vapour, I was led
Down to the postern, and we fled.

" But ere we fled, there was a voice
    Which I heard speak, and say
That many of our friends, to shun
Our fate, had left us and were gone,
And that Lord Urscelyn was one.

" That name, as was its wont, made sight
    And hearing whirl. I gave
No heed but only to the name:
I held my senses, dreading them,
And was at strife to look the same.

"We rode and rode. As the speed grew,
    The growth of some vague curse
Swarmed in my brain. It seemed to me
Numbed by the swiftness, but would be—
That still—clear knowledge certainly.

"Night lapsed. At dawn the sea was there
    And the sea-wind : afar
The ravening surge was hoarse and loud
And underneath the dim dawn-cloud
Each stalking wave shook like a shroud.

"From my drawn litter I looked out
    Unto the swarthy sea,
And knew. That voice, which late had cross'd
Mine ears, seemed with the foam uptoss'd :
I knew that Urscelyn was lost.

"Then I spake all : I turned on one
    And on the other, and spake :
My curse laughed in me to behold
Their eyes : I sat up, stricken cold,
Mad of my voice till all was told.

"Oh ! of my brothers, Hugues was mute,
    And Gilles was wild and loud,
And Raoul strained abroad his face,
As if his gnashing wrath could trace
Even there the prey that it must chase.

"And round me murmured all our train,
    Hoarse as the hoarse-tongued sea ;
Till Hugues from silence louring woke,
And cried : 'What ails the foolish folk ?
Know ye not frenzy's lightning-stroke ?'

"But my stern father came to them
    And quelled them with his look,
Silent and deadly pale. Anon
I knew that we were hastening on,
My litter closed and the light gone.

"And I remember all that day
    The barren bitter wind
Without, and the sea's moaning there
That I first moaned with unaware,
And when I knew, shook down my hair.

"Few followed us or faced our flight:
    Once only I could hear,
Far in the front, loud scornful words,
And cries I knew of hostile lords,
And crash of spears and grind of swords.

"It was soon ended. On that day
    Before the light had changed
We reached our refuge; miles of rock
Bulwarked for war; whose strength might mock
Sky, sea, or man, to storm or shock.

"Listless and feebly conscious, I
    Lay far within the night
Awake. The many pains incurred
That day,—the whole, said, seen or heard,—
Stayed by in me as things deferred.

"Not long. At dawn I slept. In dreams
    All was passed through afresh
From end to end. As the morn heaved
Towards noon, I, waking sore aggrieved,
That I might die, cursed God, and lived.

"Many days went, and I saw none
    Except my women. They
Calmed their wan faces, loving me;
And when they wept, lest I should see,
Would chaunt a desolate melody.

"Panic unthreatened shook my blood
    Each sunset, all the slow
Subsiding of the turbid light.
I would rise, sister, as I might,
And bathe my forehead through the night

"To elude madness. The stark walls
    Made chill the mirk : and when
We oped our curtains, to resume
Sun-sickness after long sick gloom,
The withering sea-wind walked the room.

"Through the gaunt windows the great gales
    Bore in the tattered clumps
Of waif-weed and the tamarisk-boughs;
And sea-mews, 'mid the storm's carouse,
Were flung, wild-clamouring, in the house.

"My hounds I had not; and my hawk,
    Which they had saved for me,
Wanting the sun and rain to beat
His wings, soon lay with gathered feet;
And my flowers faded, lacking heat.

"Such still were griefs : for grief was still
    A separate sense, untouched
Of that despair which had become
My life. Great anguish could benumb
My soul,—my heart was quarrelsome.

"Time crept. Upon a day at length
    My kinsfolk sat with me:
That which they asked was bare and plain:
I answered: the whole bitter strain
Was again said, and heard again.

"Fierce Raoul snatched his sword, and turned
    The point against my breast.
I bared it, smiling: 'To the heart
Strike home,' I said; 'another dart
Wreaks hourly there a deadlier smart.'

"'Twas then my sire struck down the sword,
    And said with shaken lips:
'She from whom all of you receive
Your life, so smiled; and I forgive.'
Thus, for my mother's sake, I live.

"But I, a mother even as she,
    Turned shuddering to the wall:
For I said: 'Great God! and what would I do,
When to the sword, with the thing I knew,
I offered not one life but two!'

"Then I fell back from them, and lay
    Outwearied. My tired sense
Soon filmed and settled, and like stone
I slept; till something made me moan,
And I woke up at night alone.

"I woke at midnight, cold and dazed;
    Because I found myself
Seated upright, with bosom bare,
Upon my bed, combing my hair,
Ready to go, I knew not where.

"It dawned light day,—the last of those
    Long months of longing days.
That noon, the change was wrought on me
In somewise,—nought to hear or see,—
Only a trance and agony."

The bride's voice failed her, from no will
    To pause. The bridesmaid leaned,
And where the window-panes were white,
Looked for the day: she knew not quite
If there were either day or night.

It seemed to Aloÿse that the whole
    Day's weight lay back on her
Like lead. The hours that did remain
Beat their dry wings upon her brain
Once in mid-flight, and passed again.

There hung a cage of burnt perfumes
    In the recess: but these,
For some hours, weak against the sun,
Had simmered in white ash. From One
The second quarter was begun.

They had not heard the stroke. The air,
    Though altered with no wind,
Breathed now by pauses, so to say:
Each breath was time that went away,—
Each pause a minute of the day.

I' the almonry, the almoner,
    Hard by, had just dispensed
Church-dole and march-dole. High and wide
Now rose the shout of thanks, which cried
On God that He should bless the bride.

Its echo thrilled within their feet,
    And in the furthest rooms
Was heard, where maidens flushed and gay
Wove with stooped necks the wreaths alway
Fair for the virgin's marriage-day.

The mother leaned along, in thought
    After her child; till tears,
Bitter, not like a wedded girl's,
Fell down her breast along her curls,
And ran in the close work of pearls.

The speech ached at her heart. She said:
    "Sweet Mary, do thou plead
This hour with thy most blessed Son
To let these shameful words atone,
That I may die when I have done."

The thought ached at her soul. Yet now:—
    "Itself—that life" (she said,)
"Out of my weary life—when sense
Unclosed, was gone. What evil men's
Most evil hands had borne it thence

"I knew, and cursed them. Still in sleep
    I have my child; and pray
To know if it indeed appear
As in my dream's perpetual sphere,
That I—death reached—may seek it there.

"Sleeping, I wept; though until dark
    A fever dried mine eyes
Kept open; save when a tear might
Be forced from the mere ache of sight.
And I nursed hatred day and night.

"Aye, and I sought revenge by spells;
    And vainly many a time
Have laid my face into the lap
Of a wise woman, and heard clap
Her thunder, the fiend's juggling trap.

"At length I feared to curse them, lest
    From evil lips the curse
Should be a blessing; and would sit
Rocking myself and stifling it
With babbled jargon of no wit.

"But this was not at first: the days
    And weeks made frenzied months
Before this came. My curses, pil'd
Then with each hour unreconcil'd,
Still wait for those who took my child."

She stopped, grown fainter. "Amelotte,
    Surely," she said, "this sun
Sheds judgment-fire from the fierce south:
It does not let me breathe: the drouth
Is like sand spread within my mouth."

The bridesmaid rose. I' the outer glare
    Gleamed her pale cheeks, and eyes
Sore troubled; and aweary weigh'd
Her brows just lifted out of shade;
And the light jarred within her head.

'Mid flowers fair-heaped there stood a bowl
    With water. She therein
Through eddying bubbles slid a cup,
And offered it, being risen up,
Close to her sister's mouth, to sup.

The freshness dwelt upon her sense,
    Yet did not the bride drink;
But she dipped in her hand anon
And cooled her temples; and all wan
With lids that held their ache, went on.

"Through those dark watches of my woe,
    Time, an ill plant, had waxed
Apace. That year was finished. Dumb
And blind, life's wheel with earth's had come
Whirled round: and we might seek our home.

'Our wealth was rendered back, with wealth
    Snatched from our foes. The house
Had more than its old strength and fame:
But still 'neath the fair outward claim
I rankled,—a fierce core of shame.

"It chilled me from their eyes and lips
    Upon a night of those
First days of triumph, as I gazed
Listless and sick, or scarcely raised
My face to mark the sports they praised.

"The endless changes of the dance
    Bewildered me: the tones
Of lute and cithern struggled tow'rds
Some sense; and still in the last chords
The music seemed to sing wild words.

"My shame possessed me in the light
    And pageant, till I swooned.
But from that hour I put my shame
From me, and cast it over them
By God's command and in God's name

"For my child's bitter sake. O thou
    Once felt against my heart
With longing of the eyes,—a pain
Since to my heart for ever,—then
Beheld not, and not felt again!"

She scarcely paused, continuing:—
    "That year drooped weak in March;
And April, finding the streams dry,
Choked, with no rain, in dust: the sky
Shall not be fainter this July.

"Men sickened; beasts lay without strength,
    The year died in the land.
But I, already desolate,
Said merely, sitting down to wait,—
'The seasons change and Time wears late.'

"For I had my hard secret told,
    In secret, to a priest;
With him I communed; and he said
The world's soul, for its sins, was sped,
And the sun's courses numberèd.

"The year slid like a corpse afloat:
    None trafficked,—who had bread
Did eat. That year our legions, come
Thinned from the place of war, at home
Found busier death, more burdensome.

"Tidings and rumours came with them,
    The first for months. The chiefs
Sat daily at our board, and in
Their speech were names of friend and kin:
One day they spoke of Urscelyn.

THE BRIDE'S PRELUDE.

" The words were light, among the rest:
    Quick glance my brothers sent
To sift the speech ; and I, struck through,
Sat sick and giddy in full view :
Yet did none gaze, so many knew.

" Because in the beginning, much
    Had caught abroad, through them
That heard my clamour on the coast :
But two were hanged ; and then the most
Held silence wisdom, as thou know'st.

" That year the convent yielded thee
    Back to our home ; and thou
Then knew'st not how I shuddered cold
To kiss thee, seeming to enfold
To my changed heart myself of old.

" Then there was showing thee the house,
    So many rooms and doors ;
Thinking the while how thou would'st start
If once I flung the doors apart
Of one dull chamber in my heart.

" And yet I longed to open it ;
    And often in that year
Of plague and want, when side by side
We've knelt to pray with them that died,
My prayer was, ' Show her what I hide ! ' "

END OF PART I.

SISTER HELEN.

"Why did you melt your waxen man,
    Sister Helen?
To-day is the third since you began."
"The time was long, yet the time ran,
    Little brother."
   (*O Mother, Mary Mother,*
Three days to-day, between Hell and Heaven!)

"But if you have done your work aright,
    Sister Helen,
You'll let me play, for you said I might."
"Be very still in your play to-night,
    Little brother."
   (*O Mother, Mary Mother,*
Third night, to-night, between Hell and Heaven!)

"You said it must melt ere vesper-bell,
    Sister Helen;
If now it be molten, all is well."
"Even so,—nay, peace! you cannot tell,
    Little brother."
   (*O Mother, Mary Mother,*
O what is this, between Hell and Heaven?)

"Oh the waxen knave was plump to-day,
    Sister Helen;
How like dead folk he has dropped away!"
"Nay now, of the dead what can you say,
    Little brother?"
   (*O Mother, Mary Mother,*
What of the dead, between Hell and Heaven?)

"See, see, the sunken pile of wood,
                    Sister Helen,
Shines through the thinned wax red as blood!"
"Nay now, when looked you yet on blood,
                    Little brother?"
            (O Mother, Mary Mother,
How pale she is, between Hell and Heaven!)

"Now close your eyes, for they're sick and sore,
                    Sister Helen,
And I'll play without the gallery door."
"Aye, let me rest,—I'll lie on the floor,
                    Little brother."
            (O Mother, Mary Mother,
What rest to-night, between Hell and Heaven?)

"Here high up in the balcony,
                    Sister Helen,
The moon flies face to face with me."
"Aye, look and say whatever you see,
                    Little brother."
            (O Mother, Mary Mother,
What sight to-night, between Hell and Heaven?)

"Outside it's merry in the wind's wake,
                    Sister Helen;
In the shaken trees the chill stars shake."
"Hush, heard you a horse-tread as you spake,
                    Little brother?"
            (O Mother, Mary Mother,
What sound to-night, between Hell and Heaven?)

"I hear a horse-tread, and I see,
                    Sister Helen,
Three horsemen that ride terribly."
"Little brother, whence come the three,
                    Little brother?"
            (O Mother, Mary Mother,
Whence should they come, between Hell and Heaven?)

"They come by the hill-verge from Boyne Bar,
    Sister Helen,
And one draws nigh, but two are afar."
"Look, look, do you know them who they are,
    Little brother?"
   (O Mother, Mary Mother,
Who should they be, between Hell and Heaven?)

"Oh, it's Keith of Eastholm rides so fast,
    Sister Helen,
For I know the white mane on the blast."
"The hour has come, has come at last,
    Little brother!"
   (O Mother, Mary Mother,
Her hour at last, between Hell and Heaven!)

"He has made a sign and called Halloo!
    Sister Helen,
And he says that he would speak with you."
"Oh tell him I fear the frozen dew,
    Little brother."
   (O Mother, Mary Mother,
Why laughs she thus, between Hell and Heaven?)

"The wind is loud, but I hear him cry,
    Sister Helen,
That Keith of Ewern's like to die."
"And he and thou, and thou and I,
    Little brother."
   (O Mother, Mary Mother,
And they and we, between Hell and Heaven!)

"Three days ago, on his marriage-morn,
    Sister Helen,
He sickened, and lies since then forlorn."
"For bridegroom's side is the bride a thorn,
    Little brother?"
   (O Mother, Mary Mother,
Cold bridal cheer, between Hell and Heaven!)

"Three days and nights he has lain abed,
    Sister Helen,
And he prays in torment to be dead."
"The thing may chance, if he have prayed,
    Little brother!"
   (O Mother, Mary Mother,
If he have prayed, between Hell and Heaven!)

"But he has not ceased to cry to-day,
    Sister Helen,
That you should take your curse away."
"*My* prayer was heard,—he need but pray,
    Little brother!"
   (O Mother, Mary Mother,
Shall God not hear, between Hell and Heaven?)

"But he says, till you take back your ban,
    Sister Helen,
His soul would pass, yet never can."
"Nay then, shall I slay a living man,
    Little brother?"
   (O Mother, Mary Mother,
A living soul, between Hell and Heaven!)

"But he calls for ever on your name,
    Sister Helen,
And says that he melts before a flame."
"My heart for his pleasure fared the same,
    Little brother."
   (O Mother, Mary Mother,
Fire at the heart, between Hell and Heaven!)

"Here's Keith of Westholm riding fast,
    Sister Helen,
For I know the white plume on the blast."
"The hour, the sweet hour I forecast,
    Little brother!"
   (O Mother, Mary Mother,
Is the hour sweet, between Hell and Heaven?)

"He stops to speak, and he stills his horse,
    Sister Helen;
But his words are drowned in the wind's course."
"Nay hear, nay hear, you must hear perforce,
    Little brother!"
   (O Mother, Mary Mother,
What word now heard, between Hell and Heaven?)

"Oh he says that Keith of Ewern's cry,
    Sister Helen,
Is ever to see you ere he die."
"In all that his soul sees, there am I,
    Little brother!"
   (O Mother, Mary Mother,
The soul's one sight, between Hell and Heaven!)

"He sends a ring and a broken coin,
    Sister Helen,
And bids you mind the banks of Boyne."
"What else he broke will he ever join,
    Little brother?"
   (O Mother, Mary Mother,
No, never joined, between Hell and Heaven!)

"He yields you these and craves full fain,
    Sister Helen,
You pardon him in his mortal pain."
"What else he took will he give again,
    Little brother?"
   (O Mother, Mary Mother,
Not twice to give, between Hell and Heaven!)

"He calls your name in an agony,
    Sister Helen,
That even dead Love must weep to see."
"Hate, born of Love, is blind as he,
    Little brother!"
   (O Mother, Mary Mother,
Love turned to hate, between Hell and Heaven!)

SISTER HELEN.

"Oh it's Keith of Keith now that rides fast,
                    Sister Helen,
For I know the white hair on the blast."
"The short short hour will soon be past,
                    Little brother!"
          (O Mother, Mary Mother,
Will soon be past, between Hell and Heaven!)

"He looks at me and he tries to speak,
                    Sister Helen,
But oh! his voice is sad and weak!"
"What here should the mighty Baron seek,
                    Little brother?"
          (O Mother, Mary Mother,
Is this the end, between Hell and Heaven?)

"Oh his son still cries, if you forgive,
                    Sister Helen,
The body dies but the soul shall live."
"Fire shall forgive me as I forgive,
                    Little brother!"
          (O Mother, Mary Mother,
As she forgives, between Hell and Heaven!)

"Oh he prays you, as his heart would rive,
                    Sister Helen,
To save his dear son's soul alive."
"Fire cannot slay it, it shall thrive,
                    Little brother!"
          (O Mother, Mary Mother,
Alas, alas, between Hell and Heaven!)

"He cries to you, kneeling in the road,
                    Sister Helen,
To go with him for the love of God!"
"The way is long to his son's abode,
                    Little brother."
          (O Mother, Mary Mother,
The way is long, between Hell and Heaven!)

SISTER HELEN.

"A lady's here, by a dark steed brought,
    Sister Helen,
So darkly clad, I saw her not."
"See her now or never see aught,
    Little brother!"
   (O Mother, Mary Mother,
What more to see, between Hell and Heaven?)

"Her hood falls back, and the moon shines fair,
    Sister Helen,
On the Lady of Ewern's golden hair."
"Blest hour of my power and her despair,
    Little brother!"
   (O Mother, Mary Mother,
Hour blest and bann'd, between Hell and Heaven!)

"Pale, pale her cheeks, that in pride did glow,
    Sister Helen,
'Neath the bridal-wreath three days ago."
"One morn for pride and three days for woe,
    Little brother!"
   (O Mother, Mary Mother,
Three days, three nights, between Hell and Heaven!)

"Her clasped hands stretch from her bending head,
    Sister Helen;
With the loud wind's wail her sobs are wed."
"What wedding-strains hath her bridal-bed,
    Little brother?"
   (O Mother, Mary Mother,
What strain but death's, between Hell and Heaven!)

"She may not speak, she sinks in a swoon,
    Sister Helen,—
She lifts her lips and gasps on the moon."
"Oh! might I but hear her soul's blithe tune,
    Little brother!"
   (O Mother, Mary Mother,
Her woe's dumb cry, between Hell and Heaven!)

SISTER HELEN.

"They've caught her to Westholm's saddle-bow,
    Sister Helen,
And her moonlit hair gleams white in its flow."
"Let it turn whiter than winter snow,
    Little brother!"
    (O Mother, Mary Mother,
Woe-withered gold, between Hell and Heaven!)

"O Sister Helen, you heard the bell,
    Sister Helen!
More loud than the vesper-chime it fell."
"No vesper-chime, but a dying knell,
    Little brother!"
    (O Mother, Mary Mother,
His dying knell, between Hell and Heaven!)

"Alas! but I fear the heavy sound,
    Sister Helen;
Is it in the sky or in the ground?"
"Say, have they turned their horses round,
    Little brother?"
    (O Mother, Mary Mother,
What would she more, between Hell and Heaven?)

"They have raised the old man from his knee,
    Sister Helen,
And they ride in silence hastily."
"More fast the naked soul doth flee,
    Little brother!"
    (O Mother, Mary Mother,
The naked soul, between Hell and Heaven!)

"Flank to flank are the three steeds gone,
    Sister Helen,
But the lady's dark steed goes alone."
"And lonely her bridegroom's soul hath flown,
    Little brother."
    (O Mother, Mary Mother,
The lonely ghost, between Hell and Heaven!)

"Oh the wind is sad in the iron chill,
     Sister Helen,
And weary sad they look by the hill."
"But he and I are sadder still,
     Little brother!"
   (*O Mother, Mary Mother,*
Most sad of all, between Hell and Heaven!)

"See, see, the wax has dropped from its place,
     Sister Helen,
And the flames are winning up apace!"
"Yet here they burn but for a space,
     Little brother!"
   (*O Mother, Mary Mother,*
Here for a space, between Hell and Heaven!)

"Ah! what white thing at the door has cross'd,
     Sister Helen?
Ah! what is this that sighs in the frost?"
"A soul that's lost as mine is lost,
     Little brother!"
   (*O Mother, Mary Mother,*
Lost, lost, all lost, between Hell and Heaven!)

THE STAFF AND SCRIP.

"Who rules these lands?" the Pilgrim said.
  "Stranger, Queen Blanchelys."
"And who has thus harried them?" he said.
  "It was Duke Luke did this:
    God's ban be his!"

The Pilgrim said: "Where is your house?
  I'll rest there, with your will."
"You've but to climb these blackened boughs
  And you'll see it over the hill,
    For it burns still."

"Which road, to seek your Queen?" said he.
  "Nay, nay, but with some wound
You'll fly back hither, it may be,
  And by your blood i' the ground
    My place be found."

"Friend, stay in peace. God keep your head,
  And mine, where I will go;
For He is here and there," he said.
  He passed the hill-side, slow,
    And stood below.

The Queen sat idle by her loom:
  She heard the arras stir,
And looked up sadly: through the room
  The sweetness sickened her
    Of musk and myrrh.

Her women, standing two and two,
  In silence combed the fleece.
The Pilgrim said, "Peace be with you,
  Lady;" and bent his knees.
    She answered, "Peace."

Her eyes were like the wave within;
  Like water-reeds the poise
Of her soft body, dainty thin;
  And like the water's noise
    Her plaintive voice.

For him, the stream had never well'd
  In desert tracts, malign
So sweet; nor had he ever felt
  So faint in the sunshine
    Of Palestine.

Right so, he knew that he saw weep
  Each night through every dream
The Queen's own face, confused in sleep
  With visages supreme
    Not known to him.

"Lady," he said, "your lands lie burnt
  And waste: to meet your foe
All fear: this I have seen and learnt.
  Say that it shall be so,
    And I will go."

She gazed at him. "Your cause is just,
  For I have heard the same,"
He said: "God's strength shall be my trust.
  Fall it to good or grame,
    'Tis in His name."

THE STAFF AND SCRIP.

"Sir, you are thanked. My cause is dead.
  Why should you toil to break
A grave, and fall therein?" she said.
  He did not pause but spake:
    "For my vow's sake."

"Can such vows be, Sir—to God's ear,
  Not to God's will?" "My vow
Remains: God heard me there as here,"
  He said with reverent brow,
    "Both then and now."

They gazed together, he and she,
  The minute while he spoke;
And when he ceased, she suddenly
  Looked round upon her folk
    As though she woke.

"Fight, Sir," she said; "my prayers in pain
  Shall be your fellowship."
He whispered one among her train,—
  "To-morrow bid her keep
    This staff and scrip."

She sent him a sharp sword, whose belt
  About his body there
As sweet as her own arms he felt.
  He kissed its blade, all bare,
    Instead of her.

She sent him a green banner wrought
  With one white lily stem,
To bind his lance with when he fought.
  He writ upon the same
    And kissed her name.

She sent him a white shield, whereon
   She bade that he should trace
His will. He blent fair hues that shone,
   And in a golden space
     He kissed her face.

Born of the day that died, that eve
   Now dying sank to rest;
As he, in likewise taking leave,
   Once with a heaving breast
     Looked to the west.

And there the sunset skies unseal'd,
   Like lands he never knew,
Beyond to-morrow's battle-field
   Lay open out of view
     To ride into.

Next day till dark the women pray'd:
   Nor any might know there
How the fight went: the Queen has bade
   That there do come to her
     No messenger.

The Queen is pale, her maidens ail;
   And to the organ-tones
They sing but faintly, who sang well
   The matin-orisons,
     The lauds and nones.

Lo, Father, is thine ear inclin'd,
   And hath thine angel pass'd?
For these thy watchers now are blind
   With vigil, and at last
     Dizzy with fast.

THE STAFF AND SCRIP.

Weak now to them the voice o' the priest
   As any trance affords;
And when each anthem failed and ceas'd,
   It seemed that the last chords
     Still sang the words.

" Oh what is the light that shines so red?
   'Tis long since the sun set;"
Quoth the youngest to the eldest maid:
   " 'Twas dim but now, and yet
     The light is great."

Quoth the other: " 'Tis our sight is dazed
   That we see flame i' the air."
But the Queen held her brows and gazed,
   And said, " It is the glare
     Of torches there."

"Oh what are the sounds that rise and spread?
   All day it was so still;"
Quoth the youngest to the eldest maid:
   " Unto the furthest hill
     The air they fill."

Quoth the other: " 'Tis our sense is blurr'd
   With all the chants gone by."
But the Queen held her breath and heard,
   And said, " It is the cry
     Of Victory."

The first of all the rout was sound,
   The next were dust and flame,
And then the horses shook the ground:
   And in the thick of them
     A still band came.

"Oh what do ye bring out of the fight,
  Thus hid beneath these boughs?"
"Thy conquering guest returns to-night,
  And yet shall not carouse,
    Queen, in thy house."

"Uncover ye his face," she said.
  "O changed in little space!"
She cried, "O pale that was so red!
  O God, O God of grace!
    Cover his face."

His sword was broken in his hand
  Where he had kissed the blade.
"O soft steel that could not withstand!
  O my hard heart unstayed,
    That prayed and prayed!"

His bloodied banner crossed his mouth
  Where he had kissed her name.
"O east, and west, and north, and south,
  Fair flew my web, for shame,
    To guide Death's aim!"

The tints were shredded from his shield
  Where he had kissed her face.
"Oh, of all gifts that I could yield,
  Death only keeps its place,
    My gift and grace!"

Then stepped a damsel to her side,
  And spoke, and needs must weep:
"For his sake, lady, if he died,
  He prayed of thee to keep
    This staff and scrip."

THE STAFF AND SCRIP. 81

That night they hung above her bed,
  Till morning wet with tears.
Year after year above her head
  Her bed his token wears,
    Five years, ten years.

That night the passion of her grief
  Shook them as there they hung.
Each year the wind that shed the leaf
  Shook them and in its tongue
    A message flung.

And once she woke with a clear mind
  That letters writ to calm
Her soul lay in the scrip; to find
  Only a torpid balm
    And dust of palm.

They shook far off with palace sport
  When joust and dance were rife;
And the hunt shook them from the court;
  For hers, in peace or strife,
    Was a Queen's life.

A Queen's death now: as now they shake
  To gusts in chapel dim,—
Hung where she sleeps, not seen to wake,
  (Carved lovely white and slim),
    With them by him.

Stand up to-day, still armed, with her,
  Good knight, before His brow
Who then as now was here and there,
  Who had in mind thy vow
    Then even as now.

The lists are set in Heaven to-day,
 The bright pavilions shine;
Fair hangs thy shield, and none gainsay
 The trumpets sound in sign
  That she is thine.

Not tithed with days' and years' decease
 He pays thy wage He owed,
But with imperishable peace
 Here in His own abode,
  Thy jealous God.

JENNY.

*Vengeance of Jenny's case!   Fie on her!   Never name
    her, child!*—(Mrs. Quickly.)

  LAZY laughing languid Jenny,
Fond of a kiss and fond of a guinea,
Whose head upon my knee to-night
Rests for a while, as if grown light
With all our dances and the sound
To which the wild tunes spun you round :
Fair Jenny mine, the thoughtless queen
Of kisses which the blush between
Could hardly make much daintier ;
Whose eyes are as blue skies, whose hair
Is countless gold incomparable :
Fresh flower, scarce touched with signs that tell
Of Love's exuberant hotbed :—Nay,
Poor flower left torn since yesterday
Until to-morrow leave you bare ;
Poor handful of bright spring-water
Flung in the whirlpool's shrieking face ;
Poor shameful Jenny, full of grace
Thus with your head upon my knee ;—
Whose person or whose purse may be
The lodestar of your reverie ?

  This room of yours, my Jenny, looks
A change from mine so full of books,
Whose serried ranks hold fast, forsooth,
So many captive hours of youth,—

The hours they thieve from day and night
To make one's cherished work come right,
And leave it wrong for all their theft,
Even as to-night my work was left:
Until I vowed that since my brain
And eyes of dancing seemed so fain,
My feet should have some dancing too:—
And thus it was I met with you.
Well, I suppose 'twas hard to part,
For here I am. And now, sweetheart,
You seem too tired to get to bed.

It was a careless life I led
When rooms like this were scarce so strange
Not long ago. What breeds the change,—
The many aims or the few years?
Because to-night it all appears
Something I do not know again.

The cloud's not danced out of my brain,—
The cloud that made it turn and swim
While hour by hour the books grew dim.
Why, Jenny, as I watch you there,—
For all your wealth of loosened hair,
Your silk ungirdled and unlac'd
And warm sweets open to the waist,
All golden in the lamplight's gleam,—
You know not what a book you seem,
Half-read by lightning in a dream!
How should you know, my Jenny? Nay,
And I should be ashamed to say:—
Poor beauty, so well worth a kiss!
But while my thought runs on like this
With wasteful whims more than enough,
I wonder what you're thinking of.

If of myself you think at all,
What is the thought?—conjectural

On sorry matters best unsolved?—
Or inly is each grace revolved
To fit me with a lure?—or (sad
To think!) perhaps you're merely glad
That I'm not drunk or ruffianly
And let you rest upon my knee.

For sometimes, were the truth confess'd,
You're thankful for a little rest,—
Glad from the crush to rest within,
From the heart-sickness and the din
Where envy's voice at virtue's pitch
Mocks you because your gown is rich;
And from the pale girl's dumb rebuke,
Whose ill-clad grace and toil-worn look
Proclaim the strength that keeps her weak,
And other nights than yours bespeak;
And from the wise unchildish elf,
To schoolmate lesser than himself
Pointing you out, what thing you are:—
Yes, from the daily jeer and jar,
From shame and shame's outbraving too,
Is rest not sometimes sweet to you?—
But most from the hatefulness of man,
Who spares not to end what he began,
Whose acts are ill and his speech ill,
Who, having used you at his will,
Thrusts you aside, as when I dine
I serve the dishes and the wine.

Well, handsome Jenny mine, sit up:
I've filled our glasses, let us sup,
And do not let me think of you,
Lest shame of yours suffice for two.
What, still so tired? Well, well then, keep
Your head there, so you do not sleep;
But that the weariness may pass
And leave you merry, take this glass.

Ah! lazy lily hand, more bless'd
If ne'er in rings it had been dress'd
Nor ever by a glove conceal'd!

Behold the lilies of the field,
They toil not neither do they spin;
(So doth the ancient text begin,—
Not of such rest as one of these
Can share.) Another rest and ease
Along each summer-sated path
From its new lord the garden hath,
Than that whose spring in blessings ran
Which praised the bounteous husbandman,
Ere yet, in days of hankering breath,
The lilies sickened unto death.

What, Jenny, are your lilies dead?
Aye, and the snow-white leaves are spread
Like winter on the garden-bed.
But you had roses left in May,—
They were not gone too. Jenny, nay,
But must your roses die, and those
Their purfled buds that should unclose?
Even so; the leaves are curled apart,
Still red as from the broken heart,
And here's the naked stem of thorns.

Nay, nay, mere words. Here nothing warns
As yet of winter. Sickness here
Or want alone could waken fear,—
Nothing but passion wrings a tear.
Except when there may rise unsought
Haply at times a passing thought
Of the old days which seem to be
Much older than any history
That is written in any book;
When she would lie in fields and look
Along the ground through the blown grass,
And wonder where the city was,

Far out of sight, whose broil and bale
They told her then for a child's tale.

  Jenny, you know the city now.
A child can tell the tale there, how
Some things which are not yet enroll'd
In market-lists are bought and sold
Even till the early Sunday light,
When Saturday night is market-night
Everywhere, be it dry or wet,
And market-night in the Haymarket.
Our learned London children know,
Poor Jenny, all your pride and woe;
Have seen your lifted silken skirt
Advertise dainties through the dirt;
Have seen your coach-wheels splash rebuke
On virtue; and have learned your look
When, wealth and health slipped past, you stare
Along the streets alone, and there,
Round the long park, across the bridge,
The cold lamps at the pavement's edge
Wind on together and apart,
A fiery serpent for your heart.

  Let the thoughts pass, an empty cloud!
Suppose I were to think aloud,—
What if to her all this were said?
Why, as a volume seldom read
Being opened halfway shuts again,
So might the pages of her brain
Be parted at such words, and thence
Close back upon the dusty sense.
For is there hue or shape defin'd
In Jenny's desecrated mind,
Where all contagious currents meet,
A Lethe of the middle street?
Nay, it reflects not any face,
Nor sound is in its sluggish pace,

But as they coil those eddies clot,
And night and day remember not.

Why, Jenny, you're asleep at last!—
Asleep, poor Jenny, hard and fast,—
So young and soft and tired; so fair,
With chin thus nestled in your hair,
Mouth quiet, eyelids almost blue
As if some sky of dreams shone through!

Just as another woman sleeps!
Enough to throw one's thoughts in heaps
Of doubt and horror,—what to say
Or think,—this awful secret sway,
The potter's power over the clay!
Of the same lump (it has been said)
For honour and dishonour made,
Two sister vessels. Here is one.

My cousin Nell is fond of fun,
And fond of dress, and change, and praise,
So mere a woman in her ways:
And if her sweet eyes rich in youth
Are like her lips that tell the truth,
My cousin Nell is fond of love.
And she's the girl I'm proudest of.
Who does not prize her, guard her well?
The love of change, in cousin Nell,
Shall find the best and hold it dear:
The unconquered mirth turn quieter
Not through her own, through others' woe:
The conscious pride of beauty glow
Beside another's pride in her,
One little part of all they share.
For Love himself shall ripen these
In a kind soil to just increase
Through years of fertilizing peace.

JENNY.

Of the same lump (as it is said)
For honour and dishonour made,
Two sister vessels.   Here is one.

It makes a goblin of the sun.

So pure,—so fall'n !   How dare to think
Of the first common kindred link ?
Yet, Jenny, till the world shall burn
It seems that all things take their turn ;
And who shall say but this fair tree
May need, in changes that may be,
Your children's children's charity ?
Scorned then, no doubt, as you are scorn'd !
Shall no man hold his pride forewarn'd
Till in the end, the Day of Days,
At Judgment, one of his own race,
As frail and lost as you, shall rise,—
His daughter, with his mother's eyes ?

How Jenny's clock ticks on the shelf !
Might not the dial scorn itself
That has such hours to register ?
Yet as to me, even so to her
Are golden sun and silver moon,
In daily largesse of earth's boon,
Counted for life-coins to one tune.
And if, as blindfold fates are toss'd,
Through some one man this life be lost,
Shall soul not somehow pay for soul ?

Fair shines the gilded aureole
In which our highest painters place
Some living woman's simple face.
And the stilled features thus descried
As Jenny's long throat droops aside,—
The shadows where the cheeks are thin,
And pure wide curve from ear to chin,—

With Raffael's, Leonardo's hand
To show them to men's souls, might stand,
Whole ages long, the whole world through,
For preachings of what God can do.
What has man done here? How atone,
Great God, for this which man has done?
And for the body and soul which by
Man's pitiless doom must now comply
With lifelong hell, what lullaby
Of sweet forgetful second birth
Remains? All dark. No sign on earth
What measure of God's rest endows
The many mansions of his house.

If but a woman's heart might see
Such erring heart unerringly
For once! But that can never be.

Like a rose shut in a book
In which pure women may not look,
For its base pages claim control
To crush the flower within the soul;
Where through each dead rose-leaf that clings,
Pale as transparent Psyche-wings,
To the vile text, are traced such things
As might make lady's cheek indeed
More than a living rose to read;
So nought save foolish foulness may
Watch with hard eyes the sure decay;
And so the life-blood of this rose,
Puddled with shameful knowledge, flows
Through leaves no chaste hand may unclose:
Yet still it keeps such faded show
Of when 'twas gathered long ago,
That the crushed petals' lovely grain,
The sweetness of the sanguine stain,
Seen of a woman's eyes, must make
Her pitiful heart, so prone to ache,

Love roses better for its sake :—
Only that this can never be :—
Even so unto her sex is she.

   Yet, Jenny, looking long at you,
The woman almost fades from view.
A cipher of man's changeless sum
Of lust, past, present, and to come,
Is left.   A riddle that one shrinks
To challenge from the scornful sphinx.

   Like a toad within a stone
Seated while Time crumbles on ;
Which sits there since the earth was curs'd
For Man's transgression at the first ;
Which, living through all centuries,
Not once has seen the sun arise ;
Whose life, to its cold circle charmed,
The earth's whole summers have not warmed ;
Which always—whitherso the stone
Be flung—sits there, deaf, blind, alone ;—
Aye, and shall not be driven out
Till that which shuts him round about
Break at the very Master's stroke,
And the dust thereof vanish as smoke,
And the seed of Man vanish as dust :—
Even so within this world is Lust.

   Come, come, what use in thoughts like this ?
Poor little Jenny, good to kiss,—
You'd not believe by what strange roads
Thought travels, when your beauty goads
A man to-night to think of toads !
Jenny, wake up . . . . Why, there's the dawn !

   And there's an early waggon drawn
To market, and some sheep that jog
Bleating before a barking dog ;
And the old streets come peering through

Another night that London knew;
And all as ghostlike as the lamps.

So on the wings of day decamps
My last night's frolic.   Glooms begin
To shiver off as lights creep in
Past the gauze curtains half drawn-to,
And the lamp's doubled shade grows blue,—
Your lamp, my Jenny, kept alight,
Like a wise virgin's, all one night!
And in the alcove coolly spread
Glimmers with dawn your empty bed;
And yonder your fair face I see
Reflected lying on my knee,
Where teems with first foreshadowings
Your pier-glass scrawled with diamond rings:
And on your bosom all night worn
Yesterday's rose now droops forlorn,
But dies not yet this summer morn.

And now without, as if some word
Had called upon them that they heard,
The London sparrows far and nigh
Clamour together suddenly;
And Jenny's cage-bird grown awake
Here in their song his part must take,
Because here too the day doth break.

And somehow in myself the dawn
Among stirred clouds and veils withdrawn
Strikes greyly on her.   Let her sleep.
But will it wake her if I heap
These cushions thus beneath her head
Where my knee was?   No,—there's your bed,
My Jenny, while you dream.   And there
I lay among your golden hair
Perhaps the subject of your dreams,
These golden coins.
     For still one deems

JENNY.

That Jenny's flattering sleep confers
New magic on the magic purse,—
Grim web, how clogged with shrivelled flies!
Between the threads fine fumes arise
And shape their pictures in the brain.
There roll no streets in glare and rain,
Nor flagrant man-swine whets his tusk;
But delicately sighs in musk
The homage of the dim boudoir;
Or like a palpitating star
Thrilled into song, the opera-night
Breathes faint in the quick pulse of light;
Or at the carriage-window shine
Rich wares for choice; or, free to dine,
Whirls through its hour of health (divine
For her) the concourse of the Park.
And though in the discounted dark
Her functions there and here are one,
Beneath the lamps and in the sun
There reigns at least the acknowledged belle
Apparelled beyond parallel.
Ah Jenny, yes, we know your dreams.

For even the Paphian Venus seems
A goddess o'er the realms of love,
When silver-shrined in shadowy grove:
Aye, or let offerings nicely plac'd
But hide Priapus to the waist,
And whoso looks on him shall see
An eligible deity.

Why, Jenny, waking here alone
May help you to remember one,
Though all the memory's long outworn
Of many a double-pillowed morn.
I think I see you when you wake,
And rub your eyes for me, and shake

My gold, in rising, from your hair,
A Danaë for a moment there.

Jenny, my love rang true! for still
Love at first sight is vague, until
That tinkling makes him audible.

And must I mock you to the last,
Ashamed of my own shame,—aghast
Because some thoughts not born amiss
Rose at a poor fair face like this?
Well, of such thoughts so much I know:
In my life, as in hers, they show,
By a far gleam which I may near,
A dark path I can strive to clear.

Only one kiss. Good-bye, my dear.

THE STREAM'S SECRET.

WHAT thing unto mine ear
Wouldst thou convey,—what secret thing,
O wandering water ever whispering?
Surely thy speech shall be of her.
Thou water, O thou whispering wanderer,
What message dost thou bring?

Say, hath not Love leaned low
This hour beside thy far well-head,
And there through jealous hollowed fingers said
The thing that most I long to know,—
Murmuring with curls all dabbled in thy flow
And washed lips rosy red?

He told it to thee there
Where thy voice hath a louder tone;
But where it welters to this little moan
His will decrees that I should hear.
Now speak: for with the silence is no fear,
And I am all alone.

Shall Time not still endow
One hour with life, and I and she
Slake in one kiss the thirst of memory?
Say, stream; lest Love should disavow
Thy service, and the bird upon the bough
Sing first to tell it me.

THE STREAM'S SECRET.

What whisperest thou? Nay, why
   Name the dead hours? I mind them well:
Their ghosts in many darkened doorways dwell
   With desolate eyes to know them by.
The hour that must be born ere it can die,—
   Of that I'd have thee tell.

But hear, before thou speak!
   Withhold, I pray, the vain behest
That while the maze hath still its bower for quest
   My burning heart should cease to seek.
Be sure that Love ordained for souls more meek
   His roadside dells of rest

Stream, when this silver thread
   In flood-time is a torrent brown
May any bulwark bind thy foaming crown?
   Shall not the waters surge and spread
And to the crannied boulders of their bed
   Still shoot the dead drift down?

Let no rebuke find place
   In speech of thine: or it shall prove
That thou dost ill expound the words of Love,
   Even as thine eddy's rippling race
Would blur the perfect image of his face.
   I will have none thereof.

O learn and understand
   That 'gainst the wrongs himself did wreak
Love sought her aid; until her shadowy cheek
   And eyes beseeching gave command;
And compassed in her close compassionate hand
   My heart must burn and speak.

THE STREAM'S SECRET.

For then at last we spoke
What eyes so oft had told to eyes
Through that long-lingering silence whose half-sighs
Alone the buried secret broke,
Which with snatched hands and lips' reverberate stroke
Then from the heart did rise.

But she is far away
Now; nor the hours of night grown hoar
Bring yet to me, long gazing from the door,
The wind-stirred robe of roseate grey
And rose-crown of the hour that leads the day
When we shall meet once more.

Dark as thy blinded wave
When brimming midnight floods the glen,—
Bright as the laughter of thy runnels when
The dawn yields all the light they crave;
Even so these hours to wound and that to save
Are sisters in Love's ken.

Oh sweet her bending grace
Then when I kneel beside her feet;
And sweet her eyes' o'erhanging heaven; and sweet
The gathering folds of her embrace;
And her fall'n hair at last shed round my face
When breaths and tears shall meet.

Beneath her sheltering hair,
In the warm silence near her breast,
Our kisses and our sobs shall sink to rest;
As in some still trance made aware
That day and night have wrought to fulness there
And Love has built our nest.

And as in the dim grove,
   When the rains cease that hushed them long,
'Mid glistening boughs the song-birds wake to song,—
   So from our hearts deep-shrined in love,
While the leaves throb beneath, around, above,
   The quivering notes shall throng.

Till tenderest words found vain
   Draw back to wonder mute and deep,
And closed lips in closed arms a silence keep,
   Subdued by memory's circling strain,—
The wind-rapt sound that the wind brings again
   While all the willows weep.

Then by her summoning art
   Shall memory conjure back the sere
Autumnal Springs, from many a dying year
   Born dead; and, bitter to the heart,
The very ways where now we walk apart
   Who then shall cling so near.

And with each thought new-grown,
   Some sweet caress or some sweet name
Low-breathed shall let me know her thought the same;
   Making me rich with every tone
And touch of the dear heaven so long unknown
   That filled my dreams with flame.

Pity and love shall burn
   In her pressed cheek and cherishing hands;
And from the living spirit of love that stands
   Between her lips to soothe and yearn,
Each separate breath shall clasp me round in turn
   And loose my spirit's bands.

THE STREAM'S SECRET.

Oh passing sweet and dear,
  Then when the worshiped form and face
Are felt at length in darkling close embrace;
  Round which so oft the sun shone clear,
With mocking light and pitiless atmosphere,
  In many an hour and place.

Ah me! with what proud growth
  Shall that hour's thirsting race be run;
While, for each several sweetness still begun
  Afresh, endures love's endless drouth:
Sweet hands, sweet hair, sweet cheeks, sweet eyes, [sweet mouth,
  Each singly wooed and won.

Yet most with the sweet soul
  Shall love's espousals then be knit;
For very passion of peace shall breathe from it
  O'er tremulous wings that touch the goal,
As on the unmeasured height of Love's control
  The lustral fires are lit.

Therefore, when breast and cheek
  Now part, from long embraces free,—
Each on the other gazing shall but see
  A self that has no need to speak:
All things unsought, yet nothing more to seek,—
  One love in unity.

O water wandering past,—
  Albeit to thee I speak this thing,
O water, thou that wanderest whispering,
  Thou keep'st thy counsel to the last.
What spell upon thy bosom should Love cast
  His message thence to wring?

THE STREAM'S SECRET.

Nay, must thou hear the tale
Of the past days,—the heavy debt
Of life that obdurate time withholds,—ere yet
To win thine ear these prayers prevail,
And by thy voice Love's self with high All-hail
Yield up the love-secret?

How should all this be told?—
All the sad sum of wayworn days;—
Heart's anguish in the impenetrable maze;
And on the waste uncoloured wold
The visible burthen of the sun grown cold
And the moon's labouring gaze?

Alas! shall hope be nurs'd
On life's all-succouring breast in vain,
And made so perfect only to be slain?
Or shall not rather the sweet thirst
Even yet rejoice the heart with warmth dispers'd
And strength grown fair again?

Stands it not by the door—
Love's Hour—till she and I shall meet;
With bodiless form and unapparent feet
That cast no shadow yet before,
Though round its head the dawn begins to pour
The breath that makes day sweet?

Its eyes invisible
Watch till the dial's thin-thrown shade
Be born,—yea, till the journeying line be laid
Upon the point that wakes the spell,
And there in lovelier light than tongue can tell
Its presence stand array'd.

Its soul remembers yet
Those sunless hours that passed it by;
And still it hears the night's disconsolate cry,
And feels the branches wringing wet
Cast on its brow, that may not once forget,
Dumb tears from the blind sky.

But oh! when now her foot
Draws near, for whose sake night and day
Were long in weary longing sighed away,—
The Hour of Love, 'mid airs grown mute,
Shall sing beside the door, and Love's own lute
Thrill to the passionate lay.

Thou know'st, for Love has told
Within thine ear, O stream, how soon
That song shall lift its sweet appointed tune
O tell me, for my lips are cold,
And in my veins the blood is waxing old
Even while I beg the boon.

So, in that hour of sighs
Assuaged, shall we beside this stone
Yield thanks for grace; while in thy mirror shown
The twofold image softly lies,
Until we kiss, and each in other's eyes
Is imaged all alone.

Still silent? Can no art
Of Love's then move thy pity? Nay,
To thee let nothing come that owns his sway:
Let happy lovers have no part
With thee; nor even so sad and poor a heart
As thou hast spurned to-day.

THE STREAM'S SECRET.

To-day? Lo! night is here.
The glen grows heavy with some veil
Risen from the earth or fall'n to make earth pale;
And all stands hushed to eye and ear,
Until the night-wind shake the shade like fear
And every covert quail.

Ah! by a colder wave
On deathlier airs the hour must come
Which to thy heart, my love, shall call me home.
Between the lips of the low cave
Against that night the lapping waters lave,
And the dark lips are dumb.

But there Love's self doth stand,
And with Life's weary wings far-flown,
And with Death's eyes that make the water moan,
Gathers the water in his hand:
And they that drink know nought of sky or land
But only love alone.

O soul-sequestered face
Far off,—O were that night but now!
So even beside that stream even I and thou
Through thirsting lips should draw Love's grace,
And in the zone of that supreme embrace
Bind aching breast and brow.

O water whispering
Still through the dark into mine ears,—
As with mine eyes, is it not now with hers?—
Mine eyes that add to thy cold spring,
Wan water, wandering water weltering,
This hidden tide of tears.

ROSE MARY.

Of her two fights with the Beryl-stone:
Lost the first, but the second won.

PART I.

"Mary mine that art Mary's Rose,
Come in to me from the garden-close.
The sun sinks fast with the rising dew,
And we marked not how the faint moon grew;
But the hidden stars are calling you.

"Tall Rose Mary, come to my side,
And read the stars if you'd be a bride.
In hours whose need was not your own,
While you were a young maid yet ungrown,
You've read the stars in the Beryl-stone.

"Daughter, once more I bid you read;
But now let it be for your own need:
Because to-morrow, at break of day,
To Holy Cross he rides on his way,
Your knight Sir James of Heronhaye.

"Ere he wed you, flower of mine,
For a heavy shrift he seeks the shrine.
Now hark to my words and do not fear;
Ill news next I have for your ear;
But be you strong, and our help is here.

"On his road, as the rumour's rife,
An ambush waits to take his life.
He needs will go, and will go alone;
Where the peril lurks may not be known;
But in this glass all things are shown."

Pale Rose Mary sank to the floor:—
"The night will come if the day is o'er!"
"Nay, heaven takes counsel, star with star,
And help shall reach your heart from afar:
A bride you'll be, as a maid you are."

The lady unbound her jewelled zone
And drew from her robe the Beryl-stone.
Shaped it was to a shadowy sphere,—
World of our world, the sun's compeer,
That bears and buries the toiling year.

With shuddering light 'twas stirred and strewn
Like the cloud-nest of the wading moon:
Freaked it was as the bubble's ball,
Rainbow-hued through a misty pall
Like the middle light of the waterfall.

Shadows dwelt in its teeming girth
Of the known and unknown things of earth;
The cloud above and the wave around,—
The central fire at the sphere's heart bound,
Like doomsday prisoned underground.

A thousand years it lay in the sea
With a treasure wrecked from Thessaly;
Deep it lay 'mid the coiled sea-wrack,
But the ocean-spirits found the track:
A soul was lost to win it back.

ROSE MARY.

The lady upheld the wondrous thing:—
"Ill fare" (she said) "with a fiend's-fairing:
But Moslem blood poured forth like wine
Can hallow Hell, 'neath the Sacred Sign;
And my lord brought this from Palestine.

"Spirits who fear the Blessed Rood
Drove forth the accursed multitude
That heathen worship housed herein,—
Never again such home to win,
Save only by a Christian's sin.

"All last night at an altar fair
I burnt strange fires and strove with prayer;
Till the flame paled to the red sunrise,
All rites I then did solemnize;
And the spell lacks nothing but your eyes."

Low spake maiden Rose Mary:—
"O mother mine, if I should not see!"
"Nay, daughter, cover your face no more,
But bend love's heart to the hidden lore,
And you shall see now as heretofore."

Paler yet were the pale cheeks grown
As the grey eyes sought the Beryl-stone:
Then over her mother's lap leaned she,
And stretched her thrilled throat passionately,
And sighed from her soul, and said, "I see."

Even as she spoke, they two were 'ware
Of music-notes that fell through the air;
A chiming shower of strange device,
Drop echoing drop, once twice and thrice,
As rain may fall in Paradise.

An instant come, in an instant gone,
No time there was to think thereon.
The mother held the sphere on her knee :—
"Lean this way and speak low to me,
And take no note but of what you see."

"I see a man with a besom grey
That sweeps the flying dust away."
"Ay, that comes first in the mystic sphere;
But now that the way is swept and clear,
Heed well what next you look on there."

"Stretched aloft and adown I see
Two roads that part in waste-country :
The glen lies deep and the ridge stands tall ;
What's great below is above seen small,
And the hill-side is the valley-wall."

"Stream-bank, daughter, or moor and moss,
Both roads will take to Holy Cross.
The hills are a weary waste to wage ;
But what of the valley-road's presage ?
That way must tend his pilgrimage."

"As 'twere the turning leaves of a book,
The road runs past me as I look ;
Or it is even as though mine eye
Should watch calm waters filled with sky
While lights and clouds and wings went by."

"In every covert seek a spear ;
They'll scarce lie close till he draws near."
"The stream has spread to a river now ;
The stiff blue sedge is deep in the slough,
But the banks are bare of shrub or bough."

"Is there any roof that near at hand
Might shelter yield to a hidden band?"
"On the further bank I see but one,
And a herdsman now in the sinking sun
Unyokes his team at the threshold-stone."

"Keep heedful watch by the water's edge,—
Some boat might lurk 'neath the shadowed sedge."
"One slid but now 'twixt the winding shores,
But a peasant woman bent to the oars
And only a young child steered its course.

"Mother, something flashed to my sight!—
Nay, it is but the lapwing's flight.—
What glints there like a lance that flees?—
Nay, the flags are stirred in the breeze,
And the water's bright through the dart-rushes.

"Ah! vainly I search from side to side:—
Woe's me! and where do the foemen hide?
Woe's me! and perchance I pass them by,
And under the new dawn's blood-red sky
Even where I gaze the dead shall lie."

Said the mother: "For dear love's sake,
Speak more low, lest the spell should break."
Said the daughter: "By love's control,
My eyes, my words, are strained to the goal;
But oh! the voice that cries in my soul!"

"Hush, sweet, hush! be calm and behold."
"I see two floodgates broken and old:
The grasses wave o'er the ruined weir,
But the bridge still leads to the breakwater;
And—mother, mother, O mother dear!"

The damsel clung to her mother's knee,
And dared not let the shriek go free;
Low she crouched by the lady's chair,
And shrank blindfold in her fallen hair,
And whispering said, "The spears are there!"

The lady stooped aghast from her place,
And cleared the locks from her daughter's face.
"More's to see, and she swoons, alas!
Look, look again, ere the moment pass!
One shadow comes but once to the glass.

"See you there what you saw but now?"
"I see eight men 'neath the willow bough.
All over the weir a wild growth's spread:
Ah me! it will hide a living head
As well as the water hides the dead.

"They lie by the broken water-gate
As men who have a while to wait.
The chief's high lance has a blazoned scroll,—
He seems some lord of tithe and toll
With seven squires to his bannerole.

"The little pennon quakes in the air,
I cannot trace the blazon there:—
Ah! now I can see the field of blue,
The spurs and the merlins two and two;—
It is the Warden of Holycleugh!"

"God be thanked for the thing we know!
You have named your good knight's mortal foe.
Last Shrovetide in the tourney-game
He sought his life by treasonous shame;
And this way now doth he seek the same.

"So, fair lord, such a thing you are!
But we too watch till the morning star.
Well, June is kind and the moon is clear:
Saint Judas send you a merry cheer
For the night you lie at Warisweir!

"Now, sweet daughter, but one more sight,
And you may lie soft and sleep to-night.
We know in the vale what perils be:
Now look once more in the glass, and see
If over the hills the road lies free."

Rose Mary pressed to her mother's cheek,
And almost smiled but did not speak;
Then turned again to the saving spell,
With eyes to search and with lips to tell
The heart of things invisible.

"Again the shape with the besom grey
Comes back to sweep the clouds away.
Again I stand where the roads divide;
But now all's near on the steep hillside,
And a thread far down is the rivertide."

"Ay, child, your road is o'er moor and moss,
Past Holycleugh to Holy Cross.
Our hunters lurk in the valley's wake,
As they knew which way the chase would take:
Yet search the hills for your true love's sake."

"Swift and swifter the waste runs by,
And nought I see but the heath and the sky;
No brake is there that could hide a spear,
And the gaps to a horseman's sight lie clear;
Still past it goes, and there's nought to fear."

"Fear no trap that you cannot see,—
They'd not lurk yet too warily.
Below by the weir they lie in sight,
And take no heed how they pass the night
Till close they crouch with the morning light."

"The road shifts ever and brings in view
Now first the heights of Holycleugh:
Dark they stand o'er the vale below,
And hide that heaven which yet shall show
The thing their master's heart doth know.

"Where the road looks to the castle steep,
There are seven hill-clefts wide and deep:
Six mine eyes can search as they list,
But the seventh hollow is brimmed with mist:
If aught were there, it might not be wist."

"Small hope, my girl, for a helm to hide
In mists that cling to a wild moorside:
Soon they melt with the wind and sun,
And scarce would wait such deeds to be done:
God send their snares be the worst to shun."

"Still the road winds ever anew
As it hastens on towards Holycleugh;
And ever the great walls loom more near,
Till the castle-shadow, steep and sheer,
Drifts like a cloud, and the sky is clear."

"Enough, my daughter," the mother said,
And took to her breast the bending head;
"Rest, poor head, with my heart below,
While love still lulls you as long ago:
For all is learnt that we need to know.

"Long the miles and many the hours
From the castle-height to the abbey-towers;
But here the journey has no more dread;
Too thick with life is the whole road spread
For murder's trembling foot to tread."

She gazed on the Beryl-stone full fain
Ere she wrapped it close in her robe again:
The flickering shades were dusk and dun,
And the lights throbbed faint in unison,
Like a high heart when a race is run.

As the globe slid to its silken gloom,
Once more a music rained through the room;
Low it splashed like a sweet star-spray,
And sobbed like tears at the heart of May,
And died as laughter dies away.

The lady held her breath for a space,
And then she looked in her daughter's face:
But wan Rose Mary had never heard;
Deep asleep like a sheltered bird
She lay with the long spell minister'd.

"Ah! and yet I must leave you, dear,
For what you have seen your knight must hear.
Within four days, by the help of God,
He comes back safe to his heart's abode:
Be sure he shall shun the valley-road."

Rose Mary sank with a broken moan,
And lay in the chair and slept alone,
Weary, lifeless, heavy as lead:
Long it was ere she raised her head
And rose up all discomforted.

She searched her brain for a vanished thing,
And clasped her brows, remembering;
Then knelt and lifted her eyes in awe,
And sighed with a long sigh sweet to draw:—
"Thank God, thank God, thank God I saw!"

The lady had left her as she lay,
To seek the Knight of Heronhaye.
But first she clomb by a secret stair,
And knelt at a carven altar fair,
And laid the precious Beryl there.

Its girth was graved with a mystic rune
In a tongue long dead 'neath sun and moon:
A priest of the Holy Sepulchre
Read that writing and did not err;
And her lord had told its sense to her.

She breathed the words in an undertone:—
"*None sees here but the pure alone.*"
"And oh!" she said, "what rose may be
In Mary's bower more pure to see
Than my own sweet maiden Rose Mary?"

Beryl-Song.

We whose home is the Beryl,
Fire-spirits of dread desire,
Who entered in
By a secret sin,
'Gainst whom all powers that strive with ours are sterile,—
We cry, Woe to thee, mother!
What hast thou taught her, the girl thy daughter,
That she and none other
Should this dark morrow to her deadly sorrow imperil?
What were her eyes
But the fiend's own spies,
O mother,
And shall We not fee her, our proper prophet and seër?
Go to her, mother,
Even thou, yea thou and none other,
Thou, from the Beryl:
Her fee must thou take her,
Her fee that We send, and make her,
Even in this hour, her sin's unsheltered avower.
Whose steed did neigh,
Riderless, bridleless,
At her gate before it was day?
Lo! where doth hover
The soul of her lover?
She sealed his doom, she, she was the sworn approver,—
Whose eyes were so wondrous wise,
Yet blind, ah! blind to his peril!
For stole not We in
Through a love-linked sin,
'Gainst whom all powers at war with ours are sterile,—
Fire-spirits of dread desire,
We whose home is the Beryl?

PART II.

"PALE Rose Mary, what shall be done
With a rose that Mary weeps upon?"
"Mother, let it fall from the tree,
And never walk where the strewn leaves be
Till winds have passed and the path is free."

"Sad Rose Mary, what shall be done
With a cankered flower beneath the sun?"
"Mother, let it wait for the night;
Be sure its shame shall be out of sight
Ere the moon pale or the east grow light."

"Lost Rose Mary, what shall be done
With a heart that is but a broken one?"
"Mother, let it lie where it must;
The blood was drained with the bitter thrust,
And dust is all that sinks in the dust."

"Poor Rose Mary, what shall I do,—
I, your mother, that lovèd you?"
"O my mother, and is love gone?
Then seek you another love anon:
Who cares what shame shall lean upon?"

Low drooped trembling Rose Mary,
Then up as though in a dream stood she.
"Come, my heart, it is time to go;
This is the hour that has whispered low
When thy pulse quailed in the nights we know.

"Yet O my heart, thy shame has a mate
Who will not leave thee desolate.
Shame for shame, yea and sin for sin:
Yet peace at length may our poor souls win
If love for love be found therein.

ROSE MARY.

"O thou who seek'st our shrift to-day,"
She cried, "O James of Heronhaye—
Thy sin and mine was for love alone;
And oh! in the sight of God 'tis known
How the heart has since made heavy moan.

"Three days yet!" she said to her heart;
"But then he comes, and we will not part
God, God be thanked that I still could see!
Oh! he shall come back assuredly,
But where, alas! must he seek for me?

"O my heart, what road shall we roam
Till my wedding-music fetch me home?
For love's shut from us and bides afar,
And scorn leans over the bitter bar
And knows us now for the thing we are."

Tall she stood with a cheek flushed high
And a gaze to burn the heart-strings by.
'Twas the lightning-flash o'er sky and plain
Ere labouring thunders heave the chain
From the floodgates of the drowning rain.

The mother looked on the daughter still
As on a hurt thing that's yet to kill.
Then wildly at length the pent tears came;
The love swelled high with the swollen shame,
And their hearts' tempest burst on them.

Closely locked, they clung without speech,
And the mirrored souls shook each to each,
As the cloud-moon and the water-moon
Shake face to face when the dim stars swoon
In stormy bowers of the night's mid-noon.

They swayed together, shuddering sore,
Till the mother's heart could bear no more.
'Twas death to feel her own breast shake
Even to the very throb and ache
Of the burdened heart she still must break.

All her sobs ceased suddenly,
And she sat straight up but scarce could see.
"O daughter, where should my speech begin?
Your heart held fast its secret sin:
How think you, child, that I read therein?"

"Ah me! but I thought not how it came
When your words showed that you knew my shame
And now that you call me still your own,
I half forget you have ever known.
Did you read my heart in the Beryl-stone?"

The lady answered her mournfully:—
"The Beryl-stone has no voice for me:
But when you charged its power to show
The truth which none but the pure may know,
Did naught speak once of a coming woe?"

Her hand was close to her daughter's heart,
And it felt the life-blood's sudden start:
A quick deep breath did the damsel draw,
Like the struck fawn in the oakenshaw:
"O mother," she cried, "but still I saw!"

"O child, my child, why held you apart
From my great love your hidden heart?
Said I not that all sin must chase
From the spell's sphere the spirits of grace,
And yield their rule to the evil race?

"Ah! would to God I had clearly told
How strong those powers, accurst of old:
Their heart is the ruined house of lies;
O girl, they can seal the sinful eyes,
Or show the truth by contraries!"

The daughter sat as cold as a stone,
And spoke no word but gazed alone,
Nor moved, though her mother strove a space
To clasp her round in a close embrace,
Because she dared not see her face.

"Oh!" at last did the mother cry,
"Be sure, as he loved you, so will I!
Ah! still and dumb is the bride, I trow;
But cold and stark as the winter snow
Is the bridegroom's heart, laid dead below!

"Daughter, daughter, remember you
That cloud in the hills by Holycleugh?
'Twas a Hell-screen hiding truth away:
There, not i' the vale, the ambush lay,
And thence was the dead borne home to-day."

Deep the flood and heavy the shock
When sea meets sea in the riven rock:
But calm is the pulse that shakes the sea
To the prisoned tide of doom set free
In the breaking heart of Rose Mary.

Once she sprang as the heifer springs
With the wolf's teeth at its red heart-strings.
First 'twas fire in her breast and brain,
And then scarce hers but the whole world's pain,
As she gave one shriek and sank again.

In the hair dark-waved the face lay white
As the moon lies in the lap of night;
And as night through which no moon may dart
Lies on a pool in the woods apart,
So lay the swoon on the weary heart.

The lady felt for the bosom's stir,
And wildly kissed and called on her;
Then turned away with a quick footfall,
And slid the secret door in the wall,
And clomb the strait stair's interval.

There above in the altar-cell
A little fountain rose and fell:
She set a flask to the water's flow,
And, backward hurrying, sprinkled now
The still cold breast and the pallid brow.

Scarce cheek that warmed or breath on the air,
Yet something told that life was there.
"Ah! not with the heart the body dies!"
The lady moaned in a bitter wise;
Then wrung her hands and hid her eyes.

"Alas! and how may I meet again
In the same poor eyes the selfsame pain?
What help can I seek, such grief to guide?
Ah! one alone might avail," she cried,—
"The priest who prays at the dead man's side."

The lady arose, and sped down all
The winding stairs to the castle-hall.
Long-known valley and wood and stream,
As the loopholes passed, naught else did seem
Than the torn threads of a broken dream.

ROSE MARY.

The hall was full of the castle-folk;
The women wept, but the men scarce spoke.
As the lady crossed the rush-strewn floor,
The throng fell backward, murmuring sore,
And pressed outside round the open door.

A stranger shadow hung on the hall
Than the dark pomp of a funeral.
'Mid common sights that were there alway,
As 'twere a chance of the passing day,
On the ingle-bench the dead man lay.

A priest who passed by Holycleugh
The tidings brought when the day was new.
He guided them who had fetched the dead;
And since that hour, unwearièd,
He knelt in prayer at the low bier's head.

Word had gone to his own domain
That in evil wise the knight was slain:
Soon the spears must gather apace
And the hunt be hard on the hunters' trace;
But all things yet lay still for a space.

As the lady's hurried step drew near,
The kneeling priest looked up to her.
"Father, death is a grievous thing;
But oh! the woe has a sharper sting
That craves by me your ministering.

"Alas for the child that should have wed
This noble knight here lying dead!
Dead in hope, with all blessed boon
Of love thus rent from her heart ere noon,
I left her laid in a heavy swoon.

"O haste to the open bower-chamber
That's topmost as you mount the stair:
Seek her, father, ere yet she wake;
Your words, not mine, be the first to slake
This poor heart's fire, for Christ's sweet sake!

"God speed!" she said as the priest passed through,
"And I ere long will be with you."
Then low on the hearth her knees sank prone;
She signed all folk from the threshold-stone,
And gazed in the dead man's face alone.

The fight for life found record yet
In the clenched lips and the teeth hard-set;
The wrath from the bent brow was not gone,
And stark in the eyes the hate still shone
Of that they last had looked upon.

The blazoned coat was rent on his breast
Where the golden field was goodliest;
But the shivered sword, close-gripped, could tell
That the blood shed round him where he fell
Was not all his in the distant dell.

The lady recked of the corpse no whit,
But saw the soul and spoke to it:
A light there was in her steadfast eyes,—
The fire of mortal tears and sighs
That pity and love immortalize.

"By thy death have I learnt to-day
Thy deed, O James of Heronhaye!
Great wrong thou hast done to me and mine;
And haply God hath wrought for a sign
By our blind deed this doom of thine.

ROSE MARY.

"Thy shrift, alas! thou wast not to win;
But may death shrive thy soul herein!
Full well do I know thy love should be
Even yet—had life but stayed with thee—
Our honour's strong security."

She stooped, and said with a sob's low stir,—
"Peace be thine,—but what peace for her?"
But ere to the brow her lips were press'd,
She marked, half-hid in the riven vest,
A packet close to the dead man's breast.

'Neath surcoat pierced and broken mail
It lay on the blood-stained bosom pale.
The clot clung round it, dull and dense,
And a faintness seized her mortal sense
As she reached her hand and drew it thence.

'Twas steeped in the heart's flood welling high
From the heart it there had rested by:
'Twas glued to a broidered fragment gay,—
A shred by spear-thrust rent away
From the heron-wings of Heronhaye.

She gazed on the thing with piteous eyne:—
"Alas, poor child, some pledge of thine!
Ah me! in this troth the hearts were twain,
And one hath ebbed to this crimson stain,
And when shall the other throb again?"

She opened the packet heedfully;
The blood was stiff, and it scarce might be.
She found but a folded paper there,
And round it, twined with tenderest care,
A long bright tress of golden hair.

Even as she looked, she saw again
That dark-haired face in its swoon of pain:
It seemed a snake with a golden sheath
Crept near, as a slow flame flickereth,
And stung her daughter's heart to death.

She loosed the tress, but her hand did shake
As though indeed she had touched a snake;
And next she undid the paper's fold,
But that too trembled in her hold,
And the sense scarce grasped the tale it told.

"My heart's sweet lord," ('twas thus she read,)
"At length our love is garlanded.
At Holy Cross, within eight days' space,
I seek my shrift; and the time and place
Shall fit thee too for thy soul's good grace.

"From Holycleugh on the seventh day
My brother rides, and bides away:
And long or e'er he is back, mine own,
Afar where the face of fear's unknown
We shall be safe with our love alone.

"Ere yet at the shrine my knees I bow,
I shear one tress for our holy vow.
As round these words these threads I wind,
So, eight days hence, shall our loves be twined
Says my lord's poor lady, JOCELIND."

She read it twice, with a brain in thrall,
And then its echo told her all.
O'er brows low-fall'n her hands she drew:—
"O God!" she said, as her hands fell too,—
"The Warden's sister of Holycleugh!"

ROSE MARY.

She rose upright with a long low moan,
And stared in the dead man's face new-known.
Had it lived indeed ? She scarce could tell :
'Twas a cloud where fiends had come to dwell,—
A mask that hung on the gate of Hell.

She lifted the lock of gleaming hair
And smote the lips and left it there.
" Here's gold that Hell shall take for thy toll !
Full well hath thy treason found its goal,
O thou dead body and damnèd soul ! "

She turned, sore dazed, for a voice was near,
And she knew that some one called to her.
On many a column fair and tall
A high court ran round the castle-hall ;
And thence it was that the priest did call.

" I sought your child where you bade me go,
And in rooms around and rooms below ;
But where, alas ! may the maiden be ?
Fear nought,—we shall find her speedily,—
But come, come hither, and seek with me."

She reached the stair like a lifelorn thing,
But hastened upward murmuring :—
" Yea, Death's is a face that's fell to see ;
But bitterer pang Life hoards for thee,
Thou broken heart of Rose Mary ! "

Beryl-Song.

*We whose throne is the Beryl,
Dire-gifted spirits of fire,
Who for a twin
Leash Sorrow to Sin,
Who on no flower refrain to lour with peril,—
We cry,—O desolate daughter!
Thou and thy mother share newer shame with each other
Than last night's slaughter.
Awake and tremble, for our curses assemble!
What more, that thou know'st not yet,—
That life nor death shall forget?
No help from Heaven,—thy woes heart-riven are sterile!
O once a maiden,
With yet worse sorrow can any morrow be laden?
It waits for thee,
It looms, it must be,
O lost among women,—
It comes and thou canst not flee.
Amen to the omen,
Says the voice of the Beryl.
Thou sleep'st? Awake,—
What dar'st thou yet for his sake,
Who each for other did God's own Future imperil?
Dost dare to live
'Mid the pangs each hour must give?
Nay, rather die,—
With him thy lover 'neath Hell's cloud-cover to fly,—
Hopeless, yet not apart,
Cling heart to heart,
And beat through the nether storm-eddying winds together?
Shall this be so?
There thou shalt meet him, but mayst thou greet him?
ah no!
He loves, but thee he hoped nevermore to see,—
He sighed as he died,*

But with never a thought for thee.
  Alone!
 Alone, for ever alone,—
Whose eyes were such wondrous spies for the fate foreshown!
  Lo! have not We leashed the twin
  Of endless Sorrow to Sin,—
Who on no flower refrain to lour with peril,—
  Dire-gifted spirits of fire,
  We whose throne is the Beryl?

PART III.

A swoon that breaks is the whelming wave
When help comes late but still can save.
With all blind throes is the instant rife,—
Hurtling clangour and clouds at strife,—
The breath of death, but the kiss of life.

The night lay deep on Rose Mary's heart,
For her swoon was death's kind counterpart:
The dawn broke dim on Rose Mary's soul,—
No hill-crown's heavenly aureole,
But a wild gleam on a shaken shoal.

Her senses gasped in the sudden air,
And she looked around, but none was there.
She felt the slackening frost distil
Through her blood the last ooze dull and chill:
Her lids were dry and her lips were still.

Her tears had flooded her heart again;
As after a long day's bitter rain,
At dusk when the wet flower-cups shrink,
The drops run in from the beaded brink,
And all the close-shut petals drink.

Again her sighs on her heart were rolled;
As the wind that long has swept the wold,—
Whose moan was made with the moaning sea,—
Beats out its breath in the last torn tree,
And sinks at length in lethargy.

She knew she had waded bosom-deep
Along death's bank in the sedge of sleep:
All else was lost to her clouded mind;
Nor, looking back, could she see defin'd
O'er the dim dumb waste what lay behind.

Slowly fades the sun from the wall
Till day lies dead on the sun-dial:
And now in Rose Mary's lifted eye
'Twas shadow alone that made reply
To the set face of the soul's dark sky

Yet still through her soul there wandered past
Dread phantoms borne on a wailing blast,—
Death and sorrow and sin and shame;
And, murmured still, to her lips there came
Her mother's and her lover's name.

How to ask, and what thing to know?
She might not stay and she dared not go.
From fires unseen these smoke-clouds curled;
But where did the hidden curse lie furled?
And how to seek through the weary world?

With toiling breath she rose from the floor
And dragged her steps to an open door:
'Twas the secret panel standing wide,
As the lady's hand had let it bide
In hastening back to her daughter's side.

She passed, but reeled with a dizzy brain
And smote the door which closed again.
She stood within by the darkling stair,
But her feet might mount more freely there,—
'Twas the open light most blinded her.

Within her mind no wonder grew
At the secret path she never knew:
All ways alike were strange to her now,—
One field bare-ridged from the spirit's plough,
One thicket black with the cypress-bough.

Once she thought that she heard her name;
And she paused, but knew not whence it came.
Down the shadowed stair a faint ray fell
That guided the weary footsteps well
Till it led her up to the altar-cell.

No change there was on Rose Mary's face
As she leaned in the portal's narrow space:
Still she stood by the pillar's stem,
Hand and bosom and garment's hem,
As the soul stands by at the requiem.

The altar-cell was a dome low-lit,
And a veil hung in the midst of it:
At the pole-points of its circling girth
Four symbols stood of the world's first birth,—
Air and water and fire and earth.

To the north, a fountain glittered free;
To the south, there glowed a red fruit-tree;
To the east, a lamp flamed high and fair;
To the west, a crystal casket rare
Held fast a cloud of the fields of air.

The painted walls were a mystic show
Of time's ebb-tide and overflow;
His hoards long-locked and conquering key,
His service-fires that in heaven be,
And earth-wheels whirled perpetually.

ROSE MARY.

Rose Mary gazed from the open door
As on idle things she cared not for,—
The fleeting shapes of an empty tale;
Then stepped with a heedless visage pale,
And lifted aside the altar-veil.

The altar stood from its curved recess
In a coiling serpent's life-likeness:
Even such a serpent evermore
Lies deep asleep at the world's dark core
Till the last Voice shake the sea and shore.

From the altar-cloth a book rose spread
And tapers burned at the altar-head;
And there in the altar-midst alone,
'Twixt wings of a sculptured beast unknown,
Rose Mary saw the Béryl-stone.

Firm it sat 'twixt the hollowed wings,
As an orb sits in the hand of kings:
And lo! for that Foe whose curse far-flown
Had bound her life with a burning zone,
Rose Mary knew the Beryl-stone.

Dread is the meteor's blazing sphere
When the poles throb to its blind career;
But not with a light more grim and ghast
Thereby is the future doom forecast,
Than now this sight brought back the past.

The hours and minutes seemed to whirr
In a clanging swarm that deafened her;
They stung her heart to a writhing flame,
And marshalled past in its glare they came,—
Death and sorrow and sin and shame.

Round the Beryl's sphere she saw them pass
And mock her eyes from the fated glass:
One by one in a fiery train
The dead hours seemed to wax and wane,
And burned till all was known again.

From the drained heart's fount there rose no cry,
There sprang no tears, for the source was dry.
Held in the hand of some heavy law,
Her eyes she might not once withdraw,
Nor shrink away from the thing she saw.

Even as she gazed, through all her blood
The flame was quenched in a coming flood:
Out of the depth of the hollow gloom
On her soul's bare sands she felt it boom,—
The measured tide of a sea of doom.

Three steps she took through the altar-gate,
And her neck reared and her arms grew straight:
The sinews clenched like a serpent's throe,
And the face was white in the dark hair's flow,
As her hate beheld what lay below.

Dumb she stood in her malisons,—
A silver statue tressed with bronze:
As the fabled head by Perseus mown,
It seemed in sooth that her gaze alone
Had turned the carven shapes to stone.

O'er the altar-sides on either hand
There hung a dinted helm and brand:
By strength thereof, 'neath the Sacred Sign,
That bitter gift o'er the salt sea-brine
Her father brought from Palestine.

Rose Mary moved with a stern accord
And reached her hand to her father's sword;
Nor did she stir her gaze one whit
From the thing whereon her brows were knit;
But gazing still, she spoke to it.

"O ye, three times accurst," she said,
" By whom this stone is tenanted!
Lo! here ye came by a strong sin's might;
Yet a sinner's hand that's weak to smite
Shall send you hence ere the day be night.

"This hour a clear voice bade me know
My hand shall work your overthrow:
Another thing in mine ear it spake,—
With the broken spell my life shall break.
I thank Thee, God, for the dear death's sake!

" And he Thy heavenly minister
Who swayed erewhile this spell-bound sphere,—
My parting soul let him haste to greet,
And none but he be guide for my feet
To where Thy rest is made complete."

Then deep she breathed, with a tender moan:—
" My love, my lord, my only one!
Even as I held the cursed clue,
When thee, through me, these foul ones slew,—
By mine own deed shall they slay me too!

" Even while they speed to Hell, my love,
Two hearts shall meet in Heaven above.
Our shrift thou sought'st, but might'st not bring:
And oh! for me 'tis a blessed thing
To work hereby our ransoming.

"One were our hearts in joy and pain,
And our souls e'en now grow one again.
And O my love, if our souls are three,
O thine and mine shall the third soul be,—
One threefold love eternally."

Her eyes were soft as she spoke apart,
And the lips smiled to the broken heart:
But the glance was dark and the forehead scored
With the bitter frown of hate restored,
As her two hands swung the heavy sword.

Three steps back from her Foe she trod :—
"Love, for thy sake! In Thy Name, O God!"
In the fair white hands small strength was shown;
Yet the blade flashed high and the edge fell prone,
And she cleft the heart of the Beryl-stone.

What living flesh in the thunder-cloud
Hath sat and felt heaven cry aloud?
Or known how the levin's pulse may beat?
Or wrapped the hour when the whirlwinds meet
About its breast for a winding-sheet?

Who hath crouched at the world's deep heart
While the earthquake rends its loins apart?
Or walked far under the seething main
While overhead the heavens ordain
The tempest-towers of the hurricane?

Who hath seen or what ear hath heard
The secret things unregister'd
Of the place where all is past and done,
And tears and laughter sound as one
In Hell's unhallowed unison?

Nay, is it writ how the fiends despair
In earth and water and fire and air?
Even so no mortal tongue may tell
How to the clang of the sword that fell
The echoes shook the altar-cell.

When all was still on the air again
The Beryl-stone lay cleft in twain;
The veil was rent from the riven dome;
And every wind that's winged to roam
Might have the ruined place for home.

The fountain no more glittered free;
The fruit hung dead on the leafless tree;
The flame of the lamp had ceased to flare;
And the crystal casket shattered there
Was emptied now of its cloud of air.

And lo! on the ground Rose Mary lay,
With a cold brow like the snows ere May,
With a cold breast like the earth till Spring,
With such a smile as the June days bring
When the year grows warm for harvesting.

The death she had won might leave no trace
On the soft sweet form and gentle face:
In a gracious sleep she seemed to lie;
And over her head her hand on high
Held fast the sword she triumphed by.

'Twas then a clear voice said in the room:—
"Behold the end of the heavy doom.
O come,—for thy bitter love's sake blest;
By a sweet path now thou journeyest,
And I will lead thee to thy rest.

"Me thy sin by Heaven's sore ban
Did chase erewhile from the talisman:
But to my heart, as a conquered home,
In glory of strength thy footsteps come
Who hast thus cast forth my foes therefrom

"Already thy heart remembereth
No more his name thou sought'st in death:
For under all deeps, all heights above,—
So wide the gulf in the midst thereof,—
Are Hell of Treason and Heaven of Love.

"Thee, true soul, shall thy truth prefer
To blessed Mary's rose-bower:
Warmed and lit is thy place afar
With guerdon-fires of the sweet Love-star
Where hearts of steadfast lovers are :—

"Though naught for the poor corpse lying here
Remain to-day but the cold white bier,
But burial-chaunt and bended knee,
But sighs and tears that heaviest be,
But rent rose-flower and rosemary."

Beryl-Song.

We, cast forth from the Beryl,
Gyre-circling spirits of fire,
 Whose pangs begin
 With God's grace to sin,
For whose spent powers the immortal hours are sterile,—
 Woe! must We behold this mother
Find grace in her dead child's face, and doubt of none other
But that perfect pardon, alas! hath assured her guerdon?
 Woe! must We behold this daughter,
Made clean from the soil of sin wherewith We had fraught her,
 Shake off a man's blood like water?
 Write up her story
 On the Gate of Heaven's glory,
Whom there We behold so fair in shining apparel,
 And beneath her the ruin
 Of our own undoing!
 Alas, the Beryl!
 We had for a foeman
 But one weak woman;
 In one day's strife,
Her hope fell dead from her life;
 And yet no iron,
 Her soul to environ,
Could this manslayer, this false soothsayer imperil!
 Lo, where she bows
 In the Holy House!
Who now shall dissever her soul from its joy for ever,
 While every ditty
 Of love and plentiful pity
 Fills the White City,
And the floor of Heaven to her feet for ever is given?
 Hark, a voice cries "Flee!"

Woe! woe! what shelter have We,
Whose pangs begin
With God's grace to sin,
For whose spent powers the immortal hours are sterile,
Gyre-circling spirits of fire,
We, cast forth from the Beryl?

THE WHITE SHIP.

Henry I. of England.—25th November 1120.

By none but me can the tale be told,
The butcher of Rouen, poor Berold.
   (*Lands are swayed by a King on a throne.*)
'Twas a royal train put forth to sea,
Yet the tale can be told by none but me.
   (*The sea hath no King but God alone.*)

King Henry held it as life's whole gain
That after his death his son should reign.

'Twas so in my youth I heard men say,
And my old age calls it back to-day.

King Henry of England's realm was he,
And Henry Duke of Normandy.

The times had changed when on either coast
"Clerkly Harry" was all his boast.

Of ruthless strokes full many an one
He had struck to crown himself and his son;
And his elder brother's eyes were gone.

And when to the chase his court would crowd,
The poor flung ploughshares on his road,
And shrieked: "Our cry is from King to God!"

But all the chiefs of the English land
Had knelt and kissed the Prince's hand.

And next with his son he sailed to France
To claim the Norman allegiance:

And every baron in Normandy
Had taken the oath of fealty.

'Twas sworn and sealed, and the day had come
When the King and the Prince might journey home:

For Christmas cheer is to home hearts dear,
And Christmas now was drawing near.

Stout Fitz-Stephen came to the King,—
A pilot famous in seafaring;

And he held to the King, in all men's sight,
A mark of gold for his tribute's right.

"Liege Lord! my father guided the ship
From whose boat your father's foot did slip
When he caught the English soil in his grip,

"And cried: 'By this clasp I claim command
O'er every rood of English land!'

"He was borne to the realm you rule o'er now
In that ship with the archer carved at her prow:

"And thither I'll bear, an it be my due,
Your father's son and his grandson too.

"The famed White Ship is mine in the bay,
From Harfleur's harbour she sails to-day,

THE WHITE SHIP.

"With masts fair-pennoned as Norman spears
And with fifty well-tried mariners."

Quoth the King: "My ships are chosen each one,
But I'll not say nay to Stephen's son.

"My son and daughter and fellowship
Shall cross the water in the White Ship."

The King set sail with the eve's south wind,
And soon he left that coast behind.

The Prince and all his, a princely show,
Remained in the good White Ship to go.

With noble knights and with ladies fair,
With courtiers and sailors gathered there,
Three hundred living souls we were:

And I Berold was the meanest hind
In all that train to the Prince assign'd.

The Prince was a lawless shameless youth;
From his father's loins he sprang without ruth:

Eighteen years till then he had seen,
And the devil's dues in him were eighteen.

And now he cried: "Bring wine from below;
Let the sailors revel ere yet they row:

"Our speed shall o'ertake my father's flight
Though we sail from the harbour at midnight."

The rowers made good cheer without check;
The lords and ladies obeyed his beck;
The night was light, and they danced on the deck.

But at midnight's stroke they cleared the bay,
And the White Ship furrowed the water-way.

The sails were set, and the oars kept tune
To the double flight of the ship and the moon:

Swifter and swifter the White Ship sped
Till she flew as the spirit flies from the dead:

As white as a lily glimmered she
Like a ship's fair ghost upon the sea.

And the Prince cried, "Friends, 'tis the hour to sing!
Is a songbird's course so swift on the wing?"

And under the winter stars' still throng,
From brown throats, white throats, merry and strong,
The knights and the ladies raised a song.

A song,—nay, a shriek that rent the sky,
That leaped o'er the deep!—the grievous cry
Of three hundred living that now must die.

An instant shriek that sprang to the shock
As the ship's keel felt the sunken rock.

'Tis said that afar—a shrill strange sigh—
The King's ships heard it and knew not why.

Pale Fitz-Stephen stood by the helm
'Mid all those folk that the waves must whelm.

A great King's heir for the waves to whelm,
And the helpless pilot pale at the helm!

THE WHITE SHIP.

The ship was eager and sucked athirst,
By the stealthy stab of the sharp reef pierc'd:

And like the moil round a sinking cup,
The waters against her crowded up.

A moment the pilot's senses spin,—
The next he snatched the Prince 'mid the din,
Cut the boat loose, and the youth leaped in.

A few friends leaped with him, standing near.
"Row! the sea's smooth and the night is clear!"

"What! none to be saved but these and I?"
"Row, row as you'd live! All here must die!"

Out of the churn of the choking ship,
Which the gulf grapples and the waves strip,
They struck with the strained oars' flash and dip.

'Twas then o'er the splitting bulwarks' brim
The Prince's sister screamed to him.

He gazed aloft, still rowing apace,
And through the whirled surf he knew her face.

To the toppling decks clave one and all
As a fly cleaves to a chamber-wall.

I Berold was clinging anear;
I prayed for myself and quaked with fear,
But I saw his eyes as he looked at her.

He knew her face and he heard her cry,
And he said, "Put back! she must not die!"

And back with the current's force they reel
Like a leaf that's drawn to a water-wheel.

'Neath the ship's travail they scarce might float,
But he rose and stood in the rocking boat.

Low the poor ship leaned on the tide:
O'er the naked keel as she best might slide,
The sister toiled to the brother's side.

He reached an oar to her from below,
And stiffened his arms to clutch her so.

But now from the ship some spied the boat,
And "Saved!" was the cry from many a throat.

And down to the boat they leaped and fell:
It turned as a bucket turns in a well,
And nothing was there but the surge and swell.

The Prince that was and the King to come,
There in an instant gone to his doom,

Despite of all England's bended knee
And maugre the Norman fealty!

He was a Prince of lust and pride;
He showed no grace till the hour he died.

When he should be King, he oft would vow,
He'd yoke the peasant to his own plough.
O'er him the ships score their furrows now.

God only knows where his soul did wake,
But I saw him die for his sister's sake.

By none but me can the tale be told,
The butcher of Rouen, poor Berold.
   (Lands are swayed by a King on a throne.)
'Twas a royal train put forth to sea,
Yet the tale can be told by none but me.
   (The sea hath no King but God alone.)

THE WHITE SHIP.

And now the end came o'er the waters' womb
Like the last great Day that's yet to come.

With prayers in vain and curses in vain,
The White Ship sundered on the mid-main:

And what were men and what was a ship
Were toys and splinters in the sea's grip.

I Berold was down in the sea;
And passing strange though the thing may be,
Of dreams then known I remember me.

Blithe is the shout on Harfleur's strand
When morning lights the sails to land:

And blithe is Honfleur's echoing gloam
When mothers call the children home:

And high do the bells of Rouen beat
When the Body of Christ goes down the street.

These things and the like were heard and shown
In a moment's trance 'neath the sea alone;

And when I rose, 'twas the sea did seem,
And not these things, to be all a dream.

The ship was gone and the crowd was gone,
And the deep shuddered and the moon shone,

And in a strait grasp my arms did span
The mainyard rent from the mast where it ran;
And on it with me was another man.

Where lands were none 'neath the dim sea-sky,
We told our names, that man and I.

"O I am Godefroy de l'Aigle hight,
And son I am to a belted knight."

"And I am Berold the butcher's son
Who slays the beasts in Rouen town."

Then cried we upon God's name, as we
Did drift on the bitter winter sea.

But lo! a third man rose o'er the wave,
And we said, "Thank God! us three may He save!"

He clutched to the yard with panting stare,
And we looked and knew Fitz-Stephen there.

He clung, and "What of the Prince?" quoth he.
"Lost, lost!" we cried. He cried, "Woe on me!"
And loosed his hold and sank through the sea.

And soul with soul again in that space
We two were together face to face:

And each knew each, as the moments sped,
Less for one living than for one dead:

And every still star overhead
Seemed an eye that knew we were but dead.

And the hours passed; till the noble's son
Sighed, "God be thy help! my strength's foredone!

"O farewell, friend, for I can no more!"
"Christ take thee!" I moaned; and his life was o'er.

Three hundred souls were all lost but one,
And I drifted over the sea alone.

THE WHITE SHIP.

At last the morning rose on the sea
Like an angel's wing that beat tow'rds me.

Sore numbed I was in my sheepskin coat;
Half dead I hung, and might nothing note,
Till I woke sun-warmed in a fisher-boat.

The sun was high o'er the eastern brim
As I praised God and gave thanks to Him.

That day I told my tale to a priest,
Who charged me, till the shrift were releas'd,
That I should keep it in mine own breast.

And with the priest I thence did fare
To King Henry's court at Winchester.

We spoke with the King's high chamberlain,
And he wept and mourned again and again,
As if his own son had been slain:

And round us ever there crowded fast
Great men with faces all aghast:

And who so bold that might tell the thing
Which now they knew to their lord the King?
Much woe I learnt in their communing.

The King had watched with a heart sore stirred
For two whole days, and this was the third:

And still to all his court would he say,
"What keeps my son so long away?"

And they said: "The ports lie far and wide
That skirt the swell of the English tide;

"And England's cliffs are not more white
Than her women are, and scarce so light
Her skies as their eyes are blue and bright;

"And in some port that he reached from France
The Prince has lingered for his pleasaùnce."

But once the King asked: "What distant cry
Was that we heard 'twixt the sea and sky?"

And one said: "With suchlike shouts, pardie!
Do the fishers fling their nets at sea."

And one: "Who knows not the shrieking quest
When the sea-mew misses its young from the nest?"

'Twas thus till now they had soothed his dread,
Albeit they knew not what they said:

But who should speak to-day of the thing
That all knew there except the King?

Then pondering much they found a way,
And met round the King's high seat that day:

And the King sat with a heart sore stirred,
And seldom he spoke and seldom heard.

'Twas then through the hall the King was 'ware
Of a little boy with golden hair,

As bright as the golden poppy is
That the beach breeds for the surf to kiss:

Yet pale his cheek as the thorn in Spring,
And his garb black like the raven's wing.

Nothing heard but his foot through the hall,
For now the lords were silent all.

And the King wondered, and said, "Alack!
Who sends me a fair boy dressed in black?

"Why, sweet heart, do you pace through the hall
As though my court were a funeral?"

Then lowly knelt the child at the dais,
And looked up weeping in the King's face.

"O wherefore black, O King, ye may say,
For white is the hue of death to-day.

"Your son and all his fellowship
Lie low in the sea with the White Ship."

King Henry fell as a man struck dead;
And speechless still he stared from his bed
When to him next day my rede I read.

There's many an hour must needs beguile
A King's high heart that he should smile,—

Full many a lordly hour, full fain
Of his realm's rule and pride of his reign:—

But this King never smiled again.

By none but me can the tale be told,
The butcher of Rouen, poor Berold.
(Lands are swayed by a King on a throne.)
'Twas a royal train put forth to sea,
Yet the tale can be told by none but me.
(The sea hath no King but God alone.)

THE KING'S TRAGEDY.

JAMES I. OF SCOTS.—20TH FEBRUARY 1437.

NOTE.

Tradition says that Catherine Douglas, in honour of her heroic act when she barred the door with her arm against the murderers of James the First of Scots, received popularly the name of "Barlass." This name remains to her descendants, the Barlas family, in Scotland, who bear for their crest a broken arm. She married Alexander Lovell of Bolunnie.

A few stanzas from King James's lovely poem, known as *The King's Quair*, are quoted in the course of this ballad. The writer must express regret for the necessity which has compelled him to shorten the ten-syllabled lines to eight syllables, in order that they might harmonize with the ballad metre.

I CATHERINE am a Douglas born,
    A name to all Scots dear;
And Kate Barlass they've called me now
    Through many a waning year.

This old arm's withered now. 'Twas once
    Most deft 'mong maidens all
To rein the steed, to wing the shaft,
    To smite the palm-play ball.

In hall adown the close-linked dance
    It has shone most white and fair,
It has been the rest for a true lord's head,
And many a sweet babe's nursing-bed,
    And the bar to a King's chambère.

THE KING'S TRAGEDY.

Aye, lasses, draw round Kate Barlass,
    And hark with bated breath
How good King James, King Robert's son,
    Was foully done to death.

Through all the days of his gallant youth
    The princely James was pent,
By his friends at first and then by his foes,
    In long imprisonment.

For the elder Prince, the kingdom's heir,
    By treason's murderous brood
Was slain; and the father quaked for the child
    With the royal mortal blood.

I' the Bass Rock fort, by his father's care,
    Was his childhood's life assured;
And Henry the subtle Bolingbroke,
Proud England's King, 'neath the southron yoke
    His youth for long years immured.

Yet in all things meet for a kingly man
    Himself did he approve;
And the nightingale through his prison-wall
    Taught him both lore and love.

For once, when the bird's song drew him close
    To the opened window-pane,
In her bower beneath a lady stood,
A light of life to his sorrowful mood,
    Like a lily amid the rain.

And for her sake, to the sweet bird's note,
    He framed a sweeter Song,
More sweet than ever a poet's heart
    Gave yet to the English tongue.

She was a lady of royal blood;
    And when, past sorrow and teen,
He stood where still through his crownless years
    His Scotish realm had been,
At Scone were the happy lovers crowned,
    A heart-wed King and Queen.

But the bird may fall from the bough of youth,
    And song be turned to moan,
And Love's storm-cloud be the shadow of Hate,
When the tempest-waves of a troubled State
    Are beating against a throne.

Yet well they loved; and the god of Love,
    Whom well the King had sung,
Might find on the earth no truer hearts
    His lowliest swains among.

From the days when first she rode abroad
    With Scotish maids in her train,
I Catherine Douglas won the trust
    Of my mistress sweet Queen Jane.

And oft she sighed, "To be born a King!"
    And oft along the way
When she saw the homely lovers pass
    She has said, "Alack the day!"

Years waned,—the loving and toiling years:
    Till England's wrong renewed
Drove James, by outrage cast on his crown,
    To the open field of feud.

'Twas when the King and his host were met
    At the leaguer of Roxbro' hold,
The Queen o' the sudden sought his camp
    With a tale of dread to be told.

And she showed him a secret letter writ
   That spoke of treasonous strife,
And how a band of his noblest lords
   Were sworn to take his life.

"And it may be here or it may be there,
   In the camp or the court," she said:
"But for my sake come to your people's arms
   And guard your royal head."

Quoth he, "'Tis the fifteenth day of the siege,
   And the castle's nigh to yield."
"O face your foes on your throne," she cried,
   "And show the power you wield;
And under your Scotish people's love
   You shall sit as under your shield."

At the fair Queen's side I stood that day
   When he bade them raise the siege,
And back to his Court he sped to know
   How the lords would meet their Liege.

But when he summoned his Parliament,
   The louring brows hung round,
Like clouds that circle the mountain-head
   Ere the first low thunders sound.

For he had tamed the nobles' lust
   And curbed their power and pride,
And reached out an arm to right the poor
   Through Scotland far and wide;
And many a lordly wrong-doer
   By the headsman's axe had died.

'Twas then upspoke Sir Robert Græme,
   The bold o'ermastering man:—
"O King, in the name of your Three Estates
   I set you under their ban!

"For, as your lords made oath to you
   Of service and fealty,
Even in like wise you pledged your oath
   Their faithful sire to be :—

"Yet all we here that are nobly sprung
   Have mourned dear kith and kin
Since first for the Scotish Barons' curse
   Did your bloody rule begin."

With that he laid his hands on his King :—
   "Is this not so, my lords?"
But of all who had sworn to league with him
   Not one spake back to his words.

Quoth the King :—"Thou speak'st but for one Estate,
   Nor doth it avow thy gage.
Let my liege lords hale this traitor hence!"
   The Græme fired dark with rage :—
"Who works for lesser men than himself,
   He earns but a witless wage!"

But soon from the dungeon where he lay
   He won by privy plots,
And forth he fled with a price on his head
   To the country of the Wild Scots.

And word there came from Sir Robert Græme
   To the King at Edinbro' :—
"No Liege of mine thou art; but I see
From this day forth alone in thee
   God's creature, my mortal foe.

"Through thee are my wife and children lost,
   My heritage and lands ;
And when my God shall show me a way,
Thyself my mortal foe will I slay
   With these my proper hands."

THE KING'S TRAGEDY.

Against the coming of Christmastide
   That year the King bade call
I' the Black Friars' Charterhouse of Perth
   A solemn festival.

And we of his household rode with him
   In a close-ranked company;
But not till the sun had sunk from his throne
   Did we reach the Scotish Sea.

That eve was clenched for a boding storm,
   'Neath a toilsome moon half seen;
The cloud stooped low and the surf rose high;
And where there was a line of the sky,
   Wild wings loomed dark between.

And on a rock of the black beach-side,
   By the veiled moon dimly lit,
There was something seemed to heave with life
   As the King drew nigh to it.

And was it only the tossing furze
   Or brake of the waste sea-wold?
Or was it an eagle bent to the blast?
When near we came, we knew it at last
   For a woman tattered and old.

But it seemed as though by a fire within
   Her writhen limbs were wrung;
And as soon as the King was close to her,
   She stood up gaunt and strong.

'Twas then the moon sailed clear of the rack
   On high in her hollow dome;
And still as aloft with hoary crest
   Each clamorous wave rang home,
Like fire in snow the moonlight blazed
   Amid the champing foam.

And the woman held his eyes with her eyes:—
"O King, thou art come at last,
But thy wraith has haunted the Scotish Sea
To my sight for four years past.

"Four years it is since first I met,
'Twixt the Duchray and the Dhu,
A shape whose feet clung close in a shroud,
And that shape for thine I knew.

"A year again, and on Inchkeith Isle
I saw thee pass in the breeze,
With the cerecloth risen above thy feet
And wound about thy knees.

"And yet a year, in the Links of Forth,
As a wanderer without rest,
Thou cam'st with both thine arms i' the shroud
That clung high up thy breast.

"And in this hour I find thee here,
And well mine eyes may note
That the winding-sheet hath passed thy breast
And risen around thy throat.

"And when I meet thee again, O King,
That of death hast such sore drouth,—
Except thou turn again on this shore,—
The winding-sheet shall have moved once more
And covered thine eyes and mouth.

"O King, whom poor men bless for their King,
Of thy fate be not so fain;
But these my words for God's message take,
And turn thy steed, O King, for her sake
Who rides beside thy rein!"

THE KING'S TRAGEDY.

While the woman spoke, the King's horse reared
   As if it would breast the sea,
And the Queen turned pale as she heard on the gale
   The voice die dolorously.

When the woman ceased, the steed was still,
   But the King gazed on her yet,
And in silence save for the wail of the sea
   His eyes and her eyes met.

At last he said :—"God's ways are His own ;
   Man is but shadow and dust.
Last night I prayed by His altar-stone ;
To-night I wend to the Feast of His Son ;
   And in Him I set my trust.

" I have held my people in sacred charge,
   And have not feared the sting
Of proud men's hate,—to His will resign'd
Who has but one same death for a hind
   And one same death for a King.

" And if God in His wisdom have brought close
   The day when I must die,
That day by water or fire or air
My feet shall fall in the destined snare
   Wherever my road may lie.

" What man can say but the Fiend hath set
   Thy sorcery on my path,
My heart with the fear of death to fill,
And turn me against God's very will
   To sink in His burning wrath ?"

The woman stood as the train rode past,
   And moved nor limb nor eye ;
And when we were shipped, we saw her there
   Still standing against the sky.

As the ship made way, the moon once more
   Sank slow in her rising pall;
And I thought of the shrouded wraith of the King,
   And I said, "The Heavens know all."

And now, ye lasses, must ye hear
   How my name is Kate Barlass:—
But a little thing, when all the tale
   Is told of the weary mass
Of crime and woe which in Scotland's realm
   God's will let come to pass.

'Twas in the Charterhouse of Perth
   That the King and all his Court
Were met, the Christmas Feast being done,
   For solace and disport.

'Twas a wind-wild eve in February,
   And against the casement-pane
The branches smote like summoning hands,
   And muttered the driving rain.

And when the wind swooped over the lift
   And made the whole heaven frown,
It seemed a grip was laid on the walls
   To tug the housetop down.

And the Queen was there, more stately fair
   Than a lily in garden set;
And the King was loth to stir from her side;
For as on the day when she was his bride,
   Even so he loved her yet.

And the Earl of Athole, the King's false friend,
   Sat with him at the board;
And Robert Stuart the chamberlain
   Who had sold his sovereign Lord.

THE KING'S TRAGEDY.

Yet the traitor Christopher Chaumber there
   Would fain have told him all,
And vainly four times that night he strove
   To reach the King through the hall.

But the wine is bright at the goblet's brim
   Though the poison lurk beneath;
And the apples still are red on the tree
Within whose shade may the adder be
   That shall turn thy life to death.

There was a knight of the King's fast friends
   Whom he called the King of Love;
And to such bright cheer and courtesy
   That name might best behove.

And the King and Queen both loved him well
   For his gentle knightliness;
And with him the King, as that eve wore on,
   Was playing at the chess.

And the King said, (for he thought to jest
   And soothe the Queen thereby;)—
"In a book 'tis writ that this same year
   A King shall in Scotland die.

"And I have pondered the matter o'er,
   And this have I found, Sir Hugh,—
There are but two Kings on Scotish ground
   And those Kings are I and you.

"And I have a wife and a newborn heir,
   And you are yourself alone;
So stand you stark at my side with me
   To guard our double throne.

"For here sit I and my wife and child,
　　As well your heart shall approve,
In full surrender and soothfastness,
　　Beneath your Kingdom of Love."

And the Knight laughed, and the Queen too smiled;
　　But I knew her heavy thought,
And I strove to find in the good King's jest
　　What cheer might thence be wrought.

And I said, "My Liege, for the Queen's dear love
　　Now sing the song that of old
You made, when a captive Prince you lay,
And the nightingale sang sweet on the spray,
　　In Windsor's castle-hold."

Then he smiled the smile I knew so well
　　When he thought to please the Queen;
The smile which under all bitter frowns
　　Of fate that rose between
For ever dwelt at the poet's heart
　　Like the bird of love unseen.

And he kissed her hand and took his harp,
　　And the music sweetly rang;
And when the song burst forth, it seemed
　　'Twas the nightingale that sang.

"Worship, ye lovers, on this May:
　　Of bliss your kalends are begun:
Sing with us, Away, Winter, away!
　　Come, Summer, the sweet season and sun!
　　Awake for shame,—your heaven is won,—
And amorously your heads lift all:
Thank Love, that you to his grace doth call!"

But when he bent to the Queen, and sang
    The speech whose praise was hers,
It seemed his voice was the voice of the Spring
    And the voice of the bygone years.

*"The fairest and the freshest flower
That ever I saw before that hour,
The which o' the sudden made to start
The blood of my body to my heart.*
    *   *   *   *   *
*Ah sweet, are ye a worldly creature
Or heavenly thing in form of nature?"*

And the song was long, and richly stored
    With wonder and beauteous things;
And the harp was tuned to every change
    Of minstrel ministerings;
But when he spoke of the Queen at the last,
    Its strings were his own heart-strings.

*"Unworthy but only of her grace,
    Upon Love's rock that's easy and sure,
In guerdon of all my love's space
    She took me her humble creäture.
    Thus fell my blissful aventure
In youth of love that from day to day
Flowereth aye new, and further I say.*

*"To reckon all the circumstance
    As it happed when lessen gan my sore,
Of my rancour and woful chance,
    It were too long,—I have done therefor.
    And of this flower I say no more,
But unto my help her heart hath tended
And even from death her man defended."*

"Aye, even from death," to myself I said;
  For I thought of the day when she
Had borne him the news, at Roxbro' siege,
  Of the fell confederacy.

But Death even then took aim as he sang
  With an arrow deadly bright;
And the grinning skull lurked grimly aloof,
And the wings were spread far over the roof
  More dark than the winter night.

Yet truly along the amorous song
  Of Love's high pomp and state,
There were words of Fortune's trackless doom
  And the dreadful face of Fate.

And oft have I heard again in dreams
  The voice of dire appeal
In which the King then sang of the pit
  That is under Fortune's wheel.

*"And under the wheel beheld I there
  An ugly Pit as deep as hell,
That to behold I quaked for fear:
  And this I heard, that who therein fell
  Came no more up, tidings to tell:
Whereat, astound of the fearful sight,
I wist not what to do for fright."*

And oft has my thought called up again
  These words of the changeful song:—
*" Wist thou thy pain and thy travàil
To come, well might'st thou weep and wail!"*
  And our wail, O God! is long.

THE KING'S TRAGEDY.

But the song's end was all of his love;
    And well his heart was grac'd
With her smiling lips and her tear-bright eyes
    As his arm went round her waist.

And on the swell of her long fair throat
    Close clung the necklet-chain
As he bent her pearl-tir'd head aside,
And in the warmth of his love and pride
    He kissed her lips full fain.

And her true face was a rosy red,
    The very red of the rose
That, couched on the happy garden-bed,
    In the summer sunlight glows.

And all the wondrous things of love
    That sang so sweet through the song
Were in the look that met in their eyes,
    And the look was deep and long.

'Twas then a knock came at the outer gate,
    And the usher sought the King.
"The woman you met by the Scotish Sea,
    My Liege, would tell you a thing;
And she says that her present need for speech
    Will bear no gainsaying."

And the King said: "The hour is late;
    To-morrow will serve, I ween."
Then he charged the usher strictly, and said:
    "No word of this to the Queen."

But the usher came again to the King.
    "Shall I call her back?" quoth he:
"For as she went on her way, she cried,
    'Woe! Woe! then the thing must be!'"

And the King paused, but he did not speak.
  Then he called for the Voidee-cup:
And as we heard the twelfth hour strike,
There by true lips and false lips alike
  Was the draught of trust drained up.

So with reverence meet to King and Queen,
  To bed went all from the board;
And the last to leave of the courtly train
Was Robert Stuart the chamberlain
  Who had sold his sovereign lord.

And all the locks of the chamber-door
  Had the traitor riven and brast;
And that Fate might win sure way from afar,
He had drawn out every bolt and bar
  That made the entrance fast.

And now at midnight he stole his way
  To the moat of the outer wall,
And laid strong hurdles closely across
  Where the traitors' tread should fall.

But we that were the Queen's bower-maids
  Alone were left behind;
And with heed we drew the curtains close
  Against the winter wind.

And now that all was still through the hall,
  More clearly we heard the rain
That clamoured ever against the glass
  And the boughs that beat on the pane.

But the fire was bright in the ingle-nook,
  And through empty space around
The shadows cast on the arras'd wall
'Mid the pictured kings stood sudden and tall
  Like spectres sprung from the ground.

THE KING'S TRAGEDY.

And the bed was dight in a deep alcove;
    And as he stood by the fire
The King was still in talk with the Queen
    While he doffed his goodly attire.

And the song had brought the image back
    Of many a bygone year;
And many a loving word they said
With hand in hand and head laid to head;
    And none of us went anear.

But Love was weeping outside the house,
    A child in the piteous rain;
And as he watched the arrow of Death,
He wailed for his own shafts close in the sheath
    That never should fly again.

And now beneath the window arose
    A wild voice suddenly:
And the King reared straight, but the Queen fell back
    As for bitter dule to dree;
And all of us knew the woman's voice
    Who spoke by the Scotish Sea.

"O King," she cried, "in an evil hour
    They drove me from thy gate;
And yet my voice must rise to thine ears;
    But alas! it comes too late!

"Last night at mid-watch, by Aberdour,
    When the moon was dead in the skies,
O King, in a death-light of thine own
    I saw thy shape arise.

"And in full season, as erst I said,
    The doom had gained its growth;
And the shroud had risen above thy neck
    And covered thine eyes and mouth.

"And no moon woke, but the pale dawn broke,
    And still thy soul stood there;
And I thought its silence cried to my soul
    As the first rays crowned its hair.

"Since then have I journeyed fast and fain
    In very despite of Fate,
Lest Hope might still be found in God's will:
    But they drove me from thy gate.

"For every man on God's ground, O King,
    His death grows up from his birth
In a shadow-plant perpetually;
And thine towers high, a black yew-tree,
    O'er the Charterhouse of Perth!"

That room was built far out from the house;
    And none but we in the room
Might hear the voice that rose beneath,
    Nor the tread of the coming doom.

For now there came a torchlight-glare,
    And a clang of arms there came;
And not a soul in that space but thought
    Of the foe Sir Robert Græme.

Yea, from the country of the Wild Scots,
    O'er mountain, valley, and glen,
He had brought with him in murderous league
    Three hundred armèd men.

The King knew all in an instant's flash;
    And like a King did he stand;
But there was no armour in all the room,
    Nor weapon lay to his hand.

And all we women flew to the door
    And thought to have made it fast;
But the bolts were gone and the bars were gone
    And the locks were riven and brast.

THE KING'S TRAGEDY.

And he caught the pale pale Queen in his arms
   As the iron footsteps fell,—
Then loosed her, standing alone, and said,
   "Our bliss was our farewell!"

And 'twixt his lips he murmured a prayer,
   And he crossed his brow and breast;
And proudly in royal hardihood
Even so with folded arms he stood,—
   The prize of the bloody quest.

Then on me leaped the Queen like a deer:—
   "O Catherine, help!" she cried.
And low at his feet we clasped his knees
   Together side by side.
"Oh! even a King, for his people's sake,
   From treasonous death must hide!"

"For *her* sake most!" I cried, and I marked
   The pang that my words could wring.
And the iron tongs from the chimney-nook
   I snatched and held to the king:—
"Wrench up the plank! and the vault beneath
   Shall yield safe harbouring."

With brows low-bent, from my eager hand
   The heavy heft did he take;
And the plank at his feet he wrenched and tore;
And as he frowned through the open floor,
   Again I said, "For her sake!"

Then he cried to the Queen, "God's will be done!"
   For her hands were clasped in prayer.
And down he sprang to the inner crypt;
And straight we closed the plank he had ripp'd
   And toiled to smooth it fair.

(Alas! in that vault a gap once was
    Wherethro' the King might have fled:
But three days since close-walled had it been
By his will; for the ball would roll therein
    When without at the palm he play'd.)

Then the Queen cried, "Catherine, keep the door,
    And I to this will suffice!"
At her word I rose all dazed to my feet,
    And my heart was fire and ice.

And louder ever the voices grew,
    And the tramp of men in mail;
Until to my brain it seemed to be
As though I tossed on a ship at sea
    In the teeth of a crashing gale.

Then back I flew to the rest; and hard
    We strove with sinews knit
To force the table against the door;
    But we might not compass it.

Then my wild gaze sped far down the hall
    To the place of the hearthstone-sill;
And the Queen bent ever above the floor,
    For the plank was rising still.

And now the rush was heard on the stair,
    And "God, what help?" was our cry.
And was I frenzied or was I bold?
I looked at each empty stanchion-hold,
    And no bar but my arm had I!

Like iron felt my arm, as through
    The staple I made it pass:—
Alack! it was flesh and bone—no more!
'Twas Catherine Douglas sprang to the door,
    But I fell back Kate Barlass.

THE KING'S TRAGEDY.

With that they all thronged into the hall,
  Half dim to my failing ken;
And the space that was but a void before
  Was a crowd of wrathful men.

Behind the door I had fall'n and lay,
  Yet my sense was wildly aware,
And for all the pain of my shattered arm
  I never fainted there.

Even as I fell, my eyes were cast
  Where the King leaped down to the pit;
And lo! the plank was smooth in its place,
  And the Queen stood far from it.

And under the litters and through the bed
  And within the presses all
The traitors sought for the King, and pierced
  The arras around the wall.

And through the chamber they ramped and stormed
  Like lions loose in the lair,
And scarce could trust to their very eyes,—
  For behold! no King was there.

Then one of them seized the Queen, and cried,—
  "Now tell us, where is thy lord?"
And he held the sharp point over her heart:
She drooped not her eyes nor did she start,
  But she answered never a word.

Then the sword half pierced the true true breast:
  But it was the Græme's own son
Cried, "This is a woman,—we seek a man!"
  And away from her girdle zone
He struck the point of the murderous steel;
  And that foul deed was not done.

And forth flowed all the throng like a sea
  And 'twas empty space once more;
And my eyes sought out the wounded Queen
  As I lay behind the door.

And I said: "Dear Lady, leave me here,
  For I cannot help you now;
But fly while you may, and none shall reck
  Of my place here lying low."

And she said, "My Catherine, God help thee!"
  Then she looked to the distant floor,
And clasping her hands, "O God help *him*,"
  She sobbed, "for we can no more!"

But God He knows what help may mean,
  If it mean to live or to die;
And what sore sorrow and mighty moan
On earth it may cost ere yet a throne
  Be filled in His house on high.

And now the ladies fled with the Queen;
  And through the open door
The night-wind wailed round the empty room
  And the rushes shook on the floor.

And the bed drooped low in the dark recess
  Whence the arras was rent away;
And the firelight still shone over the space
  Where our hidden secret lay.

And the rain had ceased, and the moonbeams lit
  The window high in the wall,—
Bright beams that on the plank that I knew
  Through the painted pane did fall,
And gleamed with the splendour of Scotland's crown
  And shield armorial.

THE KING'S TRAGEDY.

But then a great wind swept up the skies
    And the climbing moon fell back;
And the royal blazon fled from the floor,
    And nought remained on its track;
And high in the darkened window-pane
    The shield and the crown were black.

And what I say next I partly saw
    And partly I heard in sooth,
And partly since from the murderers' lips
    The torture wrung the truth.

For now again came the armèd tread,
    And fast through the hall it fell;
But the throng was less; and ere I saw,
    By the voice without I could tell
That Robert Stuart had come with them
    Who knew that chamber well.

And over the space the Græme strode dark
    With his mantle round him flung;
And in his eye was a flaming light
    But not a word on his tongue.

And Stuart held a torch to the floor,
    And he found the thing he sought;
And they slashed the plank away with their swords;
    And O God! I fainted not!

And the traitor held his torch in the gap,
    All smoking and smouldering;
And through the vapour and fire, beneath
    In the dark crypt's narrow ring,
With a shout that pealed to the room's high roof
    They saw their naked King.

Half naked he stood, but stood as one
 Who yet could do and dare :
With the crown, the King was stript away,—
The Knight was 'reft of his battle-array,—
 But still the Man was there.

From the rout then stepped a villain forth,—
 Sir John Hall was his name ;
With a knife unsheathed he leapt to the vault
 Beneath the torchlight-flame.

Of his person and stature was the King
 A man right manly strong,
And mightily by the shoulder-blades
 His foe to his feet he flung.

Then the traitor's brother, Sir Thomas Hall,
 Sprang down to work his worst ;
And the King caught the second man by the neck
 And flung him above the first.

And he smote and trampled them under him ;
 And a long month thence they bare
All black their throats with the grip of his hands
 When the hangman's hand came there.

And sore he strove to have had their knives,
 But the sharp blades gashed his hands.
Oh James ! so armed, thou hadst battled there
 Till help had come of thy bands ;
And oh ! once more thou hadst held our throne
 And ruled thy Scotish lands !

But while the King o'er his foes still raged
　　With a heart that nought could tame,
Another man sprang down to the crypt;
And with his sword in his hand hard-gripp'd,
　　There stood Sir Robert Græme.

(Now shame on the recreant traitor's heart
　　Who durst not face his King
Till the body unarmed was wearied out
　　With two-fold combating!

Ah! well might the people sing and say,
　　As oft ye have heard aright:—
"*O Robert Græme, O Robert Græme,
Who slew our King, God give thee shame!*"
　　For he slew him not as a knight.)

And the naked King turned round at bay,
　　But his strength had passed the goal,
And he could but gasp:—"Mine hour is come;
But oh! to succour thine own soul's doom,
　　Let a priest now shrive my soul!"

And the traitor looked on the King's spent strength,
　　And said:—"Have I kept my word?—
Yea, King, the mortal pledge that I gave?
No black friar's shrift thy soul shall have,
　　But the shrift of this red sword!"

With that he smote his King through the breast;
　　And all they three in that pen
Fell on him and stabbed and stabbed him there
　　Like merciless murderous men.

Yet seemed it now that Sir Robert Græme,
　　Ere the King's last breath was o'er,
Turned sick at heart with the deadly sight
　　And would have done no more.

But a cry came from the troop above :—
  "If him thou do not slay,
The price of his life that thou dost spare
  Thy forfeit life shall pay!"

O God! what more did I hear or see,
  Or how should I tell the rest?
But there at length our King lay slain
  With sixteen wounds in his breast.

O God! and now did a bell boom forth,
  And the murderers turned and fled;—
Too late, too late, O God, did it sound!—
And I heard the true men mustering round,
  And the cries and the coming tread.

But ere they came, to the black death-gap
  Somewise did I creep and steal;
And lo! or ever I swooned away,
Through the dusk I saw where the white face lay
  In the Pit of Fortune's Wheel.

And now, ye Scotish maids who have heard
  Dread things of the days grown old,—
Even at the last, of true Queen Jane
  May somewhat yet be told,
And how she dealt for her dear lord's sake
  Dire vengeance manifold.

'Twas in the Charterhouse of Perth,
  In the fair-lit Death-chapelle,
That the slain King's corpse on bier was laid
  With chaunt and requiem-knell.

THE KING'S TRAGEDY.

And all with royal wealth of balm
   Was the body purified;
And none could trace on the brow and lips
   The death that he had died.

In his robes of state he lay asleep
   With orb and sceptre in hand;
And by the crown he wore on his throne
   Was his kingly forehead spann'd.

And, girls, 'twas a sweet sad thing to see
   How the curling golden hair,
As in the day of the poet's youth,
   From the King's crown clustered there.

And if all had come to pass in the brain
   That throbbed beneath those curls,
Then Scots had said in the days to come
That this their soil was a different home
   And a different Scotland, girls!

And the Queen sat by him night and day,
   And oft she knelt in prayer,
All wan and pale in the widow's veil
   That shrouded her shining hair.

And I had got good help of my hurt:
   And only to me some sign
She made; and save the priests that were there,
   No face would she see but mine.

And the month of March wore on apace;
   And now fresh couriers fared
Still from the country of the Wild Scots
   With news of the traitors snared.

And still as I told her day by day,
  Her pallor changed to sight,
And the frost grew to a furnace-flame
  That burnt her visage white.

And evermore as I brought her word,
  She bent to her dead King James,
And in the cold ear with fire-drawn breath
  She spoke the traitors' names.

But when the name of Sir Robert Græme
  Was the one she had to give,
I ran to hold her up from the floor;
For the froth was on her lips, and sore
  I feared that she could not live.

And the month of March wore nigh to its end,
  And still was the death-pall spread;
For she would not bury her slaughtered lord
  Till his slayers all were dead.

And now of their dooms dread tidings came,
  And of torments fierce and dire;
And nought she spake,—she had ceased to speak,—
  But her eyes were a soul on fire.

But when I told her the bitter end
  Of the stern and just award,
She leaned o'er the bier, and thrice three times
  She kissed the lips of her lord.

And then she said,—"My King, they are dead!"
  And she knelt on the chapel-floor,
And whispered low with a strange proud smile,—
  "James, James, they suffered more!"

Last she stood up to her queenly height,
 But she shook like an autumn leaf,
As though the fire wherein she burned
Then left her body, and all were turned
 To winter of life-long grief.

And "O James!" she said,—"My James!" she said,—
 "Alas for the woful thing,
That a poet true and a friend of man,
In desperate days of bale and ban,
 Should needs be born a King!"

THE HOUSE OF LIFE.

A SONNET-SEQUENCE.

Part I.
YOUTH AND CHANGE.

Part II.
CHANGE AND FATE.

(The present full series of *The House of Life* consists of sonnets only. It will be evident that many among those now first added are still the work of earlier years.—1881.)

A Sonnet is a moment's monument,—
Memorial from the Soul's eternity
To one dead deathless hour. Look that it be,
Whether for lustral rite or dire portent,
Of its own arduous fulness reverent:
Carve it in ivory or in ebony,
As Day or Night may rule; and let Time see
Its flowering crest impearled and orient.

A Sonnet is a coin: its face reveals
The soul,—its converse, to what Power 'tis due:—
Whether for tribute to the august appeals
Of Life, or dower in Love's high retinue,
It serve; or, 'mid the dark wharf's cavernous breath,
In Charon's palm it pay the toll to Death.

THE HOUSE OF LIFE.

Part I.—*YOUTH AND CHANGE.*

SONNET I.
LOVE ENTHRONED.

I MARKED all kindred Powers the heart finds fair:—
   Truth, with awed lips; and Hope, with eyes upcast;
   And Fame, whose loud wings fan the ashen Past
To signal-fires, Oblivion's flight to scare;
And Youth, with still some single golden hair
   Unto his shoulder clinging, since the last
   Embrace wherein two sweet arms held him fast;
And Life, still wreathing flowers for Death to wear.

Love's throne was not with these; but far above
   All passionate wind of welcome and farewell
He sat in breathless bowers they dream not of;
   Though Truth foreknow Love's heart, and Hope foretell,
   And Fame be for Love's sake desirable,
And Youth be dear, and Life be sweet to Love.

SONNET II.
BRIDAL BIRTH.

As when desire, long darkling, dawns, and first
   The mother looks upon the newborn child,
   Even so my Lady stood at gaze and smiled
When her soul knew at length the Love it nurs'd.
Born with her life, creature of poignant thirst
   And exquisite hunger, at her heart Love lay
   Quickening in darkness, till a voice that day
Cried on him, and the bonds of birth were burst.

Now, shadowed by his wings, our faces yearn
   Together, as his full-grown feet now range
     The grove, and his warm hands our couch prepare:
Till to his song our bodiless souls in turn
   Be born his children, when Death's nuptial change
     Leaves us for light the halo of his hair.

SONNET III.

LOVE'S TESTAMENT.

O THOU who at Love's hour ecstatically
   Unto my heart dost evermore present,
   Clothed with his fire, thy heart his testament;
Whom I have neared and felt thy breath to be
The inmost incense of his sanctuary;
   Who without speech hast owned him, and, intent
   Upon his will, thy life with mine hast blent,
And murmured, " I am thine, thou'rt one with me!"

O what from thee the grace, to me the prize,
   And what to Love the glory,—when the whole
   Of the deep stair thou tread'st to the dim shoal
And weary water of the place of sighs,
And there dost work deliverance, as thine eyes
   Draw up my prisoned spirit to thy soul!

SONNET IV.

LOVESIGHT.

WHEN do I see thee most, beloved one?
   When in the light the spirits of mine eyes
   Before thy face, their altar, solemnize
The worship of that Love through thee made known?
Or when in the dusk hours, (we two alone,)
   Close-kissed and eloquent of still replies
   Thy twilight-hidden glimmering visage lies,
And my soul only sees thy soul its own?

O love, my love! if I no more should see
Thyself, nor on the earth the shadow of thee,
   Nor image of thine eyes in any spring,—
How then should sound upon Life's darkening slope
The ground-whirl of the perished leaves of Hope,
   The wind of Death's imperishable wing?

THE HOUSE OF LIFE.

SONNET V.

HEART'S HOPE.

By what word's power, the key of paths untrod,
   Shall I the difficult deeps of Love explore,
   Till parted waves of Song yield up the shore
Even as that sea which Israel crossed dryshod?
For lo! in some poor rhythmic period,
   Lady, I fain would tell how evermore
   Thy soul I know not from thy body, nor
Thee from myself, neither our love from God.

Yea, in God's name, and Love's, and thine, would I
   Draw from one loving heart such evidence
As to all hearts all things shall signify;
   Tender as dawn's first hill-fire, and intense
   As instantaneous penetrating sense,
In Spring's birth-hour, of other Springs gone by.

SONNET VI.

THE KISS.

What smouldering senses in death's sick delay
   Or seizure of malign vicissitude
   Can rob this body of honour, or denude
This soul of wedding-raiment worn to-day?
For lo! even now my lady's lips did play
   With these my lips such consonant interlude
   As laurelled Orpheus longed for when he wooed
The half-drawn hungering face with that last lay

I was a child beneath her touch,—a man
   When breast to breast we clung, even I and she,
   A spirit when her spirit looked through me,—
A god when all our life-breath met to fan
Our life-blood, till love's emulous ardours ran,
   Fire within fire, desire in deity.

SONNET VII.

SUPREME SURRENDER.

To all the spirits of Love that wander by
   Along his love-sown harvest-field of sleep
   My lady lies apparent; and the deep
Calls to the deep; and no man sees but I.
The bliss so long afar, at length so nigh,
   Rests there attained. Methinks proud Love must weep
   When Fate's control doth from his harvest reap
The sacred hour for which the years did sigh.

First touched, the hand now warm around my neck
   Taught memory long to mock desire: and lo!
   Across my breast the abandoned hair doth flow,
Where one shorn tress long stirred the longing ache:
And next the heart that trembled for its sake
   Lies the queen-heart in sovereign overthrow.

SONNET VIII.

LOVE'S LOVERS.

SOME ladies love the jewels in Love's zone,
   And gold-tipped darts he hath for painless play
   In idle scornful hours he flings away;
And some that listen to his lute's soft tone
Do love to vaunt the silver praise their own;
   Some prize his blindfold sight; and there be they
   Who kissed his wings which brought him yesterday
And thank his wings to-day that he is flown.

My lady only loves the heart of Love:
   Therefore Love's heart, my lady, hath for thee
   His bower of unimagined flower and tree:
There kneels he now, and all-anhungered of
Thine eyes grey-lit in shadowing hair above,
   Seals with thy mouth his immortality.

SONNET IX.

PASSION AND WORSHIP.

One flame-winged brought a white-winged harp-player
   Even where my lady and I lay all alone;
   Saying: "Behold, this minstrel is unknown;
Bid him depart, for I am minstrel here:
Only my strains are to Love's dear ones dear."
   Then said I: "Through thine hautboy's rapturous tone
   Unto my lady still this harp makes moan,
And still she deems the cadence deep and clear."

Then said my lady: "Thou art Passion of Love,
   And this Love's Worship: both he plights to me.
   Thy mastering music walks the sunlit sea:
But where wan water trembles in the grove
And the wan moon is all the light thereof,
   This harp still makes my name its voluntary."

SONNET X.

THE PORTRAIT.

O Lord of all compassionate control,
   O Love! let this my lady's picture glow
   Under my hand to praise her name, and show
Even of her inner self the perfect whole:
That he who seeks her beauty's furthest goal,
   Beyond the light that the sweet glances throw
   And refluent wave of the sweet smile, may know
The very sky and sea-line of her soul.

Lo! it is done. Above the enthroning throat
   The mouth's mould testifies of voice and kiss,
     The shadowed eyes remember and foresee.
Her face is made her shrine. Let all men note
   That in all years (O Love, thy gift is this!)
     They that would look on her must come to me.

SONNET XI.
THE LOVE-LETTER.

Warmed by her hand and shadowed by her hair
   As close she leaned and poured her heart through thee,
   Whereof the articulate throbs accompany
The smooth black stream that makes thy whiteness fair,—
Sweet fluttering sheet, even of her breath aware,—
   Oh let thy silent song disclose to me
   That soul wherewith her lips and eyes agree
Like married music in Love's answering air.

Fain had I watched her when, at some fond thought,
   Her bosom to the writing closelier press'd,
   And her breast's secrets peered into her breast;
When, through eyes raised an instant, her soul sought
My soul, and from the sudden confluence caught
   The words that made her love the loveliest.

SONNET XII.
THE LOVERS' WALK.

Sweet twining hedgeflowers wind-stirred in no wise
   On this June day; and hand that clings in hand :-
   Still glades; and meeting faces scarcely fann'd :—
An osier-odoured stream that draws the skies
Deep to its heart; and mirrored eyes in eyes :—
   Fresh hourly wonder o'er the Summer land
   Of light and cloud; and two souls softly spann'd
With one o'erarching heaven of smiles and sighs :—

Even such their path, whose bodies lean unto
   Each other's visible sweetness amorously,—
   Whose passionate hearts lean by Love's high decree
Together on his heart for ever true,
As the cloud-foaming firmamental blue
   Rests on the blue line of a foamless sea.

SONNET XIII.
YOUTH'S ANTIPHONY.

" I LOVE you, sweet: how can you ever learn
   How much I love you?" "You I love even so,
   And so I learn it." "Sweet, you cannot know
How fair you are." "If fair enough to earn
Your love, so much is all my love's concern."
   "My love grows hourly, sweet." "Mine too doth grow,
   Yet love seemed full so many hours ago!"
Thus lovers speak, till kisses claim their turn.

Ah! happy they to whom such words as these
   In youth have served for speech the whole day long,
   Hour after hour, remote from the world's throng,
Work, contest, fame, all life's confederate pleas,—
What while Love breathed in sighs and silences
   Through two blent souls one rapturous undersong.

SONNET XIV.
YOUTH'S SPRING-TRIBUTE.

ON this sweet bank your head thrice sweet and dear
   I lay, and spread your hair on either side,
   And see the newborn woodflowers bashful-eyed
Look through the golden tresses here and there.
On these debateable borders of the year
   Spring's foot half falters; scarce she yet may know
   The leafless blackthorn-blossom from the snow;
And through her bowers the wind's way still is clear.

But April's sun strikes down the glades to-day;
   So shut your eyes upturned, and feel my kiss
Creep, as the Spring now thrills through every spray,
   Up your warm throat to your warm lips: for this
   Is even the hour of Love's sworn suitservice,
With whom cold hearts are counted castaway.

SONNET XV.

THE BIRTH-BOND.

Have you not noted, in some family
  Where two were born of a first marriage-bed,
  How still they own their gracious bond, though fed
And nursed on the forgotten breast and knee?—
How to their father's children they shall be
  In act and thought of one goodwill; but each
  Shall for the other have, in silence speech,
And in a word complete community?

Even so, when first I saw you, seemed it, love,
  That among souls allied to mine was yet
One nearer kindred than life hinted of.
  O born with me somewhere that men forget,
  And though in years of sight and sound unmet,
Known for my soul's birth-partner well enough!

SONNET XVI.

A DAY OF LOVE.

Those envied places which do know her well,
  And are so scornful of this lonely place,
  Even now for once are emptied of her grace:
Nowhere but here she is: and while Love's spell
From his predominant presence doth compel
  All alien hours, an outworn populace,
  The hours of Love fill full the echoing space
With sweet confederate music favourable.

Now many memories make solicitous
  The delicate love-lines of her mouth, till, lit
  With quivering fire, the words take wing from it;
As here between our kisses we sit thus
  Speaking of things remembered, and so sit
Speechless while things forgotten call to us.

SONNET XVII.

BEAUTY'S PAGEANT.

WHAT dawn-pulse at the heart of heaven, or last
   Incarnate flower of culminating day,—
   What marshalled marvels on the skirts of May,
Or song full-quired, sweet June's encomiast;
What glory of change by Nature's hand amass'd
   Can vie with all those moods of varying grace
   Which o'er one loveliest woman's form and face
Within this hour, within this room, have pass'd?

Love's very vesture and elect disguise
   Was each fine movement,—wonder new-begot
   Of lily or swan or swan-stemmed galiot;
Joy to his sight who now the sadlier sighs,
Parted again; and sorrow yet for eyes
   Unborn, that read these words and saw her not.

SONNET XVIII.

GENIUS IN BEAUTY.

BEAUTY like hers is genius. Not the call
   Of Homer's or of Dante's heart sublime,—
   Not Michael's hand furrowing the zones of time,—
Is more with compassed mysteries musical;
Nay, not in Spring's or Summer's sweet footfall
   More gathered gifts exuberant Life bequeaths
   Than doth this sovereign face, whose love-spell breathes
Even from its shadowed contour on the wall.

As many men are poets in their youth,
   But for one sweet-strung soul the wires prolong
   Even through all change the indomitable song;
So in likewise the envenomed years, whose tooth
Rends shallower grace with ruin void of ruth,
   Upon this beauty's power shall wreak no wrong.

SONNET XIX.

SILENT NOON.

Your hands lie open in the long fresh grass,—
    The finger-points look through like rosy blooms:
    Your eyes smile peace. The pasture gleams and glooms
'Neath billowing skies that scatter and amass.
All round our nest, far as the eye can pass,
    Are golden kingcup-fields with silver edge
    Where the cow-parsley skirts the hawthorn-hedge.
'Tis visible silence, still as the hour-glass.

Deep in the sun-searched growths the dragon-fly
Hangs like a blue thread loosened from the sky:—
    So this wing'd hour is dropt to us from above.
Oh! clasp we to our hearts, for deathless dower,
This close-companioned inarticulate hour
    When twofold silence was the song of love.

SONNET XX.

GRACIOUS MOONLIGHT.

Even as the moon grows queenlier in mid-space
    When the sky darkens, and her cloud-rapt car
    Thrills with intenser radiance from afar,—
So lambent, lady, beams thy sovereign grace
When the drear soul desires thee. Of that face
    What shall be said,—which, like a governing star,
    Gathers and garners from all things that are
Their silent penetrative loveliness?

O'er water-daisies and wild waifs of Spring,
    There where the iris rears its gold-crowned sheaf
    With flowering rush and sceptred arrow-leaf,
So have I marked Queen Dian, in bright ring
Of cloud above and wave below, take wing
    And chase night's gloom, as thou the spirit's grief.

SONNET XXI.

LOVE-SWEETNESS.

Sweet dimness of her loosened hair's downfall
   About thy face; her sweet hands round thy head
   In gracious fostering union garlanded;
Her tremulous smiles; her glances' sweet recall
Of love; her murmuring sighs memorial;
   Her mouth's culled sweetness by thy kisses shed
   On cheeks and neck and eyelids, and so led
Back to her mouth which answers there for all :—

What sweeter than these things, except the thing
   In lacking which all these would lose their sweet:—
   The confident heart's still fervour: the swift beat
And soft subsidence of the spirit's wing,
Then when it feels, in cloud-girt wayfaring,
   The breath of kindred plumes against its feet?

SONNET XXII.

HEART'S HAVEN.

Sometimes she is a child within mine arms,
   Cowering beneath dark wings that love must chase,—
   With still tears showering and averted face,
Inexplicably filled with faint alarms :
And oft from mine own spirit's hurtling harms
   I crave the refuge of her deep embrace,—
   Against all ills the fortified strong place
And sweet reserve of sovereign counter-charms.

And Love, our light at night and shade at noon,
   Lulls us to rest with songs, and turns away
   All shafts of shelterless tumultuous day.
Like the moon's growth, his face gleams through his tune;
And as soft waters warble to the moon,
   Our answering spirits chime one roundelay.

SONNET XXIII.

LOVE'S BAUBLES.

I STOOD where Love in brimming armfuls bore
   Slight wanton flowers and foolish toys of fruit:
   And round him ladies thronged in warm pursuit,
Fingered and lipped and proffered the strange store.
And from one hand the petal and the core
   Savoured of sleep; and cluster and curled shoot
   Seemed from another hand like shame's salute,—
Gifts that I felt my cheek was blushing for.

At last Love bade my Lady give the same:
   And as I looked, the dew was light thereon;
   And as I took them, at her touch they shone
With inmost heaven-hue of the heart of flame.
And then Love said: "Lo! when the hand is hers,
Follies of love are love's true ministers."

SONNET XXIV.

PRIDE OF YOUTH.

EVEN as a child, of sorrow that we give
   The dead, but little in his heart can find,
   Since without need of thought to his clear mind
Their turn it is to die and his to live:—
Even so the winged New Love smiles to receive
   Along his eddying plumes the auroral wind,
   Nor, forward glorying, casts one look behind
Where night-rack shrouds the Old Love fugitive.

There is a change in every hour's recall,
   And the last cowslip in the fields we see
   On the same day with the first corn-poppy.
Alas for hourly change! Alas for all
The loves that from his hand proud Youth lets fall,
   Even as the beads of a told rosary!

SONNET XXV.

WINGED HOURS.

Each hour until we meet is as a bird
    That wings from far his gradual way along
    The rustling covert of my soul,—his song
Still loudlier trilled through leaves more deeply stirr'd:
But at the hour of meeting, a clear word
    Is every note he sings, in Love's own tongue;
    Yet, Love, thou know'st the sweet strain suffers wrong,
Full oft through our contending joys unheard.

What of that hour at last, when for her sake
    No wing may fly to me nor song may flow;
    When, wandering round my life unleaved, I know
The bloodied feathers scattered in the brake,
And think how she, far from me, with like eyes
Sees through the untuneful bough the wingless skies?

SONNET XXVI.

MID-RAPTURE.

Thou lovely and beloved, thou my love;
    Whose kiss seems still the first; whose summoning eyes,
    Even now, as for our love-world's new sunrise,
Shed very dawn; whose voice, attuned above
All modulation of the deep-bowered dove,
    Is like a hand laid softly on the soul;
    Whose hand is like a sweet voice to control
Those worn tired brows it hath the keeping of:—

What word can answer to thy word,—what gaze
    To thine, which now absorbs within its sphere
    My worshiping face, till I am mirrored there
Light-circled in a heaven of deep-drawn rays?
What clasp, what kiss mine inmost heart can prove,
O lovely and beloved, O my love?

SONNET XXVII.
HEART'S COMPASS.

Sometimes thou seem'st not as thyself alone,
  But as the meaning of all things that are;
  A breathless wonder, shadowing forth afar
Some heavenly solstice hushed and halcyon;
Whose unstirred lips are music's visible tone;
  Whose eyes the sun-gate of the soul unbar,
  Being of its furthest fires oracular;—
The evident heart of all life sown and mown.

Even such Love is; and is not thy name Love?
  Yea, by thy hand the Love-god rends apart
  All gathering clouds of Night's ambiguous art;
Flings them far down, and sets thine eyes above;
And simply, as some gage of flower or glove,
  Stakes with a smile the world against thy heart.

SONNET XXVIII.
SOUL-LIGHT.

What other woman could be loved like you,
  Or how of you should love possess his fill?
  After the fulness of all rapture, still,—
As at the end of some deep avenue
A tender glamour of day,—there comes to view
  Far in your eyes a yet more hungering thrill,—
  Such fire as Love's soul-winnowing hands distil
Even from his inmost arc of light and dew.

And as the traveller triumphs with the sun,
  Glorying in heat's mid-height, yet startide brings
  Wonder new-born, and still fresh transport springs
From limpid lambent hours of day begun;—
Even so, through eyes and voice, your soul doth move
My soul with changeful light of infinite love.

THE HOUSE OF LIFE.

SONNET XXIX.

THE MOONSTAR.

Lady, I thank thee for thy loveliness,
    Because my lady is more lovely still.
    Glorying I gaze, and yield with glad goodwill
To thee thy tribute; by whose sweet-spun dress
Of delicate life Love labours to assess
    My lady's absolute queendom; saying, "Lo!
    How high this beauty is, which yet doth show
But as that beauty's sovereign votaress."

Lady, I saw thee with her, side by side;
    And as, when night's fair fires their queen surround,
An emulous star too near the moon will ride,—
    Even so thy rays within her luminous bound
    Were traced no more; and by the light so drown'd,
Lady, not thou but she was glorified.

SONNET XXX.

LAST FIRE.

Love, through your spirit and mine what summer eve
    Now glows with glory of all things possess'd,
    Since this day's sun of rapture filled the west
And the light sweetened as the fire took leave?
Awhile now softlier let your bosom heave,
    As in Love's harbour, even that loving breast,
    All care takes refuge while we sink to rest,
And mutual dreams the bygone bliss retrieve.

Many the days that Winter keeps in store,
    Sunless throughout, or whose brief sun-glimpses
    Scarce shed the heaped snow through the naked trees.
This day at least was Summer's paramour,
Sun-coloured to the imperishable core
    With sweet well-being of love and full heart's ease.

SONNET XXXI.
HER GIFTS.

High grace, the dower of queens; and therewithal
  Some wood-born wonder's sweet simplicity
  A glance like water brimming with the sky
Or hyacinth-light where forest-shadows fall;
Such thrilling pallor of cheek as doth enthral
  The heart; a mouth whose passionate forms imply
  All music and all silence held thereby;
Deep golden locks, her sovereign coronal;
A round reared neck, meet column of Love's shrine
  To cling to when the heart takes sanctuary;
  Hands which for ever at Love's bidding be,
And soft-stirred feet still answering to his sign :—
These are her gifts, as tongue may tell them o'er.
Breathe low her name, my soul; for that means more.

SONNET XXXII.
EQUAL TROTH.

Not by one measure mayst thou mete our love;
  For how should I be loved as I love thee ?—
  I, graceless, joyless, lacking absolutely
All gifts that with thy queenship best behove ;—
Thou, throned in every heart's elect alcove,
  And crowned with garlands culled from every tree,
  Which for no head but thine, by Love's decree,
All beauties and all mysteries interwove.

But here thine eyes and lips yield soft rebuke :—
  "Then only" (say'st thou) "could I love thee less,
  When thou couldst doubt my love's equality."
Peace, sweet! If not to sum but worth we look,—
  Thy heart's transcendence, not my heart's excess,—
  Then more a thousandfold thou lov'st than I.

SONNET XXXIII.

VENUS VICTRIX.

Could Juno's self more sovereign presence wear
   Than thou, 'mid other ladies throned in grace?—
   Or Pallas, when thou bend'st with soul-stilled face
O'er poet's page gold-shadowed in thy hair?
Dost thou than Venus seem less heavenly fair
   When o'er the sea of love's tumultuous trance
   Hovers thy smile, and mingles with thy glance
That sweet voice like the last wave murmuring there?

Before such triune loveliness divine
   Awestruck I ask, which goddess here most claims
The prize that, howsoe'er adjudged, is thine?
   Then Love breathes low the sweetest of thy names;
And Venus Victrix to my heart doth bring
Herself, the Helen of her guerdoning.

SONNET XXXIV.

THE DARK GLASS.

Not I myself know all my love for thee:
   How should I reach so far, who cannot weigh
   To-morrow's dower by gage of yesterday?
Shall birth and death, and all dark names that be
As doors and windows bared to some loud sea,
   Lash deaf mine ears and blind my face with spray;
   And shall my sense pierce love,—the last relay
And ultimate outpost of eternity?

Lo! what am I to Love, the lord of all?
   One murmuring shell he gathers from the sand,—
   One little heart-flame sheltered in his hand.
Yet through thine eyes he grants me clearest call
And veriest touch of powers primordial
   That any hour-girt life may understand.

SONNET XXXV.

THE LAMP'S SHRINE.

Sometimes I fain would find in thee some fault,
    That I might love thee still in spite of it:
    Yet how should our Lord Love curtail one whit
Thy perfect praise whom most he would exalt?
Alas! he can but make my heart's low vault
    Even in men's sight unworthier, being lit
    By thee, who thereby show'st more exquisite
Like fiery chrysoprase in deep basalt.

Yet will I nowise shrink; but at Love's shrine
    Myself within the beams his brow doth dart
    Will set the flashing jewel of thy heart
In that dull chamber where it deigns to shine:
For lo! in honour of thine excellencies
My heart takes pride to show how poor it is.

SONNET XXXVI.

LIFE-IN-LOVE.

Not in thy body is thy life at all,
    But in this lady's lips and hands and eyes;
    Through these she yields thee life that vivifies
What else were sorrow's servant and death's thrall.
Look on thyself without her, and recall
    The waste remembrance and forlorn surmise
    That lived but in a dead-drawn breath of sighs
O'er vanished hours and hours eventual.

Even so much life hath the poor tress of hair
    Which, stored apart, is all love hath to show
    For heart-beats and for fire-heats long ago;
Even so much life endures unknown, even where,
'Mid change the changeless night environeth,
Lies all that golden hair undimmed in death.

THE HOUSE OF LIFE.

SONNET XXXVII.

THE LOVE-MOON.

"When that dead face, bowered in the furthest years,
    Which once was all the life years held for thee,
    Can now scarce bid the tides of memory
Cast on thy soul a little spray of tears,—
How canst thou gaze into these eyes of hers
    Whom now thy heart delights in, and not see
    Within each orb Love's philtred euphrasy
Make them of buried troth remembrancers?"

"Nay, pitiful Love, nay, loving Pity! Well
    Thou knowest that in these twain I have confess'd
Two very voices of thy summoning bell.
    Nay, Master, shall not Death make manifest
In these the culminant changes which approve
The love-moon that must light my soul to Love?"

SONNET XXXVIII.

THE MORROW'S MESSAGE.

"Thou Ghost," I said, "and is thy name To-day?—
    Yesterday's son, with such an abject brow!—
    And can To-morrow be more pale than thou?"
While yet I spoke, the silence answered: "Yea,
Henceforth our issue is all grieved and grey,
    And each beforehand makes such poor avow
    As of old leaves beneath the budding bough
Or night-drift that the sundawn shreds away."

Then cried I: "Mother of many malisons,
    O Earth, receive me to thy dusty bed!"
    But therewithal the tremulous silence said:
"Lo! Love yet bids thy lady greet thee once:—
Yea, twice,—whereby thy life is still the sun's;
    And thrice,—whereby the shadow of death is dead."

SONNET XXXIX.

SLEEPLESS DREAMS.

Girt in dark growths, yet glimmering with one star
    O night desirous as the nights of youth!
    Why should my heart within thy spell, forsooth,
Now beat, as the bride's finger-pulses are
Quickened within the girdling golden bar?
    What wings are these that fan my pillow smooth?
    And why does Sleep, waved back by Joy and Ruth,
Tread softly round and gaze at me from far?

Nay, night deep-leaved! And would Love feign in thee
    Some shadowy palpitating grove that bears
    Rest for man's eyes and music for his ears?
O lonely night! art thou not known to me,
A thicket hung with masks of mockery
    And watered with the wasteful warmth of tears?

SONNET XL.

SEVERED SELVES.

Two separate divided silences,
    Which, brought together, would find loving voice;
    Two glances which together would rejoice
In love, now lost like stars beyond dark trees;
Two hands apart whose touch alone gives ease;
    Two bosoms which, heart-shrined with mutual flame,
    Would, meeting in one clasp, be made the same;
Two souls, the shores wave-mocked of sundering seas:—

Such are we now. Ah! may our hope forecast
    Indeed one hour again, when on this stream
    Of darkened love once more the light shall gleam?—
An hour how slow to come, how quickly past,—
Which blooms and fades, and only leaves at last,
    Faint as shed flowers, the attenuated dream.

SONNET XLI.

THROUGH DEATH TO LOVE.

Like labour-laden moonclouds faint to flee
   From winds that sweep the winter-bitten wold,—
   Like multiform circumfluence manifold
Of night's flood-tide,—like terrors that agree
Of hoarse-tongued fire and inarticulate sea,—
   Even such, within some glass dimmed by our breath,
   Our hearts discern wild images of Death,
Shadows and shoals that edge eternity.

Howbeit athwart Death's imminent shade doth soar
   One Power, than flow of stream or flight of dove
   Sweeter to glide around, to brood above.
Tell me, my heart,—what angel-greeted door
Or threshold of wing-winnowed threshing-floor
   Hath guest fire-fledged as thine, whose lord is Love?

SONNET XLII.

HOPE OVERTAKEN.

I deemed thy garments, O my Hope, were grey,
   So far I viewed thee. Now the space between
   Is passed at length; and garmented in green
Even as in days of yore thou stand'st to-day.
Ah God! and but for lingering dull dismay,
   On all that road our footsteps erst had been
   Even thus commingled, and our shadows seen
Blent on the hedgerows and the water-way.

O Hope of mine whose eyes are living love,
   No eyes but hers,—O Love and Hope the same!—
   Lean close to me, for now the sinking sun
That warmed our feet scarce gilds our hair above.
   O hers thy voice and very hers thy name!
   Alas, cling round me, for the day is done!

SONNET XLIII.

LOVE AND HOPE.

BLESS love and hope. Full many a withered year
   Whirled past us, eddying to its chill doomsday;
   And clasped together where the blown leaves lay
We long have knelt and wept full many a tear.
Yet lo! one hour at last, the Spring's compeer,
   Flutes softly to us from some green byeway:
   Those years, those tears are dead, but only they:—
Bless love and hope, true soul; for we are here.

Cling heart to heart; nor of this hour demand
   Whether in very truth, when we are dead,
   Our hearts shall wake to know Love's golden head
Sole sunshine of the imperishable land;
Or but discern, through night's unfeatured scope,
Scorn-fired at length the illusive eyes of Hope.

SONNET XLIV.

CLOUD AND WIND.

LOVE, should I fear death most for you or me?
   Yet if you die, can I not follow you,
   Forcing the straits of change? Alas! but who
Shall wrest a bond from night's inveteracy,
Ere yet my hazardous soul put forth, to be
   Her warrant against all her haste might rue?—
   Ah! in your eyes so reached what dumb adieu,
What unsunned gyres of waste eternity?

And if I die the first, shall death be then
   A lampless watchtower whence I see you weep?—
   Or (woe is me!) a bed wherein my sleep
Ne'er notes (as death's dear cup at last you drain)
The hour when you too learn that all is vain
   And that Hope sows what Love shall never reap?

SONNET XLV.
SECRET PARTING.

Because our talk was of the cloud-control
   And moon-track of the journeying face of Fate,
   Her tremulous kisses faltered at love's gate
And her eyes dreamed against a distant goal:
But soon, remembering her how brief the whole
   Of joy, which its own hours annihilate,
   Her set gaze gathered, thirstier than of late,
And as she kissed, her mouth became her soul.

Thence in what ways we wandered, and how strove
   To build with fire-tried vows the piteous home
   Which memory haunts and whither sleep may roam,—
They only know for whom the roof of Love
Is the still-seated secret of the grove,
   Nor spire may rise nor bell be heard therefrom.

SONNET XLVI.
PARTED LOVE.

What shall be said of this embattled day
   And armèd occupation of this night
   By all thy foes beleaguered,—now when sight
Nor sound denotes the loved one far away?
Of these thy vanquished hours what shalt thou say,—
   As every sense to which she dealt delight
   Now labours lonely o'er the stark noon-height
To reach the sunset's desolate disarray?

Stand still, fond fettered wretch! while Memory's art
   Parades the Past before thy face, and lures
   Thy spirit to her passionate portraitures:
Till the tempestuous tide-gates flung apart
Flood with wild will the hollows of thy heart,
   And thy heart rends thee, and thy body endures.

SONNET XLVII.

BROKEN MUSIC.

The mother will not turn, who thinks she hears
   Her nursling's speech first grow articulate;
   But breathless with averted eyes elate
She sits, with open lips and open ears,
That it may call her twice. 'Mid doubts and fears
   Thus oft my soul has hearkened; till the song,
   A central moan for days, at length found tongue,
And the sweet music welled and the sweet tears.

But now, whatever while the soul is fain
   To list that wonted murmur, as it were
The speech-bound sea-shell's low importunate strain,—
   No breath of song, thy voice alone is there,
O bitterly beloved! and all her gain
   Is but the pang of unpermitted prayer.

SONNET XLVIII.

DEATH-IN-LOVE.

There came an image in Life's retinue
   That had Love's wings and bore his gonfalon:
   Fair was the web, and nobly wrought thereon,
O soul-sequestered face, thy form and hue!
Bewildering sounds, such as Spring wakens to,
   Shook in its folds; and through my heart its power
   Sped trackless as the immemorable hour
When birth's dark portal groaned and all was new.

But a veiled woman followed, and she caught
   The banner round its staff, to furl and cling,—
   Then plucked a feather from the bearer's wing,
And held it to his lips that stirred it not,
And said to me, "Behold, there is no breath:
I and this Love are one, and I am Death."

THE HOUSE OF LIFE

SONNETS XLIX, L, LI, LII.

WILLOWWOOD.

I.

I SAT with Love upon a woodside well,
   Leaning across the water, I and he;
   Nor ever did he speak nor looked at me,
But touched his lute wherein was audible
The certain secret thing he had to tell:
   Only our mirrored eyes met silently
   In the low wave; and that sound came to be
The passionate voice I knew; and my tears fell.

And at their fall, his eyes beneath grew hers;
And with his foot and with his wing-feathers
   He swept the spring that watered my heart's drouth.
Then the dark ripples spread to waving hair,
And as I stooped, her own lips rising there
   Bubbled with brimming kisses at my mouth.

II.

AND now Love sang: but his was such a song
   So meshed with half-remembrance hard to free,
   As souls disused in death's sterility
May sing when the new birthday tarries long.
And I was made aware of a dumb throng
   That stood aloof, one form by every tree,
   All mournful forms, for each was I or she,
The shades of those our days that had no tongue.

They looked on us, and knew us and were known;
   While fast together, alive from the abyss,
   Clung the soul-wrung implacable close kiss;
And pity of self through all made broken moan
Which said, "For once, for once, for once alone!"
   And still Love sang, and what he sang was this:—

III.

" O YE, all ye that walk in Willowwood,
    That walk with hollow faces burning white;
What fathom-depth of soul-struck widowhood,
    What long, what longer hours, one lifelong night,
Ere ye again, who so in vain have wooed
    Your last hope lost, who so in vain invite
Your lips to that their unforgotten food,
    Ere ye, ere ye again shall see the light!

Alas! the bitter banks in Willowwood,
    With tear-spurge wan, with blood-wort burning red:
Alas! if ever such a pillow could
    Steep deep the soul in sleep till she were dead,—
Better all life forget her than this thing,
That Willowwood should hold her wandering!"

IV.

So sang he: and as meeting rose and rose
    Together cling through the wind's wellaway
    Nor change at once, yet near the end of day
The leaves drop loosened where the heart-stain glows,—
So when the song died did the kiss unclose;
    And her face fell back drowned, and was as grey
    As its grey eyes; and if it ever may
Meet mine again I know not if Love knows.

Only I know that I leaned low and drank
A long draught from the water where she sank,
    Her breath and all her tears and all her soul:
And as I leaned, I know I felt Love's face
Pressed on my neck with moan of pity and grace,
    Till both our heads were in his aureole.

SONNET LIII.
WITHOUT HER.

WHAT of her glass without her ? The blank grey
  There where the pool is blind of the moon's face.
  Her dress without her ? The tossed empty space
Of cloud-rack whence the moon has passed away.
Her paths without her ? Day's appointed sway
  Usurped by desolate night. Her pillowed place
  Without her ? Tears, ah me ! for love's good grace,
And cold forgetfulness of night or day.

What of the heart without her ? Nay, poor heart,
  Of thee what word remains ere speech be still ?
  A wayfarer by barren ways and chill,
Steep ways and weary, without her thou art,
Where the long cloud, the long wood's counterpart,
  Sheds doubled darkness up the labouring hill.

SONNET LIV.
LOVE'S FATALITY.

SWEET Love,—but oh ! most dread Desire of Love
  Life-thwarted. Linked in gyves I saw them stand,
  Love shackled with Vain-longing, hand to hand :
And one was eyed as the blue vault above :
But hope tempestuous like a fire-cloud hove
  I' the other's gaze, even as in his whose wand
  Vainly all night with spell-wrought power has spann'd
The unyielding caves of some deep treasure-trove.

Also his lips, two writhen flakes of flame,
  Made moan : " Alas O Love, thus leashed with me !
  Wing-footed thou, wing-shouldered, once born free :
And I, thy cowering self, in chains grown tame,—
Bound to thy body and soul, named with thy name,—
  Life's iron heart, even Love's Fatality."

SONNET LV.
STILLBORN LOVE.

The hour which might have been yet might not be,
    Which man's and woman's heart conceived and bore
    Yet whereof life was barren,—on what shore
Bides it the breaking of Time's weary sea?
Bondchild of all consummate joys set free,
    It somewhere sighs and serves, and mute before
    The house of Love, hears through the echoing door
His hours elect in choral consonancy.

But lo! what wedded souls now hand in hand
Together tread at last the immortal strand
    With eyes where burning memory lights love home?
Lo! how the little outcast hour has turned
And leaped to them and in their faces yearned:—
    "I am your child: O parents, ye have come!"

SONNETS LVI, LVII, LVIII.
TRUE WOMAN.
I. HERSELF.

To be a sweetness more desired than Spring;
    A bodily beauty more acceptable
    Than the wild rose-tree's arch that crowns the fell;
To be an essence more environing
Than wine's drained juice; a music ravishing
    More than the passionate pulse of Philomel;—
    To be all this 'neath one soft bosom's swell
That is the flower of life:—how strange a thing!

How strange a thing to be what Man can know
    But as a sacred secret! Heaven's own screen
Hides her soul's purest depth and loveliest glow;
    Closely withheld, as all things most unseen,—
    The wave-bowered pearl,—the heart-shaped seal of green
That flecks the snowdrop underneath the snow.

II. HER LOVE.

She loves him; for her infinite soul is Love,
    And he her lodestar. Passion in her is
    A glass facing his fire, where the bright bliss
Is mirrored, and the heat returned. Yet move
That glass, a stranger's amorous flame to prove,
    And it shall turn, by instant contraries,
    Ice to the moon; while her pure fire to his
For whom it burns, clings close i' the heart's alcove.

Lo! they are one. With wifely breast to breast
    And circling arms, she welcomes all command
    Of love,—her soul to answering ardours fann'd:
Yet as morn springs or twilight sinks to rest,
Ah! who shall say she deems not loveliest
    The hour of sisterly sweet hand-in-hand?

III. HER HEAVEN.

If to grow old in Heaven is to grow young,
    (As the Seer saw and said,) then blest were he
    With youth for evermore, whose heaven should be
True Woman, she whom these weak notes have sung,
Here and hereafter,—choir-strains of her tongue,—
    Sky-spaces of her eyes,—sweet signs that flee
    About her soul's immediate sanctuary,—
Were Paradise all uttermost worlds among.

The sunrise blooms and withers on the hill
    Like any hillflower; and the noblest troth
    Dies here to dust. Yet shall Heaven's promise clothe
Even yet those lovers who have cherished still
This test for love:—in every kiss sealed fast
To feel the first kiss and forebode the last.

SONNET LIX.

LOVE'S LAST GIFT.

Love to his singer held a glistening leaf,
    And said : " The rose-tree and the apple-tree
    Have fruits to vaunt or flowers to lure the bee ;
And golden shafts are in the feathered sheaf
Of the great harvest-marshal, the year's chief,
    Victorious Summer ; aye, and 'neath warm sea
    Strange secret grasses lurk inviolably
Between the filtering channels of sunk reef.

All are my blooms ; and all sweet blooms of love
    To thee I gave while Spring and Summer sang ;
    But Autumn stops to listen, with some pang
From those worse things the wind is moaning of.
Only this laurel dreads no winter days :
Take my last gift ; thy heart hath sung my praise."

Part II.—*CHANGE AND FATE.*

SONNET LX.
TRANSFIGURED LIFE.

As growth of form or momentary glance
   In a child's features will recall to mind
   The father's with the mother's face combin'd,—
Sweet interchange that memories still enhance:
And yet, as childhood's years and youth's advance,
   The gradual mouldings leave one stamp behind,
   Till in the blended likeness now we find
A separate man's or woman's countenance :—

So in the Song, the singer's Joy and Pain,
   Its very parents, evermore expand
To bid the passion's fullgrown birth remain,
   By Art's transfiguring essence subtly spann'd;
   And from that song-cloud shaped as a man's hand
There comes the sound as of abundant rain.

SONNET LXI.
THE SONG-THROE.

By thine own tears thy song must tears beget,
   O Singer! Magic mirror thou hast none
   Except thy manifest heart; and save thine own
Anguish or ardour, else no amulet.
Cisterned in Pride, verse is the feathery jet
   Of soulless air-flung fountains; nay, more dry
   Than the Dead Sea for throats that thirst and sigh,
That song o'er which no singer's lids grew wet.

The Song-god—He the Sun-god—is no slave
   Of thine : thy Hunter he, who for thy soul
   Fledges his shaft : to no august control
Of thy skilled hand his quivered store he gave :
But if thy lips' loud cry leap to his smart,
The inspir'd recoil shall pierce thy brother's heart.

SONNET LXII.

THE SOUL'S SPHERE.

Some prisoned moon in steep cloud-fastnesses,—
    Throned queen and thralled; some dying sun whose pyre
    Blazed with momentous memorable fire;—
Who hath not yearned and fed his heart with these?
Who, sleepless, hath not anguished to appease
    Tragical shadow's realm of sound and sight
    Conjectured in the lamentable night? . . . . .
Lo! the soul's sphere of infinite images!

What sense shall count them? Whether it forecast
    The rose-winged hours that flutter in the van
    Of Love's unquestioning unrevealèd span,—
Visions of golden futures: or that last
Wild pageant of the accumulated past
    That clangs and flashes for a drowning man.

SONNET LXIII.

INCLUSIVENESS.

The changing guests, each in a different mood,
    Sit at the roadside table and arise:
    And every life among them in likewise
Is a soul's board set daily with new food.
What man has bent o'er his son's sleep, to brood
    How that face shall watch his when cold it lies?—
    Or thought, as his own mother kissed his eyes,
Of what her kiss was when his father wooed?

May not this ancient room thou sitt'st in dwell
    In separate living souls for joy or pain?
    Nay, all its corners may be painted plain
Where Heaven shows pictures of some life spent well,
    And may be stamped, a memory all in vain,
Upon the sight of lidless eyes in Hell.

SONNET LXIV.

ARDOUR AND MEMORY.

The cuckoo-throb, the heartbeat of the Spring;
   The rosebud's blush that leaves it as it grows
   Into the full-eyed fair unblushing rose;
The summer clouds that visit every wing
With fires of sunrise and of sunsetting;
   The furtive flickering streams to light re-born
   'Mid airs new-fledged and valorous lusts of morn,
While all the daughters of the daybreak sing:—

These ardour loves, and memory: and when flown
   All joys, and through dark forest-boughs in flight
   The wind swoops onward brandishing the light,
Even yet the rose-tree's verdure left alone
Will flush all ruddy though the rose be gone;
   With ditties and with dirges infinite.

SONNET LXV.

KNOWN IN VAIN.

As two whose love, first foolish, widening scope,
   Knows suddenly, to music high and soft,
   The Holy of holies; who because they scoff'd
Are now amazed with shame, nor dare to cope
With the whole truth aloud, lest heaven should ope;
   Yet, at their meetings, laugh not as they laugh'd
   In speech; nor speak, at length; but sitting oft
Together, within hopeless sight of hope
For hours are silent:—So it happeneth
   When Work and Will awake too late, to gaze
After their life sailed by, and hold their breath.
   Ah! who shall dare to search through what sad maze
   Thenceforth their incommunicable ways
Follow the desultory feet of Death?

SONNET LXVI.

THE HEART OF THE NIGHT.

From child to youth; from youth to arduous man;
   From lethargy to fever of the heart;
   From faithful life to dream-dowered days apart;
From trust to doubt; from doubt to brink of ban;—
Thus much of change in one swift cycle ran
   Till now. Alas, the soul!—how soon must she
   Accept her primal immortality,—
The flesh resume its dust whence it began?

O Lord of work and peace! O Lord of life!
   O Lord, the awful Lord of will! though late,
      Even yet renew this soul with duteous breath .
That when the peace is garnered in from strife,
   The work retrieved, the will regenerate,
      This soul may see thy face, O Lord of death!

SONNET LXVII.

THE LANDMARK.

Was *that* the landmark? What,—the foolish well
   Whose wave, low down, I did not stoop to drink,
   But sat and flung the pebbles from its brink
In sport to send its imaged skies pell-mell,
(And mine own image, had I noted well!)—
   Was that my point of turning?—I had thought
   The stations of my course should rise unsought,
As altar-stone or ensigned citadel.

But lo! the path is missed, I must go back,
   And thirst to drink when next I reach the spring
Which once I stained, which since may have grown
     black.
   Yet though no light be left nor bird now sing
   As here I turn, I'll thank God, hastening,
That the same goal is still on the same track.

SONNET LXVIII.

A DARK DAY.

The gloom that breathes upon me with these airs
   Is like the drops which strike the traveller's brow
   Who knows not, darkling, if they bring him now
Fresh storm, or be old rain the covert bears.
Ah! bodes this hour some harvest of new tares,
   Or hath but memory of the day whose plough
   Sowed hunger once,—the night at length when thou,
O prayer found vain, didst fall from out my prayers?

How prickly were the growths which yet how smooth,
   Along the hedgerows of this journey shed,
Lie by Time's grace till night and sleep may soothe!
   Even as the thistledown from pathsides dead
Gleaned by a girl in autumns of her youth,
   Which one new year makes soft her marriage-bed.

SONNET LXIX.

AUTUMN IDLENESS.

This sunlight shames November where he grieves
   In dead red leaves, and will not let him shun
   The day, though bough with bough be over-run.
But with a blessing every glade receives
High salutation; while from hillock-eaves
   The deer gaze calling, dappled white and dun,
   As if, being foresters of old, the sun
Had marked them with the shade of forest-leaves.

Here dawn to-day unveiled her magic glass;
   Here noon now gives the thirst and takes the dew;
Till eve bring rest when other good things pass.
   And here the lost hours the lost hours renew
While I still lead my shadow o'er the grass,
   Nor know, for longing, that which I should do.

SONNET LXX.

THE HILL SUMMIT.

This feast-day of the sun, his altar there
   In the broad west has blazed for vesper-song;
   And I have loitered in the vale too long
And gaze now a belated worshiper.
Yet may I not forget that I was 'ware,
   So journeying, of his face at intervals
   Transfigured where the fringed horizon falls,—
A fiery bush with coruscating hair.

And now that I have climbed and won this height,
   I must tread downward through the sloping shade
And travel the bewildered tracks till night.
   Yet for this hour I still may here be stayed
   And see the gold air and the silver fade
And the last bird fly into the last light.

SONNETS LXXI, LXXII, LXXIII.

THE CHOICE.

I.

Eat thou and drink; to-morrow thou shalt die.
   Surely the earth, that's wise being very old,
   Needs not our help. Then loose me, love, and hold
Thy sultry hair up from my face; that I
May pour for thee this golden wine, brim-high,
   Till round the glass thy fingers glow like gold.
   We'll drown all hours: thy song, while hours are toll'd,
Shall leap, as fountains veil the changing sky.

Now kiss, and think that there are really those,
   My own high-bosomed beauty, who increase
     Vain gold, vain lore, and yet might choose our way!
     Through many years they toil; then on a day
   They die not,—for their life was death,—but cease;
And round their narrow lips the mould falls close.

II.

Watch thou and fear; to-morrow thou shalt die.
  Or art thou sure thou shalt have time for death?
  Is not the day which God's word promiseth
To come man knows not when? In yonder sky,
Now while we speak, the sun speeds forth: can I
  Or thou assure him of his goal? God's breath
  Even at this moment haply quickeneth
The air to a flame; till spirits, always nigh
Though screened and hid, shall walk the daylight here.
  And dost thou prate of all that man shall do?
    Canst thou, who hast but plagues, presume to be
    Glad in his gladness that comes after thee?
  Will *his* strength slay *thy* worm in Hell? Go to ·
Cover thy countenance, and watch, and fear.

III.

Think thou and act; to-morrow thou shalt die.
  Outstretched in the sun's warmth upon the shore,
  Thou say'st: "Man's measured path is all gone o'er:
Up all his years, steeply, with strain and sigh,
Man clomb until he touched the truth; and I,
  Even I, am he whom it was destined for."
  How should this be? Art thou then so much more
Than they who sowed, that thou shouldst reap thereby?

Nay, come up hither. From this wave-washed mound
  Unto the furthest flood-brim look with me;
Then reach on with thy thought till it be drown'd.
  Miles and miles distant though the last line be,
And though thy soul sail leagues and leagues beyond,—
  Still, leagues beyond those leagues, there is more sea.

SONNETS LXXIV, LXXV, LXXVI.

OLD AND NEW ART.

I. ST. LUKE THE PAINTER.

Give honour unto Luke Evangelist;
   For he it was (the aged legends say)
   Who first taught Art to fold her hands and pray.
Scarcely at once she dared to rend the mist
Of devious symbols: but soon having wist
   How sky-breadth and field-silence and this day
   Are symbols also in some deeper way,
She looked through these to God and was God's priest.

And if, past noon, her toil began to irk,
   And she sought talismans, and turned in vain
   To soulless self-reflections of man's skill,—
   Yet now, in this the twilight, she might still
   Kneel in the latter grass to pray again,
Ere the night cometh and she may not work.

II. NOT AS THESE.

"I am not as these are," the poet saith
   In youth's pride, and the painter, among men
   At bay, where never pencil comes nor pen,
And shut about with his own frozen breath.
To others, for whom only rhyme wins faith
   As poets,—only paint as painters,—then
   He turns in the cold silence; and again
Shrinking, "I am not as these are," he saith.

And say that this is so, what follows it?
   For were thine eyes set backwards in thine head,
   Such words were well; but they see on, and far.
Unto the lights of the great Past, new-lit
   Fair for the Future's track, look thou instead,—
   Say thou instead, "I am not as *these* are."

III. THE HUSBANDMEN.

Though God, as one that is an householder,
   Called these to labour in His vineyard first,
   Before the husk of darkness was well burst
Bidding them grope their way out and bestir,
(Who, questioned of their wages, answered, "Sir,
   Unto each man a penny":) though the worst
   Burthen of heat was theirs and the dry thirst:
Though God has since found none such as these were
To do their work like them:—Because of this
   Stand not ye idle in the market-place.
     Which of ye knoweth *he* is not that last
Who may be first by faith and will?—yea, his
   The hand which after the appointed days
     And hours shall give a Future to their Past?

SONNET LXXVII.

SOUL'S BEAUTY.

Under the arch of Life, where love and death,
   Terror and mystery, guard her shrine, I saw
   Beauty enthroned; and though her gaze struck awe,
I drew it in as simply as my breath.
Hers are the eyes which, over and beneath,
   The sky and sea bend on thee,—which can draw,
   By sea or sky or woman, to one law,
The allotted bondman of her palm and wreath.

This is that Lady Beauty, in whose praise
   Thy voice and hand shake still,—long known to thee
     By flying hair and fluttering hem,—the beat
     Following her daily of thy heart and feet,
   How passionately and irretrievably,
In what fond flight, how many ways and days!

SONNET LXXVIII.

BODY'S BEAUTY.

Of Adam's first wife, Lilith, it is told
  (The witch he loved before the gift of Eve,)
  That, ere the snake's, her sweet tongue could deceive,
And her enchanted hair was the first gold.
And still she sits, young while the earth is old,
  And, subtly of herself contemplative,
  Draws men to watch the bright web she can weave,
Till heart and body and life are in its hold.

The rose and poppy are her flowers; for where
  Is he not found, O Lilith, whom shed scent
And soft-shed kisses and soft sleep shall snare?
  Lo! as that youth's eyes burned at thine, so went
  Thy spell through him, and left his straight neck bent
And round his heart one strangling golden hair

SONNET LXXIX.

THE MONOCHORD.

Is it this sky's vast vault or ocean's sound
  That is Life's self and draws my life from me,
  And by instinct ineffable decree
Holds my breath quailing on the bitter bound?
Nay, is it Life or Death, thus thunder-crown'd,
  That 'mid the tide of all emergency
  Now notes my separate wave, and to what sea
Its difficult eddies labour in the ground?

Oh! what is this that knows the road I came,
The flame turned cloud, the cloud returned to flame,
  The lifted shifted steeps and all the way?—
That draws round me at last this wind-warm space,
And in regenerate rapture turns my face
  Upon the devious coverts of dismay?

SONNET LXXX.

FROM DAWN TO NOON.

As the child knows not if his mother's face
  Be fair; nor of his elders yet can deem
  What each most is; but as of hill or stream
At dawn, all glimmering life surrounds his place:
Who yet, tow'rd noon of his half-weary race,
  Pausing awhile beneath the high sun-beam
  And gazing steadily back,—as through a dream,
In things long past new features now can trace:—

Even so the thought that is at length fullgrown
  Turns back to note the sun-smit paths, all grey
And marvellous once, where first it walked alone;
  And haply doubts, amid the unblenching day,
  Which most or least impelled its onward way,—
Those unknown things or these things overknown.

SONNET LXXXI.

MEMORIAL THRESHOLDS.

What place so strange,—though unrevealèd snow
  With unimaginable fires arise
  At the earth's end,—what passion of surprise
Like frost-bound fire-girt scenes of long ago?
Lo! this is none but I this hour; and lo!
  This is the very place which to mine eyes
  Those mortal hours in vain immortalize,
'Mid hurrying crowds, with what alone I know.

City, of thine a single simple door,
  By some new Power reduplicate, must be
  Even yet my life-porch in eternity,
Even with one presence filled, as once of yore:
Or mocking winds whirl round a chaff-strown floor
  Thee and thy years and these my words and me.

SONNET LXXXII.

HOARDED JOY.

I SAID : " Nay, pluck not,—let the first fruit be:
　　Even as thou sayest, it is sweet and red,
　　But let it ripen still.　The tree's bent head
Sees in the stream its own fecundity
And bides the day of fulness.　Shall not we
　　At the sun's hour that day possess the shade,
　　And claim our fruit before its ripeness fade,
And eat it from the branch and praise the tree ? "

I say : " Alas ! our fruit hath wooed the sun
　　Too long,—'tis fallen and floats adown the stream.
Lo, the last clusters !　Pluck them every one,
　　And let us sup with summer ; ere the gleam
Of autumn set the year's pent sorrow free,
And the woods wail like echoes from the sea."

SONNET LXXXIII.

BARREN SPRING.

ONCE more the changed year's turning wheel returns :
　　And as a girl sails balanced in the wind,
　　And now before and now again behind
Stoops as it swoops, with cheek that laughs and burns,—
So Spring comes merry towards me here, but earns
　　No answering smile from me, whose life is twin'd
　　With the dead boughs that winter still must bind,
And whom to-day the Spring no more concerns.

Behold, this crocus is a withering flame ;
　　This snowdrop, snow ; this apple-blossom's part
　　To breed the fruit that breeds the serpent's art.
Nay, for these Spring-flowers, turn thy face from them,
Nor stay till on the year's last lily-stem
　　The white cup shrivels round the golden heart.

SONNET LXXXIV.

FAREWELL TO THE GLEN.

Sweet stream-fed glen, why say "farewell" to thee
  Who far'st so well and find'st for ever smooth
  The brow of Time where man may read no ruth?
Nay, do thou rather say "farewell" to me,
Who now fare forth in bitterer fantasy
  Than erst was mine where other shade might soothe
  By other streams, what while in fragrant youth
The bliss of being sad made melancholy.

And yet, farewell! For better shalt thou fare
  When children bathe sweet faces in thy flow
And happy lovers blend sweet shadows there
  In hours to come, than when an hour ago
Thine echoes had but one man's sighs to bear
  And thy trees whispered what he feared to know.

SONNET LXXXV.

VAIN VIRTUES.

What is the sorriest thing that enters Hell?
  None of the sins,—but this and that fair deed
  Which a soul's sin at length could supersede.
These yet are virgins, whom death's timely knell
Might once have sainted; whom the fiends compel
  Together now, in snake-bound shuddering sheaves
  Of anguish, while the pit's pollution leaves
Their refuse maidenhood abominable.

Night sucks them down, the tribute of the pit,
  Whose names, half entered in the book of Life,
    Were God's desire at noon. And as their hair
And eyes sink last, the Torturer deigns no whit
  To gaze, but, yearning, waits his destined wife,
    The Sin still blithe on earth that sent them there.

SONNET LXXXVI.

LOST DAYS.

The lost days of my life until to-day,
  What were they, could I see them on the street
  Lie as they fell? Would they be ears of wheat
Sown once for food but trodden into clay?
Or golden coins squandered and still to pay?
  Or drops of blood dabbling the guilty feet?
  Or such spilt water as in dreams must cheat
The undying throats of Hell, athirst alway?

I do not see them here; but after death
  God knows I know the faces I shall see,
Each one a murdered self, with low last breath.
  "I am thyself,—what hast thou done to me?"
  "And I—and I—thyself," (lo! each one saith,)
  "And thou thyself to all eternity!"

SONNET LXXXVII.

DEATH'S SONGSTERS.

When first that horse, within whose populous womb
  The birth was death, o'ershadowed Troy with fate,
  Her elders, dubious of its Grecian freight,
Brought Helen there to sing the songs of home;
She whispered, "Friends, I am alone; come, come!"
  Then, crouched within, Ulysses waxed afraid,
  And on his comrades' quivering mouths he laid
His hands, and held them till the voice was dumb.

The same was he who, lashed to his own mast,
  There where the sea-flowers screen the charnel-caves,
Beside the sirens' singing island pass'd,
  Till sweetness failed along the inveterate waves. . . .
Say, soul,—are songs of Death no heaven to thee,
Nor shames her lip the cheek of Victory?

SONNET LXXXVIII.
HERO'S LAMP.[1]

That lamp thou fill'st in Eros' name to-night,
  O Hero, shall the Sestian augurs take
  To-morrow, and for drowned Leander's sake
To Anteros its fireless lip shall plight.
Aye, waft the unspoken vow : yet dawn's first light
  On ebbing storm and life twice ebb'd must break;
  While 'neath no sunrise, by the Avernian Lake,
Lo where Love walks, Death's pallid neophyte.

That lamp within Anteros' shadowy shrine
  Shall stand unlit (for so the gods decree)
  Till some one man the happy issue see
Of a life's love, and bid its flame to shine :
Which still may rest unfir'd ; for, theirs or thine,
  O brother, what brought love to them or thee ?

SONNET LXXXIX.
THE TREES OF THE GARDEN.

Ye who have passed Death's haggard hills ; and ye
  Whom trees that knew your sires shall cease to know
  And still stand silent :—is it all a show,—
A wisp that laughs upon the wall ?—decree
Of some inexorable supremacy
  Which ever, as man strains his blind surmise
  From depth to ominous depth, looks past his eyes,
Sphinx-faced with unabashèd augury ?

Nay, rather question the Earth's self. Invoke
  The storm-felled forest-trees moss-grown to-day
  Whose roots are hillocks where the children play ;
Or ask the silver sapling 'neath what yoke   [wage
  Those stars, his spray-crown's clustering gems, shall
  Their journey still when his boughs shrink with age.

---

[1] After the deaths of Leander and of Hero, the signal-lamp was dedicated to Anteros, with the edict that no man should light it unless his love had proved fortunate.

SONNET XC.

"RETRO ME, SATHANA!"

GET thee behind me. Even as, heavy-curled,
   Stooping against the wind, a charioteer
   Is snatched from out his chariot by the hair,
So shall Time be; and as the void car, hurled
Abroad by reinless steeds, even so the world:
   Yea, even as chariot-dust upon the air,
   It shall be sought and not found anywhere.
Get thee behind me, Satan. Oft unfurled,
Thy perilous wings can beat and break like lath
   Much mightiness of men to win thee praise.
   Leave these weak feet to tread in narrow ways.
Thou still, upon the broad vine-sheltered path,
Mayst wait the turning of the phials of wrath
   For certain years, for certain months and days.

SONNET XCI.

LOST ON BOTH SIDES.

As when two men have loved a woman well,
   Each hating each, through Love's and Death's deceit;
   Since not for either this stark marriage-sheet
And the long pauses of this wedding-bell;
   Yet o'er her grave the night and day dispel
   At last their feud forlorn, with cold and heat;
   Nor other than dear friends to death may fleet
The two lives left that most of her can tell:—

So separate hopes, which in a soul had wooed
   The one same Peace, strove with each other long,
     And Peace before their faces perished since:
So through that soul, in restless brotherhood,
   They roam together now, and wind among
     Its bye-streets, knocking at the dusty inns.

SONNETS XCII, XCIII.

THE SUN'S SHAME.

I.

Beholding youth and hope in mockery caught
   From life; and mocking pulses that remain
    When the soul's death of bodily death is fain;
Honour unknown, and honour known unsought;
And penury's sedulous self-torturing thought
   On gold, whose master therewith buys his bane,
   And longed-for woman longing all in vain
For lonely man with love's desire distraught;
And wealth, and strength, and power, and pleasantness,
   Given unto bodies of whose souls men say,
    None poor and weak, slavish and foul, as they:—
Beholding these things, I behold no less
The blushing morn and blushing eve confess
   The shame that loads the intolerable day.

II.

As some true chief of men, bowed down with stress
   Of life's disastrous eld, on blossoming youth
   May gaze, and murmur with self-pity and ruth,—
"Might I thy fruitless treasure but possess,
Such blessing of mine all coming years should bless;"—
   Then sends one sigh forth to the unknown goal,
   And bitterly feels breathe against his soul
The hour swift-winged of nearer nothingness:—

Even so the World's grey Soul to the green World
   Perchance one hour must cry: "Woe's me, for whom
   Inveteracy of ill portends the doom,—
Whose heart's old fire in shadow of shame is furl'd:
While thou even as of yore art journeying,
All soulless now, yet merry with the Spring!"

SONNET XCIV.

MICHELANGELO'S KISS.

GREAT Michelangelo, with age grown bleak
    And uttermost labours, having once o'ersaid
    All grievous memories on his long life shed,
This worst regret to one true heart could speak :—
That when, with sorrowing love and reverence meek,
    He stooped o'er sweet Colonna's dying bed,
    His Muse and dominant Lady, spirit-wed,—
Her hand he kissed, but not her brow or cheek.

O Buonarruoti,—good at Art's fire-wheels
    To urge her chariot!—even thus the Soul,
    Touching at length some sorely-chastened goal,
Earns oftenest but a little : her appeals
Were deep and mute,—lowly her claim. Let be :
What holds for her Death's garner ? And for thee ?

SONNET XCV.

THE VASE OF LIFE.

AROUND the vase of Life at your slow pace
    He has not crept, but turned it with his hands,
    And all its sides already understands.
There, girt, one breathes alert for some great race ;
Whose road runs far by sands and fruitful space ;
    Who laughs, yet through the jolly throng has pass'd ;
    Who weeps, nor stays for weeping ; who at last,
A youth, stands somewhere crowned, with silent face.

And he has filled this vase with wine for blood,
    With blood for tears, with spice for burning vow,
        With watered flowers for buried love most fit ;
And would have cast it shattered to the flood,
    Yet in Fate's name has kept it whole ; which now
        Stands empty till his ashes fall in it.

SONNET XCVI.
LIFE THE BELOVED.

As thy friend's face, with shadow of soul o'erspread,
   Somewhile unto thy sight perchance hath been
   Ghastly and strange, yet never so is seen
In thought, but to all fortunate favour wed;
As thy love's death-bound features never dead
   To memory's glass return, but contravene
   Frail fugitive days, and alway keep, I ween,
Than all new life a livelier lovelihead :—

So Life herself, thy spirit's friend and love,
   Even still as Spring's authentic harbinger
     Glows with fresh hours for hope to glorify;
Though pale she lay when in the winter grove
   Her funeral flowers were snow-flakes shed on her
     And the red wings of frost-fire rent the sky.

SONNET XCVII.
A SUPERSCRIPTION.

Look in my face; my name is Might-have-been;
   I am also called No-more, Too-late, Farewell;
   Unto thine ear I hold the dead-sea shell
Cast up thy Life's foam-fretted feet between;
Unto thine eyes the glass where that is seen
   Which had Life's form and Love's, but by my spell
   Is now a shaken shadow intolerable,
Of ultimate things unuttered the frail screen.

Mark me, how still I am! But should there dart
   One moment through thy soul the soft surprise
     Of that winged Peace which lulls the breath of sighs,—
Then shalt thou see me smile, and turn apart
Thy visage to mine ambush at thy heart
     Sleepless with cold commemorative eyes.

SONNET XCVIII.

HE AND I.

Whence came his feet into my field, and why?
   How is it that he sees it all so drear?
   How do I see his seeing, and how hear
The name his bitter silence knows it by?
This was the little fold of separate sky
   Whose pasturing clouds in the soul's atmosphere
   Drew living light from one continual year:
How should he find it lifeless? He, or I?

Lo! this new Self now wanders round my field,
   With plaints for every flower, and for each tree
   A moan, the sighing wind's auxiliary:
And o'er sweet waters of my life, that yield
Unto his lips no draught but tears unseal'd,
   Even in my place he weeps. Even I, not he.

SONNETS XCIX, C.

NEWBORN DEATH.

I.

To-day Death seems to me an infant child
   Which her worn mother Life upon my knee
   Has set to grow my friend and play with me;
If haply so my heart might be beguil'd
To find no terrors in a face so mild,—
   If haply so my weary heart might be
   Unto the newborn milky eyes of thee,
O Death, before resentment reconcil'd.

How long, O Death? And shall thy feet depart
   Still a young child's with mine, or wilt thou stand
Fullgrown the helpful daughter of my heart,
   What time with thee indeed I reach the strand
Of the pale wave which knows thee what thou art,
   And drink it in the hollow of thy hand?

II.

And thou, O Life, the lady of all bliss,
  With whom, when our first heart beat full and fast
  I wandered till the haunts of men were pass'd,
And in fair places found all bowers amiss
Till only woods and waves might hear our kiss,
  While to the winds all thought of Death we cast :—
  Ah, Life! and must I have from thee at last
No smile to greet me and no babe but this?

Lo! Love, the child once ours; and Song, whose hair
  Blew like a flame and blossomed like a wreath;
And Art, whose eyes were worlds by God found fair:
  These o'er the book of Nature mixed their breath
With neck-twined arms, as oft we watched them there;
  And did these die that thou mightst bear me Death?

SONNET CI.

THE ONE HOPE.

When vain desire at last and vain regret
  Go hand in hand to death, and all is vain,
  What shall assuage the unforgotten pain
And teach the unforgetful to forget?
Shall Peace be still a sunk stream long unmet,—
  Or may the soul at once in a green plain
  Stoop through the spray of some sweet life-fountain
And cull the dew-drenched flowering amulet?

Ah! when the wan soul in that golden air
  Between the scriptured petals softly blown
  Peers breathless for the gift of grace unknown,—
Ah! let none other alien spell soe'er
But only the one Hope's one name be there,—
  Not less nor more, but even that word alone.

II.—*MISCELLANEOUS POEMS.*

MY SISTER'S SLEEP.

She fell asleep on Christmas Eve.
   At length the long-ungranted shade
   Of weary eyelids overweigh'd
The pain nought else might yet relieve.

Our mother, who had leaned all day
   Over the bed from chime to chime,
   Then raised herself for the first time,
And as she sat her down, did pray.

Her little work-table was spread
   With work to finish. For the glare
   Made by her candle, she had care
To work some distance from the bed.

Without, there was a cold moon up,
   Of winter radiance sheer and thin;
   The hollow halo it was in
Was like an icy crystal cup.

Through the small room, with subtle sound
   Of flame, by vents the fireshine drove
   And reddened. In its dim alcove
The mirror shed a clearness round.

I had been sitting up some nights,
   And my tired mind felt weak and blank;
   Like a sharp strengthening wine it drank
The stillness and the broken lights.

Twelve struck. That sound, by dwindling years
   Heard in each hour, crept off; and then
   The ruffled silence spread again,
Like water that a pebble stirs.

Our mother rose from where she sat:
   Her needles, as she laid them down,
   Met lightly, and her silken gown
Settled: no other noise than that.

"Glory unto the Newly Born!"
   So, as said angels, she did say;
   Because we were in Christmas Day,
Though it would still be long till morn.

Just then in the room over us
   There was a pushing back of chairs,
   As some who had sat unawares
So late, now heard the hour, and rose.

With anxious softly-stepping haste
   Our mother went where Margaret lay,
   Fearing the sounds o'erhead—should they
Have broken her long watched-for rest!

She stopped an instant, calm, and turned;
   But suddenly turned back again;
   And all her features seemed in pain
With woe, and her eyes gazed and yearned.

For my part, I but hid my face,
   And held my breath, and spoke no word:
   There was none spoken; but I heard
The silence for a little space.

Our mother bowed herself and wept:
    And both my arms fell, and I said,
    "God knows I knew that she was dead."
And there, all white, my sister slept.

Then kneeling, upon Christmas morn
    A little after twelve o'clock,
    We said, ere the first quarter struck,
"Christ's blessing on the newly born!"

THE BLESSED DAMOZEL.

The blessed damozel leaned out
   From the gold bar of Heaven;
Her eyes were deeper than the depth
   Of waters stilled at even;
She had three lilies in her hand,
   And the stars in her hair were seven.

Her robe, ungirt from clasp to hem,
   No wrought flowers did adorn,
But a white rose of Mary's gift,
   For service meetly worn;
Her hair that lay along her back
   Was yellow like ripe corn.

Herseemed she scarce had been a day
   One of God's choristers;
The wonder was not yet quite gone
   From that still look of hers;
Albeit, to them she left, her day
   Had counted as ten years.

(To one, it is ten years of years.
   . . . Yet now, and in this place,
Surely she leaned o'er me—her hair
   Fell all about my face. . . .
Nothing: the autumn-fall of leaves.
   The whole year sets apace.)

THE BLESSED DAMOZEL.

It was the rampart of God's house
   That she was standing on;
By God built over the sheer depth
   The which is Space begun;
So high, that looking downward thence
   She scarce could see the sun.

It lies in Heaven, across the flood
   Of ether, as a bridge.
Beneath, the tides of day and night
   With flame and darkness ridge
The void, as low as where this earth
   Spins like a fretful midge.

Around her, lovers, newly met
   'Mid deathless love's acclaims,
Spoke evermore among themselves
   Their heart-remembered names;
And the souls mounting up to God
   Went by her like thin flames.

And still she bowed herself and stooped
   Out of the circling charm;
Until her bosom must have made
   The bar she leaned on warm,
And the lilies lay as if asleep
   Along her bended arm.

From the fixed place of Heaven she saw
   Time like a pulse shake fierce
Through all the worlds. Her gaze still strove
   Within the gulf to pierce
Its path; and now she spoke as when
   The stars sang in their spheres

The sun was gone now; the curled moon
  Was like a little feather
Fluttering far down the gulf; and now
  She spoke through the still weather.
Her voice was like the voice the stars
  Had when they sang together.

(Ah sweet! Even now, in that bird's song,
  Strove not her accents there,
Fain to be hearkened? When those bells
  Possessed the mid-day air,
Strove not her steps to reach my side
  Down all the echoing stair?)

"I wish that he were come to me,
  For he will come," she said.
"Have I not prayed in Heaven?—on earth,
  Lord, Lord, has he not pray'd?
Are not two prayers a perfect strength?
  And shall I feel afraid?

"When round his head the aureole clings,
  And he is clothed in white,
I'll take his hand and go with him
  To the deep wells of light;
As unto a stream we will step down,
  And bathe there in God's sight.

"We two will stand beside that shrine,
  Occult, withheld, untrod,
Whose lamps are stirred continually
  With prayer sent up to God;
And see our old prayers, granted, melt
  Each like a little cloud.

THE BLESSED DAMOZEL.

"We two will lie i' the shadow of
   That living mystic tree
Within whose secret growth the Dove
   Is sometimes felt to be,
While every leaf that His plumes touch
   Saith His Name audibly.

"And I myself will teach to him,
   I myself, lying so,
The songs I sing here; which his voice
   Shall pause in, hushed and slow,
And find some knowledge at each pause,
   Or some new thing to know."

(Alas! we two, we two, thou say'st!
   Yea, one wast thou with me
That once of old. But shall God lift
   To endless unity
The soul whose likeness with thy soul
   Was but its love for thee?)

"We two," she said, "will seek the groves
   Where the lady Mary is,
With her five handmaidens, whose names
   Are five sweet symphonies,
Cecily, Gertrude, Magdalen,
   Margaret and Rosalys.

"Circlewise sit they, with bound locks
   And foreheads garlanded;
Into the fine cloth white like flame
   Weaving the golden thread,
To fashion the birth-robes for them
   Who are just born, being dead.

THE BLESSED DAMOZEL.

"He shall fear, haply, and be dumb:
  Then will I lay my cheek
To his, and tell about our love,
  Not once abashed or weak:
And the dear Mother will approve
  My pride, and let me speak.

"Herself shall bring us, hand in hand,
  To Him round whom all souls
Kneel, the clear-ranged unnumbered heads
  Bowed with their aureoles:
And angels meeting us shall sing
  To their citherns and citoles.

"There will I ask of Christ the Lord
  Thus much for him and me:—
Only to live as once on earth
  With Love,—only to be,
As then awhile, for ever now
  Together, I and he."

She gazed and listened and then said,
  Less sad of speech than mild,—
"All this is when he comes." She ceased.
  The light thrilled towards her, fill'd
With angels in strong level flight.
  Her eyes prayed, and she smil'd.

(I saw her smile.) But soon their path
  Was vague in distant spheres:
And then she cast her arms along
  The golden barriers,
And laid her face between her hands,
  And wept. (I heard her tears.)

AT THE SUN-RISE IN 1848.

God said, Let there be light; and there was light.
   Then heard we sounds as though the Earth did sing
   And the Earth's angel cried upon the wing:
We saw priests fall together and turn white:
And covered in the dust from the sun's sight,
   A king was spied, and yet another king.
   We said: "The round world keeps its balancing;
On this globe, they and we are opposite,—
If it is day with us, with them 'tis night.
   Still, Man, in thy just pride, remember this:—
      Thou hadst not made that thy sons' sons shall ask
      What the word *king* may mean in their day's task,
   But for the light that led: and if light is,
It is because God said, Let there be light.

AUTUMN SONG.

Know'st thou not at the fall of the leaf
How the heart feels a languid grief
    Laid on it for a covering,
    And how sleep seems a goodly thing
In Autumn at the fall of the leaf?

And how the swift beat of the brain
Falters because it is in vain,
    In Autumn at the fall of the leaf
    Knowest thou not? and how the chief
Of joys seems—not to suffer pain?

Know'st thou not at the fall of the leaf
How the soul feels like a dried sheaf
    Bound up at length for harvesting,
    And how death seems a comely thing
In Autumn at the fall of the leaf?

THE LADY'S LAMENT.

Never happy any more!
Aye, turn the saying o'er and o'er,
It says but what it said before,
And heart and life are just as sore.
The wet leaves blow aslant the floor
In the rain through the open door.
    No, no more.

Never happy any more!
The eyes are weary and give o'er,
But still the soul weeps as before.
And always must each one deplore
Each once, nor bear what others bore?
This is now as it was of yore.
    No, no more.

Never happy any more!
Is it not but a sorry lore
That says, "Take strength, the worst is o'er"?
Shall the stars seem as heretofore?
The day wears on more and more—
While I was weeping the day wore.
    No, no more.

Never happy any more!
In the cold behind the door
That was the dial striking four:
One for joy the past hours bore,
Two for hope and will cast o'er,
One for the naked dark before.
    No, no more.

THE LADY'S LAMENT.

Never happy any more!
Put the light out, shut the door,
Sweep the wet leaves from the floor.
Even thus Fate's hand has swept her floor,
Even thus Love's hand has shut the door
Through which his warm feet passed of yore.
Shall it be opened any more?
      No, no, no more.

THE PORTRAIT.

This is her picture as she was:
  It seems a thing to wonder on,
As though mine image in the glass
  Should tarry when myself am gone.
I gaze until she seems to stir,—
Until mine eyes almost aver
  That now, even now, the sweet lips part
  To breathe the words of the sweet heart:—
And yet the earth is over her.

Alas! even such the thin-drawn ray
  That makes the prison-depths more rude,—
The drip of water night and day
  Giving a tongue to solitude.
Yet only this, of love's whole prize,
Remains; save what in mournful guise
  Takes counsel with my soul alone,—
  Save what is secret and unknown,
Below the earth, above the skies.

In painting her I shrined her face
  'Mid mystic trees, where light falls in
Hardly at all; a covert place
  Where you might think to find a din
Of doubtful talk, and a live flame
Wandering, and many a shape whose name
  Not itself knoweth, and old dew,
  And your own footsteps meeting you,
And all things going as they came.

THE PORTRAIT.

A deep dim wood; and there she stands
   As in that wood that day: for so
Was the still movement of her hands
   And such the pure line's gracious flow.
And passing fair the type must seem,
Unknown the presence and the dream.
   'Tis she: though of herself, alas!
   Less than her shadow on the grass
Or than her image in the stream.

That day we met there, I and she
   One with the other all alone;
And we were blithe; yet memory
   Saddens those hours, as when the moon
Looks upon daylight. And with her
I stooped to drink the spring-water,
   Athirst where other waters sprang:
   And where the echo is, she sang,—
My soul another echo there.

But when that hour my soul won strength
   For words whose silence wastes and kills,
Dull raindrops smote us, and at length
   Thundered the heat within the hills.
That eve I spoke those words again
Beside the pelted window-pane;
   And there she hearkened what I said,
   With under-glances that surveyed
The empty pastures blind with rain.

Next day the memories of these things,
   Like leaves through which a bird has flown,
Still vibrated with Love's warm wings;
   Till I must make them all my own
And paint this picture. So, 'twixt ease
Of talk and sweet long silences,
   She stood among the plants in bloom
   At windows of a summer room,
To feign the shadow of the trees.

THE PORTRAIT.

And as I wrought, while all above
    And all around was fragrant air,
In the sick burthen of my love
    It seemed each sun-thrilled blossom there
Beat like a heart among the leaves.
O heart that never beats nor heaves,
    In that one darkness lying still,
    What now to thee my love's great will
Or the fine web the sunshine weaves?

For now doth daylight disavow
    Those days—nought left to see or hear.
Only in solemn whispers now
    At night-time these things reach mine ear;
When the leaf-shadows at a breath
Shrink in the road, and all the heath,
    Forest and water, far and wide,
    In limpid starlight glorified,
Lie like the mystery of death.

Last night at last I could have slept,
    And yet delayed my sleep till dawn,
Still wandering. Then it was I wept:
    For unawares I came upon
Those glades where once she walked with me:
And as I stood there suddenly,
    All wan with traversing the night,
    Upon the desolate verge of light
Yearned loud the iron-bosomed sea.

Even so, where Heaven holds breath and hears
    The beating heart of Love's own breast,—
Where round the secret of all spheres
    All angels lay their wings to rest,—
How shall my soul stand rapt and awed,
When, by the new birth borne abroad
    Throughout the music of the suns,
    It enters in her soul at once
And knows the silence there for God!

THE PORTRAIT.

Here with her face doth memory sit
    Meanwhile, and wait the day's decline,
Till other eyes shall look from it,
    Eyes of the spirit's Palestine,
Even than the old gaze tenderer:
While hopes and aims long lost with her
    Stand round her image side by side,
    Like tombs of pilgrims that have died
About the Holy Sepulchre.

AVE.

Mother of the Fair Delight,
Thou handmaid perfect in God's sight,
Now sitting fourth beside the Three,
Thyself a woman-Trinity,—
Being a daughter born to God,
Mother of Christ from stall to rood,
And wife unto the Holy Ghost:—
Oh when our need is uttermost,
Think that to such as death may strike
Thou once wert sister sisterlike!
Thou headstone of humanity,
Groundstone of the great Mystery,
Fashioned like us, yet more than we!

Mind'st thou not (when June's heavy breath
Warmed the long days in Nazareth,)
That eve thou didst go forth to give
Thy flowers some drink that they might live
One faint night more amid the sands?
Far off the trees were as pale wands
Against the fervid sky: the sea
Sighed further off eternally
As human sorrow sighs in sleep.
Then suddenly the awe grew deep,
As of a day to which all days
Were footsteps in God's secret ways:
Until a folding sense, like prayer,
Which is, as God is, everywhere,
Gathered about thee; and a voice
Spake to thee without any noise,

Being of the silence :—" Hail," it said,
"Thou that art highly favourèd ;
The Lord is with thee here and now ;
Blessed among all women thou."

Ah ! knew'st thou of the end, when first
That Babe was on thy bosom nurs'd ?
Or when He tottered round thy knee
Did thy great sorrow dawn on thee ?—
And through His boyhood, year by year
Eating with Him the Passover,
Didst thou discern confusedly
That holier sacrament, when He,
The bitter cup about to quaff,
Should break the bread and eat thereof ?—
Or came not yet the knowledge, even
Till on some day forecast in Heaven
His feet passed through thy door to press
Upon His Father's business ?—
Or still was God's high secret kept ?

Nay, but I think the whisper crept
Like growth through childhood. Work and play,
Things common to the course of day,
Awed thee with meanings unfulfill'd ;
And all through girlhood, something still'd
Thy senses like the birth of light,
When thou hast trimmed thy lamp at night
Or washed thy garments in the stream ;
To whose white bed had come the dream
That He was thine and thou wast His
Who feeds among the field-lilies.
O solemn shadow of the end
In that wise spirit long contain'd !
O awful end ! and those unsaid
Long years when It was Finishèd !

Mind'st thou not (when the twilight gone
Left darkness in the house of John,)
Between the naked window-bars
That spacious vigil of the stars?—
For thou, a watcher even as they,
Wouldst rise from where throughout the day
Thou wroughtest raiment for His poor;
And, finding the fixed terms endure
Of day and night which never brought
Sounds of His coming chariot,
Wouldst lift through cloud-waste unexplor'd
Those eyes which said, "How long, O Lord?"
Then that disciple whom He loved,
Well heeding, haply would be moved
To ask thy blessing in His name;
And that one thought in both, the same
Though silent, then would clasp ye round
To weep together,—tears long bound,
Sick tears of patience, dumb and slow.
Yet, "Surely I come quickly,"—so
He said, from life and death gone home.
Amen: even so, Lord Jesus, come!

But oh! what human tongue can speak
That day when Michael came * to break
From the tir'd spirit, like a veil,
Its covenant with Gabriel
Endured at length unto the end?
What human thought can apprehend
That mystery of motherhood
When thy Beloved at length renew'd
The sweet communion severèd,—
His left hand underneath thine head
And His right hand embracing thee?—
Lo! He was thine, and this is He!

* A Church legend of the Blessed Virgin's death.

Soul, is it Faith, or Love, or Hope,
That lets me see her standing up
Where the light of the Throne is bright?
Unto the left, unto the right,
The cherubim, succinct, conjoint,
Float inward to a golden point,
And from between the seraphim
The glory issues for a hymn.
O Mary Mother, be not loth
To listen,—thou whom the stars clothe,
Who seëst and mayst not be seen!
Hear us at last, O Mary Queen!
Into our shadow bend thy face,
Bowing thee from the secret place,
O Mary Virgin, full of grace!

THE CARD-DEALER.

COULD you not drink her gaze like wine?
   Yet though its splendour swoon
Into the silence languidly
   As a tune into a tune,
Those eyes unravel the coiled night
   And know the stars at noon.

The gold that's heaped beside her hand,
   In truth rich prize it were;
And rich the dreams that wreathe her brows
   With magic stillness there;
And he were rich who should unwind
   That woven golden hair.

Around her, where she sits, the dance
   Now breathes its eager heat;
And not more lightly or more true
   Fall there the dancers' feet
Than fall her cards on the bright board
   As 'twere a heart that beat.

Her fingers let them softly through,
   Smooth polished silent things;
And each one as it falls reflects
   In swift light-shadowings,
Blood-red and purple, green and blue,
   The great eyes of her rings.

THE CARD-DEALER.

Whom plays she with? With thee, who lov'st
   Those gems upon her hand;
With me, who search her secret brows;
   With all men, bless'd or bann'd.
We play together, she and we,
   Within a vain strange land:

A land without any order,—
   Day even as night, (one saith,)—
Where who lieth down ariseth not
   Nor the sleeper awakeneth;
A land of darkness as darkness itself
   And of the shadow of death.

What be her cards, you ask? Even these:—
   The heart, that doth but crave
More, having fed; the diamond,
   Skilled to make base seem brave;
The club, for smiting in the dark;
   The spade, to dig a grave.

And do you ask what game she plays?
   With me 'tis lost or won;
With thee it is playing still; with him
   It is not well begun;
But 'tis a game she plays with all
   Beneath the sway o' the sun.

Thou seest the card that falls,—she knows
   The card that followeth:
Her game in thy tongue is called Life,
   As ebbs thy daily breath:
When she shall speak, thou'lt learn her tongue
   And know she calls it Death.

WORLD'S WORTH.

'Tis of the Father Hilary.
   He strove, but could not pray ; so took
   The steep-coiled stair, where his feet shook
A sad blind echo. Ever up
   He toiled. 'Twas a sick sway of air
   That autumn noon within the stair,
As dizzy as a turning cup.
   His brain benumbed him, void and thin ;
   He shut his eyes and felt it spin ;
   The obscure deafness hemmed him in.
He said : " O world, what world for me ? "

He leaned unto the balcony
   Where the chime keeps the night and day ;
   It hurt his brain, he could not pray.
He had his face upon the stone :
   Deep 'twixt the narrow shafts, his eye
   Passed all the roofs to the stark sky,
Swept with no wing, with wind alone.
   Close to his feet the sky did shake
   With wind in pools that the rains make :
   The ripple set his eyes to ache.
He said : " O world, what world for me ? "

He stood within the mystery
   Girding God's blessed Eucharist:
   The organ and the chaunt had ceas'd.
The last words paused against his ear
   Said from the altar: drawn round him
   The gathering rest was dumb and dim.
And now the sacring-bell rang clear
   And ceased; and all was awe,—the breath
   Of God in man that warranteth
   The inmost utmost things of faith.
He said: "O God, my world in Thee!"

ON REFUSAL OF AID BETWEEN NATIONS.

Not that the earth is changing, O my God!
   Nor that the seasons totter in their walk,—
   Not that the virulent ill of act and talk
Seethes ever as a winepress ever trod,—
Not therefore are we certain that the rod
   Weighs in thine hand to smite thy world; though now
   Beneath thine hand so many nations bow,
So many kings :—not therefore, O my God!—

But because Man is parcelled out in men
   To-day; because, for any wrongful blow
     No man not stricken asks, "I would be told
Why thou dost thus;" but his heart whispers then,
   "He is he, I am I." By this we know
     That our earth falls asunder, being old.

ON THE VITA NUOVA OF DANTE.

As he that loves oft looks on the dear form
   And guesses how it grew to womanhood,
   And gladly would have watched the beauties bud
And the mild fire of precious life wax warm:
So I, long bound within the threefold charm
   Of Dante's love sublimed to heavenly mood,
   Had marvelled, touching his Beatitude,
How grew such presence from man's shameful swarm.

At length within this book I found pourtrayed
   Newborn that Paradisal Love of his,
And simple like a child; with whose clear aid
   I understood. To such a child as this,
Christ, charging well His chosen ones, forbade
   Offence: "for lo! of such my kingdom is."

SONG AND MUSIC.

O LEAVE your hand where it lies cool
    Upon the eyes whose lids are hot:
Its rosy shade is bountiful
    Of silence, and assuages thought.
O lay your lips against your hand
    And let me feel your breath through it,
While through the sense your song shall fit
    The soul to understand.

The music lives upon my brain
    Between your hands within mine eyes;
It stirs your lifted throat like pain,
    An aching pulse of melodies.
Lean nearer, let the music pause:
    The soul may better understand
Your music, shadowed in your hand,
    Now while the song withdraws.

THE SEA-LIMITS.

Consider the sea's listless chime:
   Time's self it is, made audible,—
   The murmur of the earth's own shell.
Secret continuance sublime
   Is the sea's end: our sight may pass
   No furlong further. Since time was,
This sound hath told the lapse of time.

No quiet, which is death's,—it hath
   The mournfulness of ancient life,
   Enduring always at dull strife.
As the world's heart of rest and wrath,
   Its painful pulse is in the sands.
   Last utterly, the whole sky stands,
Grey and not known, along its path.

Listen alone beside the sea,
   Listen alone among the woods;
   Those voices of twin solitudes
Shall have one sound alike to thee:
   Hark where the murmurs of thronged men
   Surge and sink back and surge again,—
Still the one voice of wave and tree.

Gather a shell from the strown beach
   And listen at its lips: they sigh
   The same desire and mystery,
The echo of the whole sea's speech.
   And all mankind is thus at heart
   Not anything but what thou art:
And Earth, Sea, Man, are all in each.

A TRIP TO PARIS AND BELGIUM.

I.

LONDON TO FOLKESTONE.

A CONSTANT keeping-past of shaken trees,
And a bewildered glitter of loose road;
Banks of bright growth, with single blades atop
Against white sky: and wires—a constant chain—
That seem to draw the clouds along with them
(Things which one stoops against the light to see
Through the low window; shaking by at rest,
Or fierce like water as the swiftness grows);
And, seen through fences or a bridge far off,
Trees that in moving keep their intervals
Still one 'twixt bar and bar; and then at times
Long reaches of green level, where one cow,
Feeding among her fellows that feed on,
Lifts her slow neck, and gazes for the sound.

Fields mown in ridges; and close garden-crops
Of the earth's increase; and a constant sky
Still with clear trees that let you see the wind;
And snatches of the engine-smoke, by fits
Tossed to the wind against the landscape, where
Rooks stooping heave their wings upon the day.

Brick walls we pass between, passed so at once
That for the suddenness I cannot know
Or what, or where begun, or where at end.
Sometimes a station in grey quiet; whence,
With a short gathered champing of pent sound,
We are let out upon the air again.
Pauses of water soon, at intervals,
That has the sky in it;—the reflexes

O' the trees move towards the bank as we go by,
Leaving the water's surface plain.   I now
Lie back and close my eyes a space; for they
Smart from the open forwardness of thought
Fronting the wind.

  *   *   *   *   *

      I did not scribble more,
Be certain, after this; but yawned, and read,
And nearly dozed a little, I believe;
Till, stretching up against the carriage-back,
I was roused altogether, and looked out
To where the pale sea brooded murmuring.

II.

BOULOGNE TO AMIENS AND PARIS.

Strong extreme speed, that the brain hurries with,
Further than trees, and hedges, and green grass
Whitened by distance,—further than small pools
Held among fields and gardens, further than
Haystacks, and wind-mill-sails, and roofs and herds,—
The sea's last margin ceases at the sun.

The sea has left us, but the sun remains.
Sometimes the country spreads aloof in tracts
Smooth from the harvest; sometimes sky and land
Are shut from the square space the window leaves
By a dense crowd of trees, stem behind stem
Passing across each other as we pass:
Sometimes tall poplar-wands stand white, their heads
Outmeasuring the distant hills.   Sometimes
The ground has a deep greenness; sometimes brown
In stubble; and sometimes no ground at all,
For the close strength of crops that stand unreaped.
The water-plots are sometimes all the sun's,—
Sometimes quite green through shadows filling them,
Or islanded with growths of reeds,—or else
Masked in grey dust like the wide face o' the fields.

And still the swiftness lasts; that to our speed
The trees seem shaken like a press of spears.

There is some count of us:—folks travelling capped,
Priesthood, and lank hard-featured soldiery,
Females (no women), blouses, Hunt, and I.

We are relayed at Amiens. The steam
Snorts, chafes, and bridles, like three hundred horse,
And flings its dusky mane upon the air.
Our company is thinned, and lamps alight.
But still there are the folks in travelling-caps,
No priesthood now, but always soldiery,
And babies to make up for show in noise;
Females (no women), blouses, Hunt, and I.

Our windows at one side are shut for warmth;
Upon the other side, a leaden sky,
Hung in blank glare, makes all the country dim,
Which too seems bald and meagre,—be it truth,
Or of the waxing darkness. Here and there
The shade takes light, where in thin patches stand
The unstirred dregs of water.

III.

THE PARIS RAILWAY-STATION.

In France, (to baffle thieves and murderers)
A journey takes two days of passport work
At least. The plan's sometimes a tedious one,
But bears its fruit. Because, the other day,
In passing by the Morgue, we saw a man
(The thing is common, and we never should
Have known of it, only we passed that way)

Who had been stabbed and tumbled in the Seine,
Where he had stayed some days.   The face was black,
And, like a negro's, swollen ; all the flesh
Had furred, and broken into a green mould.

   Now, very likely, he who did the job
Was standing among those who stood with us,
To look upon the corpse.   You fancy him—
Smoking an early pipe, and watching, as
An artist, the effect of his last work.-
This always if it had not struck him that
'Twere best to leave while yet the body took
Its crust of rot beneath the Seine.   It may :
But, if it did not, he can now remain
Without much fear.   *Only*, if he should want
To travel, and have not his passport yet,
(Deep dogs these French police !) he may be caught.

   Therefore you see (lest, being murderers,
We should not have the sense to go before
The thing were known, or to stay afterwards)
There is good reason why—having resolved
To start for Belgium—we were kept three days
To learn about the passports first, then do
As we had learned.   This notwithstanding, in
The fulness of the time 'tis come to pass.

IV.

REACHING BRUSSELS.

   There is small change of country ; but the sun
Is out, and it seems shame this were not said.
For upon all the grass the warmth has caught ;
And betwixt distant whitened poplar-stems
Makes greener darkness ; and in dells of trees
Shows spaces of a verdure that was hid ;

And the sky has its blue floated with white,
And crossed with falls of the sun's glory aslant
To lay upon the waters of the world;
And from the road men stand with shaded eyes
To look; and flowers in gardens have grown strong;
And our own shadows here within the coach
Are brighter; and all colour has more bloom.

So, after the sore torments of the route;—
Toothache, and headache, and the ache of wind,
And huddled sleep, and smarting wakefulness,
And night, and day, and hunger sick at food,
And twenty-fold relays, and packages
To be unlocked, and passports to be found,
And heavy well-kept landscape;—we were glad
Because we entered Brussels in the sun.

v.

ANTWERP TO GHENT.

We are upon the Scheldt. We know we move
Because there is a floating at our eyes
Whatso they seek; and because all the things
Which on our outset were distinct and large
Are smaller and much weaker and quite grey,
And at last gone from us. No motion else.

We are upon the road. The thin swift moon
Runs with the running clouds that are the sky,
And with the running water runs—at whiles
Weak 'neath the film and heavy growth of reeds.
The country swims with motion. Time itself
Is consciously beside us, and perceived.
Our speed is such the sparks our engine leaves
Are burning after the whole train has passed.

The darkness is a tumult. We tear on,
The roll behind us and the cry before,
Constantly, in a lull of intense speed
And thunder. Any other sound is known
Merely by sight. The shrubs, the trees your eye
Scans for their growth, are far along in haze.
The sky has lost its clouds, and lies away
Oppressively at calm: the moon has failed:
Our speed has set the wind against us. Now
Our engine's heat is fiercer, and flings up
Great glares alongside. Wind and steam and speed
And clamour and the night. We are in Ghent.

THE STAIRCASE OF NOTRE DAME, PARIS.

As one who, groping in a narrow stair,
　Hath a strong sound of bells upon his ears,
　Which, being at a distance off, appears
Quite close to him because of the pent air:
So with this France. She stumbles file and square
　Darkling and without space for breath: each one
　Who hears the thunder says: "It shall anon
Be in among her ranks to scatter her."

This may be; and it may be that the storm
　Is spent in rain upon the unscathed seas,
　　Or wasteth other countries ere it die:
Till she,—having climbed always through the swarm
　Of darkness and of hurtling sound,—from these
　　Shall step forth on the light in a still sky.

PLACE DE LA BASTILLE, PARIS.

How dear the sky has been above this place!
　Small treasures of this sky that we see here
　Seen weak through prison-bars from year to year;
Eyed with a painful prayer upon God's grace
To save, and tears that stayed along the face
　Lifted at sunset. Yea, how passing dear,
　Those nights when through the bars a wind left clear
The heaven, and moonlight soothed the limpid space!

So was it, till one night the secret kept
　Safe in low vault and stealthy corridor
　　Was blown abroad on gospel-tongues of flame.
　O ways of God, mysterious evermore!
How many on this spot have cursed and wept
　　That all might stand here now and own Thy Name.

NEAR BRUSSELS—A HALF-WAY PAUSE.

THE turn of noontide has begun.
   In the weak breeze the sunshine yields.
   There is a bell upon the fields.
On the long hedgerow's tangled run
   A low white cottage intervenes:
   Against the wall a blind man leans,
And sways his face to have the sun.

Our horses' hoofs stir in the road,
   Quiet and sharp.   Light hath a song
   Whose silence, being heard, seems long.
The point of noon maketh abode,
   And will not be at once gone through.
   The sky's deep colour saddens you,
And the heat weighs a dreamy load.

ANTWERP AND BRUGES.

I CLIMBED the stair in Antwerp church,
   What time the circling thews of sound
   At sunset seem to heave it round.
Far up, the carillon did search
The wind, and the birds came to perch
   Far under, where the gables wound.

In Antwerp harbour on the Scheldt
   I stood along, a certain space
   Of night. The mist was near my face;
Deep on, the flow was heard and felt.
The carillon kept pause, and dwelt
   In music through the silent place.

John Memmeling and John van Eyck
   Hold state at Bruges. In sore shame
   I scanned the works that keep their name.
The carillon, which then did strike
Mine ears, was heard of theirs alike:
   It set me closer unto them.

I climbed at Bruges all the flight
   The belfry has of ancient stone.
   For leagues I saw the east wind blown;
The earth was grey, the sky was white.
I stood so near upon the height
   That my flesh felt the carillon.

ON LEAVING BRUGES.

THE city's steeple-towers remove away,
   Each singly; as each vain infatuate Faith
   Leaves God in heaven, and passes. A mere breath
Each soon appears, so far. Yet that which lay
The first is now scarce further or more grey
   Than the last is. Now all are wholly gone.
   The sunless sky has not once had the sun
Since the first weak beginning of the day.

The air falls back as the wind finishes,
   And the clouds stagnate. On the water's face
    The current breathes along, but is not stirred.
   There is no branch that thrills with any bird.
Winter is to possess the earth a space,
And have its will upon the extreme seas.

VOX ECCLESIÆ, VOX CHRISTI.

I saw under the altar the souls of them that were slain for the word of God, and for the testimony which they held; and they cried with a loud voice, saying, How long, O Lord, holy and true, dost Thou not judge and avenge our blood on them that dwell on the earth?—REV. vi. 9, 10.

NOT 'neath the altar only,—yet, in sooth,
  There more than elsewhere,—is the cry, "How long?"
  The right sown there hath still borne fruit in wrong—
The wrong waxed fourfold. Thence, (in hate of truth)
O'er weapons blessed for carnage, to fierce youth
  From evil age, the word hath hissed along:—
  "Ye are the Lord's: go forth, destroy, be strong:
Christ's Church absolves ye from Christ's law of ruth."

Therefore the wine-cup at the altar is
  As Christ's own blood indeed, and as the blood
    Of Christ's elect, at divers seasons spilt
On the altar-stone, that to man's church, for this,
  Shall prove a stone of stumbling,—whence it stood
    To be rent up ere the true Church be built.

THE BURDEN OF NINEVEH.

In our Museum galleries
To-day I lingered o'er the prize
Dead Greece vouchsafes to living eyes,—
Her Art for ever in fresh wise
　From hour to hour rejoicing me.
Sighing I turned at last to win
Once more the London dirt and din;
And as I made the swing-door spin
And issued, they were hoisting in
　A wingèd beast from Nineveh.

A human face the creature wore,
And hoofs behind and hoofs before,
And flanks with dark runes fretted o'er.
'Twas bull, 'twas mitred Minotaur,
　A dead disbowelled mystery:
The mummy of a buried faith
Stark from the charnel without scathe,
Its wings stood for the light to bathe,—
Such fossil cerements as might swathe
　The very corpse of Nineveh.

The print of its first rush-wrapping,
Wound ere it dried, still ribbed the thing.
What song did the brown maidens sing,
From purple mouths alternating,
　When that was woven languidly?
What vows, what rites, what prayers preferr'd,
What songs has the strange image heard?
In what blind vigil stood interr'd
For ages, till an English word
　Broke silence first at Nineveh?

THE BURDEN OF NINEVEH.

Oh when upon each sculptured court,
Where even the wind might not resort,—
O'er which Time passed, of like import
With the wild Arab boys at sport,—
  A living face looked in to see:—
Oh seemed it not—the spell once broke—
As though the carven warriors woke,
As though the shaft the string forsook,
The cymbals clashed, the chariots shook,
  And there was life in Nineveh?

On London stones our sun anew
The beast's recovered shadow threw.
(No shade that plague of darkness knew,
No light, no shade, while older grew
  By ages the old earth and sea.)
Lo thou! could all thy priests have shown
Such proof to make thy godhead known?
From their dead Past thou liv'st alone;
And still thy shadow is thine own,
  Even as of yore in Nineveh.

That day whereof we keep record,
When near thy city-gates the Lord
Sheltered His Jonah with a gourd,
This sun, (I said) here present, pour'd
  Even thus this shadow that I see.
This shadow has been shed the same
From sun and moon,—from lamps which came
For prayer,—from fifteen days of flame,
The last, while smouldered to a name
  Sardanapalus' Nineveh.

Within thy shadow, haply, once
Sennacherib has knelt, whose sons
Smote him between the altar-stones:
Or pale Semiramis her zones
  Of gold, her incense brought to thee,

THE BURDEN OF NINEVEH.

In love for grace, in war for aid : . . . .
Ay, and who else ? . . . . till 'neath thy shade
Within his trenches newly made
Last year the Christian knelt and pray'd—
    Not to thy strength—in Nineveh.*

Now, thou poor god, within this hall
Where the blank windows blind the wall
From pedestal to pedestal,
The kind of light shall on thee fall
    Which London takes the day to be :
While school-foundations in the act
Of holiday, three files compact,
Shall learn to view thee as a fact
Connected with that zealous tract :
    "ROME,—Babylon and Nineveh."

Deemed they of this, those worshipers,
When, in some mythic chain of verse
Which man shall not again rehearse,
The faces of thy ministers
    Yearned pale with bitter ecstasy ?
Greece, Egypt, Rome,—did any god
Before whose feet men knelt unshod
Deem that in this unblest abode
Another scarce more unknown god
    Should house with him, from Nineveh ?

Ah! in what quarries lay the stone
From which this pillared pile has grown,
Unto man's need how long unknown,
Since those thy temples, court and cone,
    Rose far in desert history ?

---

* During the excavations, the Tiyari workmen held their services in the shadow of the great bulls.—(*Layard's* "*Nineveh*," ch. ix.)

THE BURDEN OF NINEVEH.

Ah! what is here that does not lie
All strange to thine awakened eye?
Ah! what is here can testify
(Save that dumb presence of the sky)
   Unto thy day and Nineveh?

Why, of those mummies in the room
Above, there might indeed have come
One out of Egypt to thy home,
An alien. Nay, but were not some
   Of these thine own "antiquity"?
And now,—they and their gods and thou
All relics here together,—now
Whose profit? whether bull or cow,
Isis or Ibis, who or how,
   Whether of Thebes or Nineveh?

The consecrated metals found,
And ivory tablets, underground,
Winged teraphim and creatures crown'd,
When air and daylight filled the mound,
   Fell into dust immediately.
And even as these, the images
Of awe and worship,—even as these,—
So, smitten with the sun's increase,
Her glory mouldered and did cease
   From immemorial Nineveh.

The day her builders made their halt,
Those cities of the lake of salt
Stood firmly 'stablished without fault,
Made proud with pillars of basalt,
   With sardonyx and porphyry.
The day that Jonah bore abroad
To Nineveh the voice of God,
A brackish lake lay in his road,
Where erst Pride fixed her sure abode,
   As then in royal Nineveh.

The day when he, Pride's lord and Man's,
Showed all the kingdoms at a glance
To Him before whose countenance
The years recede, the years advance,
　　And said, Fall down and worship me:—
'Mid all the pomp beneath that look,
Then stirred there, haply, some rebuke,
Where to the wind the Salt Pools shook,
And in those tracts, of life forsook,
　　That knew thee not O Nineveh!

Delicate harlot! On thy throne
Thou with a world beneath thee prone
In state for ages sat'st alone;
And needs were years and lustres flown
　　Ere strength of man could vanquish thee:
Whom even thy victor foes must bring,
Still royal, among maids that sing
As with doves' voices, taboring
Upon their breasts, unto the King,—
　　A kingly conquest, Nineveh!

. . . Here woke my thought. The wind's slow sway
Had waxed; and like the human play
Of scorn that smiling spreads away,
The sunshine shivered off the day:
　　The callous wind, it seemed to me,
Swept up the shadow from the ground:
And pale as whom the Fates astound,
The god forlorn stood winged and crown'd:
Within I knew the cry lay bound
　　Of the dumb soul of Nineveh.

And as I turned, my sense half shut
Still saw the crowds of kerb and rut
Go past as marshalled to the strut
Of ranks in gypsum quaintly cut.
　　It seemed in one same pageantry

THE BURDEN OF NINEVEH.

They followed forms which had been erst;
To pass, till on my sight should burst
That future of the best or worst
When some may question which was first,
   Of London or of Nineveh.

For as that Bull-god once did stand
And watched the burial-clouds of sand,
Till these at last without a hand
Rose o'er his eyes, another land,
   And blinded him with destiny :—
So may he stand again; till now,
In ships of unknown sail and prow,
Some tribe of the Australian plough
Bear him afar,—a relic now
   Of London, not of Nineveh!

Or it may chance indeed that when
Man's age is hoary among men,—
His centuries threescore and ten,—
His furthest childhood shall seem then
   More clear than later times may be:
Who, finding in this desert place
This form, shall hold us for some race
That walked not in Christ's lowly ways,
But bowed its pride and vowed its praise
   Unto the God of Nineveh.

The smile rose first,—anon drew nigh
The thought : . . Those heavy wings spread high,
So sure of flight, which do not fly;
That set gaze never on the sky;
   Those scriptured flanks it cannot see;
Its crown, a brow-contracting load;
Its planted feet which trust the sod : . . .
(So grew the image as I trod :)
O Nineveh, was this thy God,—
   Thine also, mighty Nineveh?

THE CHURCH-PORCH.

Sister, first shake we off the dust we have
  Upon our feet, lest it defile the stones
  Inscriptured, covering their sacred bones
Who lie i' the aisles which keep the names they gave,
Their trust abiding round them in the grave;
  Whom painters paint for visible orisons,
  And to whom sculptors pray in stone and bronze;
Their voices echo still like a spent wave.

Without here, the church-bells are but a tune,
And on the carven church-door this hot noon
  Lays all its heavy sunshine here without:
But having entered in, we shall find there
Silence, and sudden dimness, and deep prayer,
  And faces of crowned angels all about.

THE MIRROR.

  She knew it not:—most perfect pain
    To learn : this too she knew not. Strife
      For me, calm hers, as from the first.
      'Twas but another bubble burst
    Upon the curdling draught of life,—
  My silent patience mine again.

  As who, of forms that crowd unknown
    Within a distant mirror's shade,
      Deems such an one himself, and makes
      Some sign ; but when the image shakes
    No whit, he finds his thought betray'd,
And must seek elsewhere for his own.

A YOUNG FIR-WOOD.

These little firs to-day are things
   To clasp into a giant's cap,
   Or fans to suit his lady's lap.
From many winters many springs
   Shall cherish them in strength and sap
   Till they be marked upon the map,
A wood for the wind's wanderings.

All seed is in the sower's hands:
   And what at first was trained to spread
   Its shelter for some single head,—
Yea, even such fellowship of wands,—
   May hide the sunset, and the shade
   Of its great multitude be laid
Upon the earth and elder sands.

DURING MUSIC.

O cool unto the sense of pain
   That last night's sleep could not destroy;
   O warm unto the sense of joy,
That dreams its life within the brain.

What though I lean o'er thee to scan
   The written music cramped and stiff;—
   'Tis dark to me, as hieroglyph
On those weird bulks Egyptian.

But as from those, dumb now and strange,
   A glory wanders on the earth,
   Even so thy tones can call a birth
From these, to shake my soul with change.

O swift, as in melodious haste
   Float o'er the keys thy fingers small;
   O soft, as is the rise and fall
Which stirs that shade within thy breast.

STRATTON WATER.

"O HAVE you seen the Stratton flood
  That's great with rain to-day?
It runs beneath your wall, Lord Sands,
  Full of the new-mown hay.

"I led your hounds to Hutton bank
  To bathe at early morn:
They got their bath by Borrowbrake
  Above the standing corn."

Out from the castle-stair Lord Sands
  Looked up the western lea;
The rook was grieving on her nest,
  The flood was round her tree.

Over the castle-wall Lord Sands
  Looked down the eastern hill:
The stakes swam free among the boats,
  The flood was rising still.

"What's yonder far below that lies
  So white against the slope?"
"O it's a sail o' your bonny barks
  The waters have washed up."

"But I have never a sail so white,
  And the water's not yet there."
"O it's the swans o' your bonny lake
  The rising flood doth scare."

STRATTON WATER.

"The swans they would not hold so still,
   So high they would not win."
"O it's Joyce my wife has spread her smock
   And fears to fetch it in."

"Nay, knave, it's neither sail nor swans,
   Nor aught that you can say;
For though your wife might leave her smock,
   Herself she'd bring away."

Lord Sands has passed the turret-stair,
   The court, and yard, and all;
The kine were in the byre that day,
   The nags were in the stall.

Lord Sands has won the weltering slope
   Whereon the white shape lay:
The clouds were still above the hill,
   And the shape was still as they.

Oh pleasant is the gaze of life
   And sad is death's blind head;
But awful are the living eyes
   In the face of one thought dead!

"In God's name, Janet, is it me
   Thy ghost has come to seek?"
"Nay, wait another hour, Lord Sands,—
   Be sure my ghost shall speak."

A moment stood he as a stone,
   Then grovelled to his knee.
"O Janet, O my love, my love,
   Rise up and come with me!"
"O once before you bade me come,
   And it's here you have brought me!

"O many's the sweet word, Lord Sands,
  You've spoken oft to me;
But all that I have from you to-day
  Is the rain on my body.

"And many's the good gift, Lord Sands,
  You've promised oft to me;
But the gift of yours I keep to-day
  Is the babe in my body.

"O it's not in any earthly bed
  That first my babe I'll see;
For I have brought my body here
  That the flood may cover me."

His face was close against her face,
  His hands of hers were fain:
O her wet cheeks were hot with tears,
  Her wet hands cold with rain.

"They told me you were dead, Janet,—
  How could I guess the lie?"
"They told me you were false, Lord Sands,—
  What could I do but die?"

"Now keep you well, my brother Giles,—
  Through you I deemed her dead!
As wan as your towers seem to-day,
  To-morrow they'll be red.

"Look down, look down, my false mother,
  That bade me not to grieve:
You'll look up when our marriage fires
  Are lit to-morrow eve:

"O more than one and more than two
  The sorrow of this shall see:
But it's to-morrow, love, for them,—
  To-day's for thee and me."

He's drawn her face between his hands
    And her pale mouth to his:
No bird that was so still that day
    Chirps sweeter than his kiss.

The flood was creeping round their feet.
    "O Janet, come away!
The hall is warm for the marriage-rite,
    The bed for the birthday."

"Nay, but I hear your mother cry,
    'Go bring this bride to bed!
And would she christen her babe unborn,
    So wet she comes to wed?'

"I'll be your wife to cross your door
    And meet your mother's e'e.
We plighted troth to wed i' the kirk,
    And it's there you'll wed with me."

He's ta'en her by the short girdle
    And by the dripping sleeve:
"Go fetch Sir Jock my mother's priest,—
    You'll ask of him no leave.

"O it's one half-hour to reach the kirk
    And one for the marriage-rite;
And kirk and castle and castle-lands
    Shall be our babe's to-night."

"The flood's in the kirkyard, Lord Sands,
    And round the belfry-stair."
"I bade you fetch the priest," he said,
    "Myself shall bring him there.

"It's for the lilt of wedding bells
    We'll have the hail to pour,
And for the clink of bridle-reins
    The plashing of the oar."

Beneath them on the nether hill
  A boat was floating wide:
Lord Sands swam out and caught the oars
  And rowed to the hill-side.

He's wrapped her in a green mantle
  And set her softly in;
Her hair was wet upon her face,
  Her face was grey and thin;
And "Oh!" she said, "lie still, my babe,
  It's out you must not win!"

But woe's my heart for Father John
  As hard as he might pray,
There seemed no help but Noah's ark
  Or Jonah's fish that day.

The first strokes that the oars struck
  Were over the broad leas;
The next strokes that the oars struck
  They pushed beneath the trees;

The last stroke that the oars struck,
  The good boat's head was met,
And there the gate of the kirkyard
  Stood like a ferry-gate.

He's set his hand upon the bar
  And lightly leaped within:
He's lifted her to his left shoulder,
  Her knees beside his chin.

The graves lay deep beneath the flood
  Under the rain alone;
And when the foot-stone made him slip,
  He held by the head-stone.

The empty boat thrawed i' the wind,
    Against the postern tied.
" Hold still, you've brought my love with me,
    You shall take back my bride."

But woe's my heart for Father John
    And the saints he clamoured to !
There's never a saint but Christopher
    Might hale such buttocks through !

And " Oh ! " she said, " on men's shoulders
    I well had thought to wend,
And well to travel with a priest,
    But not to have cared or ken'd.

" And oh ! " she said, " it's well this way
    That I thought to have fared,—
Not to have lighted at the kirk
    But stopped in the kirkyard.

" For it's oh and oh I prayed to God,
    Whose rest I hoped to win,
That when to-night at your board-head
    You'd bid the feast begin,
This water past your window-sill
    Might bear my body in."

Now make the white bed warm and soft
    And greet the merry morn.
The night the mother should have died,
    The young son shall be born.

WELLINGTON'S FUNERAL.

18th November 1852.

"Victory!"
So once more the cry must be.
Duteous mourning we fulfil
In God's name; but by God's will,
Doubt not, the last word is still
"Victory!"

Funeral,
In the music round this pall,
Solemn grief yields earth to earth;
But what tones of solemn mirth
In the pageant of new birth
Rise and fall?

For indeed,
If our eyes were openèd,
Who shall say what escort floats
Here, which breath nor gleam denotes,—
Fiery horses, chariots
Fire-footed?

Trumpeter,
Even thy call he may not hear;
Long-known voice for ever past,
Till with one more trumpet-blast
God's assuring word at last
Reach his ear.

WELLINGTON'S FUNERAL.

   Multitude,
Hold your breath in reverent mood:
For while earth's whole kindred stand
Mute even thus on either hand,
This soul's labour shall be scann'd
    And found good.

   Cherubim,
Lift ye not even now your hymn?
Lo! once lent for human lack,
Michael's sword is rendered back.
Thrills not now the starry track,
    Seraphim?

   Gabriel,
Since the gift of thine "All hail!"
Out of Heaven no time hath brought
Gift with fuller blessing fraught
Than the peace which this man wrought
    Passing well.

   Be no word
Raised of bloodshed Christ-abhorr'd.
Say: "'Twas thus in His decrees
Who Himself, the Prince of Peace,
For His harvest's high increase
    Sent a sword."

   Veterans,
He by whom the neck of France
Then was given unto your heel,
Timely sought, may lend as well
To your sons his terrible
    Countenance.

Waterloo!
As the last grave must renew,
Ere fresh death, the banshee-strain,—
So methinks upon thy plain
Falls some presage in the rain,
    In the dew.

And O thou,
Watching with an exile's brow
Unappeased, o'er death's dumb flood:—
Lo! the saving strength of God
In some new heart's English blood
    Slumbers now.

Emperor,
Is this all thy work was for?—
Thus to see thy self-sought aim,
Yea thy titles, yea thy name,
In another's shame, to shame
    Bandied o'er?*

Wellington,
Thy great work is but begun.
With quick seed his end is rife
Whose long tale of conquering strife
Shows no triumph like his life
    Lost and won

* Date of the *Coup d'État*: 2nd December 1851.

PENUMBRA.

I DID not look upon her eyes,
(Though scarcely seen, with no surprise,
'Mid many eyes a single look,)
Because they should not gaze rebuke,
At night, from stars in sky and brook.

I did not take her by the hand,
(Though little was to understand
From touch of hand all friends might take,)
Because it should not prove a flake
Burnt in my palm to boil and ache.

I did not listen to her voice,
(Though none had noted, where at choice
All might rejoice in listening,)
Because no such a thing should cling
In the wood's moan at evening.

I did not cross her shadow once,
(Though from the hollow west the sun's
Last shadow runs along so far,)
Because in June it should not bar
My ways, at noon when fevers are.

They told me she was sad that day,
(Though wherefore tell what love's soothsay,
Sooner than they, did register?)
And my heart leapt and wept to her,
And yet I did not speak nor stir.

So shall the tongues of the sea's foam
(Though many voices therewith come
From drowned hope's home to cry to me,)
Bewail one hour the more, when sea
And wind are one with memory.

ON THE SITE OF A MULBERRY-TREE;

Planted by Wm. Shakspeare; felled by the Rev. F. Gastrell.

This tree, here fall'n, no common birth or death
   Shared with its kind. The world's enfranchised son,
   Who found the trees of Life and Knowledge one,
Here set it, frailer than his laurel-wreath.
Shall not the wretch whose hand it fell beneath
   Rank also singly—the supreme unhung?
   Lo! Sheppard, Turpin, pleading with black tongue
This viler thief's unsuffocated breath!

We'll search thy glossary, Shakspeare! whence almost,
   And whence alone, some name shall be reveal'd
      For this deaf drudge, to whom no length of ears
      Sufficed to catch the music of the spheres;
   Whose soul is carrion now,—too mean to yield
Some Starveling's ninth allotment of a ghost.

ON CERTAIN ELIZABETHAN REVIVALS.

O ruff-embastioned vast Elizabeth,
   Bush to these bushel-bellied casks of wine,
   Home-growth, 'tis true, but rank as turpentine—
What would we with such skittle-plays at death?
Say, must we watch these brawlers' brandished lathe,
   Or to their reeking wit our ears incline,
   Because all Castaly flowed crystalline
In gentle Shakspeare's modulated breath?

What! must our drama with the rat-pit vie,
   Nor the scene close while one is left to kill?
      Shall this be poetry?   And thou—thou man
      Of blood, thou cannibalic Caliban,
What shall be said of thee?   A poet?—Fie!
   "An honourable murderer, if you will."

ENGLISH MAY.

WOULD God your health were as this month of May
    Should be, were this not England,—and your face
    Abroad, to give the gracious sunshine grace
And laugh beneath the budding hawthorn-spray.
But here the hedgerows pine from green to grey
    While yet May's lyre is tuning, and her song
    Is weak in shade that should in sun be strong ;
And your pulse springs not to so faint a lay.

If in my life be breath of Italy,
    Would God that I might yield it all to you !
    So, when such grafted warmth had burgeoned through
The languor of your Maytime's hawthorn-tree,
My spirit at rest should walk unseen and see
    The garland of your beauty bloom anew.

BEAUTY AND THE BIRD.

SHE fluted with her mouth as when one sips,
    And gently waved her golden head, inclin'd
    Outside his cage close to the window-blind ;
Till her fond bird, with little turns and dips,
Piped low to her of sweet companionships.
    And when he made an end, some seed took she
    And fed him from her tongue, which rosily
Peeped as a piercing bud between her lips.

And like the child in Chaucer, on whose tongue
    The Blessed Mary laid, when he was dead,
A grain,—who straightway praised her name in song :
    Even so, when she, a little lightly red,
Now turned on me and laughed, I heard the throng
    Of inner voices praise her golden head.

A MATCH WITH THE MOON.

WEARY already, weary miles to-night
   I walked for bed: and so, to get some ease,
   I dogged the flying moon with similes.
And like a wisp she doubled on my sight
In ponds; and caught in tree-tops like a kite
   And in a globe of film all liquorish
   Swam full-faced like a silly silver fish;—
Last like a bubble shot the welkin's height
Where my road turned, and got behind me, and sent
   My wizened shadow craning round at me,
   And jeered," So, step the measure,—one two three!"—
And if I faced on her, looked innocent.
But just at parting, halfway down a dell,
She kissed me for good-night. So you'll not tell.

LOVE'S NOCTURN.

Master of the murmuring courts
 Where the shapes of sleep convene!—
Lo! my spirit here exhorts
 All the powers of thy demesne
 For their aid to woo my queen.
  What reports
 Yield thy jealous courts unseen?

Vaporous, unaccountable,
 Dreamworld lies forlorn of light,
Hollow like a breathing shell.
 Ah! that from all dreams I might
 Choose one dream and guide its flight!
  I know well
 What her sleep should tell to-night.

There the dreams are multitudes:
 Some that will not wait for sleep,
Deep within the August woods;
 Some that hum while rest may steep
 Weary labour laid a-heap;
  Interludes,
 Some, of grievous moods that weep.

Poets' fancies all are there:
 There the elf-girls flood with wings
Valleys full of plaintive air;
 There breathe perfumes; there in rings
 Whirl the foam-bewildered springs;
  Siren there
 Winds her dizzy hair and sings.

LOVE'S NOCTURN.

Thence the one dream mutually
   Dreamed in bridal unison,
Less than waking ecstasy;
    Half-formed visions that make moan
    In the house of birth alone;
      And what we
At death's wicket see, unknown.

But for mine own sleep, it lies
   In one gracious form's control,
Fair with honourable eyes,
    Lamps of a translucent soul:
    O their glance is loftiest dole,
      Sweet and wise,
Wherein Love descries his goal.

Reft of her, my dreams are all
   Clammy trance that fears the sky:
Changing footpaths shift and fall;
    From polluted coverts nigh,
    Miserable phantoms sigh;
      Quakes the pall,
And the funeral goes by.

Master, is it soothly said
   That, as echoes of man's speech
Far in secret clefts are made,
    So do all men's bodies reach
    Shadows o'er thy sunken beach,—
      Shape or shade
In those halls pourtrayed of each?

Ah! might I, by thy good grace
   Groping in the windy stair,
(Darkness and the breath of space
    Like loud waters everywhere,)
    Meeting mine own image there
      Face to face,
Send it from that place to her!

Nay, not I ; but oh ! do thou,
　Master, from thy shadowkind
Call my body's phantom now :
　　Bid it bear its face declin'd
　　Till its flight her slumbers find,
　　　　And her brow
　　Feel its presence bow like wind.

Where in groves the gracile Spring
　Trembles, with mute orison
Confidently strengthening,
　　Water's voice and wind's as one
　　Shed an echo in the sun.
　　　　Soft as Spring,
　　Master, bid it sing and moan.

Song shall tell how glad and strong
　Is the night she soothes alway ;
Moan shall grieve with that parched tongue
　　Of the brazen hours of day :
　　Sounds as of the springtide they,
　　　　Moan and song,
　　While the chill months long for May.

Not the prayers which with all leave
　The world's fluent woes prefer,—
Not the praise the world doth give,
　　Dulcet fulsome whisperer ;—
　　Let it yield my love to her,
　　　　And achieve
　　Strength that shall not grieve or err.

Wheresoe'er my dreams befall,
　Both at night-watch, (let it say,)
And where round the sundial
　　The reluctant hours of day,
　　Heartless, hopeless of their way,
　　　　Rest and call ;—
　　There her glance doth fall and stay.

Suddenly her face is there:
  So do mounting vapours wreathe
Subtle-scented transports where
    The black firwood sets its teeth.
    Part the boughs and look beneath,—
      Lilies share
    Secret waters there, and breathe.

Master, bid my shadow bend
  Whispering thus till birth of light,
Lest new shapes that sleep may send
    Scatter all its work to flight;—
    Master, master of the night,
      Bid it spend
    Speech, song, prayer, and end aright.

Yet, ah me! if at her head
  There another phantom lean
Murmuring o'er the fragrant bed,—
    Ah! and if my spirit's queen
    Smile those alien prayers between,—
      Ah! poor shade!
    Shall it strive, or fade unseen?

How should love's own messenger
  Strive with love and be love's foe?
Master, nay! If thus, in her,
    Sleep a wedded heart should show,—
    Silent let mine image go,
      Its old share
    Of thy spell-bound air to know.

Like a vapour wan and mute,
  Like a flame, so let it pass;
One low sigh across her lute,
    One dull breath against her glass;
    And to my sad soul, alas!
      One salute
    Cold as when death's foot shall pass.

Then, too, let all hopes of mine,
  All vain hopes by night and day,
Slowly at thy summoning sign
  Rise up pallid and obey.
  Dreams, if this is thus, were they:—
    Be they thine,
  And to dreamworld pine away.

Yet from old time, life, not death,
  Master, in thy rule is rife:
Lo! through thee, with mingling breath,
  Adam woke beside his wife.
  O Love bring me so, for strife,
    Force and faith,
  Bring me so not death but life!

Yea, to Love himself is pour'd
  This frail song of hope and fear.
Thou art Love, of one accord
  With kind Sleep to bring her near,
  Still-eyed, deep-eyed, ah how dear!
    Master, Lord,
  In her name implor'd, O hear!

FIRST LOVE REMEMBERED.

Peace in her chamber, wheresoe'er
    It be, a holy place:
The thought still brings my soul such grace
    As morning meadows wear.

Whether it still be small and light,
    A maid's who dreams alone,
As from her orchard-gate the moon
    Its ceiling showed at night:

Or whether, in a shadow dense
    As nuptial hymns invoke,
Innocent maidenhood awoke
    To married innocence:

There still the thanks unheard await
    The unconscious gift bequeathed:
For there my soul this hour has breathed
    An air inviolate.

PLIGHTED PROMISE.

In a soft-complexioned sky,
   Fleeting rose and kindling grey,
Have you seen Aurora fly
   At the break of day?
So my maiden, so my plighted may
   Blushing cheek and gleaming eye
     Lifts to look my way.

Where the inmost leaf is stirred
   With the heart-beat of the grove,
Have you heard a hidden bird
   Cast her note above?
So my lady, so my lovely love,
   Echoing Cupid's prompted word,
     Makes a tune thereof.

Have you seen, at heaven's mid-height,
   In the moon-rack's ebb and tide,
Venus leap forth burning white,
   Dian pale and hide?
So my bright breast-jewel, so my bride,
   One sweet night, when fear takes flight,
     Shall leap against my side.

SUDDEN LIGHT.

I have been here before,
   But when or how I cannot tell:
I know the grass beyond the door,
   The sweet keen smell,
The sighing sound, the lights around the shore.

You have been mine before,—
   How long ago I may not know:
But just when at that swallow's soar
   Your neck turned so,
Some veil did fall,—I knew it all of yore.

Has this been thus before?
   And shall not thus time's eddying flight
Still with our lives our love restore
   In death's despite,
And day and night yield one delight once more?

A NEW-YEAR'S BURDEN.

Along the grass sweet airs are blown
  Our way this day in Spring.
Of all the songs that we have known
  Now which one shall we sing?
          Not that, my love, ah no!—
          Not this, my love? why, so!—
Yet both were ours, but hours will come and go.

The grove is all a pale frail mist,
  The new year sucks the sun.
Of all the kisses that we kissed
  Now which shall be the one?
          Not that, my love, ah no!—
          Not this, my love?—heigh-ho
For all the sweets that all the winds can blow!

The branches cross above our eyes,
  The skies are in a net:
And what's the thing beneath the skies
  We two would most forget?
          Not birth, my love, no, no,—
          Not death, my love, no, no,—
The love once ours, but ours long hours ago.

EVEN SO.

So it is, my dear.
All such things touch secret strings
    For heavy hearts to hear.
    So it is, my dear.

    Very like indeed :
Sea and sky, afar, on high,
    Sand and strewn seaweed,—
    Very like indeed.

But the sea stands spread
As one wall with the flat skies,
Where the lean black craft like flies
    Seem well-nigh stagnated,
    Soon to drop off dead.

    Seemed it so to us
When I was thine and thou wast mine,
    And all these things were thus,
    But all our world in us?

    Could we be so now?
Not if all beneath heaven's pall
    Lay dead but I and thou,
    Could we be so now!

THE WOODSPURGE.

The wind flapped loose, the wind was still,
Shaken out dead from tree and hill ·
I had walked on at the wind's will,—
I sat now, for the wind was still.

Between my knees my forehead was,—
My lips, drawn in, said not Alas!
My hair was over in the grass,
My naked ears heard the day pass.

My eyes, wide open, had the run
Of some ten weeds to fix upon;
Among those few, out of the sun,
The woodspurge flowered, three cups in one.

From perfect grief there need not be
Wisdom or even memory:
One thing then learnt remains to me,—
The woodspurge has a cup of three.

THE HONEYSUCKLE.

I plucked a honeysuckle where
   The hedge on high is quick with thorn,
   And climbing for the prize, was torn,
And fouled my feet in quag-water;
   And by the thorns and by the wind
   The blossom that I took was thinn'd,
And yet I found it sweet and fair.

Thence to a richer growth I came,
   Where, nursed in mellow intercourse,
   The honeysuckles sprang by scores,
Not harried like my single stem,
   All virgin lamps of scent and dew.
   So from my hand that first I threw,
Yet plucked not any more of them.

DANTIS TENEBRÆ.

(In Memory of my Father.)

AND didst thou know indeed, when at the font
  Together with thy name thou gav'st me his,
  That also on thy son must Beatrice
Decline her eyes according to her wont,
Accepting me to be of those that haunt
  The vale of magical dark mysteries
  Where to the hills her poet's foot-track lies
And wisdom's living fountain to his chaunt
Trembles in music? This is that steep land
  Where he that holds his journey stands at gaze
    Tow'rd sunset, when the clouds like a new height
Seem piled to climb. These things I understand:
  For here, where day still soothes my lifted face,
    On thy bowed head, my father, fell the night.

WORDS ON THE WINDOW-PANE.*

DID she in summer write it, or in spring,
  Or with this wail of autumn at her ears,
  Or in some winter left among old years
Scratched it through tettered cark? A certain thing
That round her heart the frost was hardening,
  Not to be thawed of tears, which on this pane
  Channelled the rime, perchance, in fevered rain,
For false man's sake and love's most bitter sting.

Howbeit, between this last word and the next
  Unwritten, subtly seasoned was the smart,
    And here at least the grace to weep: if she,
Rather, midway in her disconsolate text,
  Rebelled not, loathing from the trodden heart
    That thing which she had found man's love to be.

    * For a woman's fragmentary inscription.

AN OLD SONG ENDED.

*"How should I your true love know
From another one?"*
*"By his cockle-hat and staff
And his sandal-shoon."*

"And what signs have told you now
That he hastens home?"
"Lo! the spring is nearly gone,
He is nearly come."

"For a token is there nought,
Say, that he should bring?"
"He will bear a ring I gave
And another ring."

"How may I, when he shall ask,
Tell him who lies there?"
"Nay, but leave my face unveiled
And unbound my hair."

"Can you say to me some word
I shall say to him?"
"Say I'm looking in his eyes
Though my eyes are dim."

THE SONG OF THE BOWER.

Say, is it day, is it dusk in thy bower,
    Thou whom I long for, who longest for me?
Oh! be it light, be it night, 'tis Love's hour,
    Love's that is fettered as Love's that is free.
Free Love has leaped to that innermost chamber,
    Oh! the last time, and the hundred before:
Fettered Love, motionless, can but remember,
    Yet something that sighs from him passes the door.

Nay, but my heart when it flies to thy bower,
    What does it find there that knows it again?
There it must droop like a shower-beaten flower,
    Red at the rent core and dark with the rain.
Ah! yet what shelter is still shed above it,—
    What waters still image its leaves torn apart?
Thy soul is the shade that clings round it to love it,
    And tears are its mirror deep down in thy heart.

What were my prize, could I enter thy bower,
    This day, to-morrow, at eve or at morn?
Large lovely arms and a neck like a tower,
    Bosom then heaving that now lies forlorn.
Kindled with love-breath, (the sun's kiss is colder!)
    Thy sweetness all near me, so distant to-day;
My hand round thy neck and thy hand on my shoulder
    My mouth to thy mouth as the world melts away.

What is it keeps me afar from thy bower,—
    My spirit, my body, so fain to be there?
Waters engulfing or fires that devour?—
    Earth heaped against me or death in the air?

Nay, but in day-dreams, for terror, for pity,
  The trees wave their heads with an omen to tell;
Nay, but in night-dreams, throughout the dark city,
  The hours, clashed together, lose count in the bell.

Shall I not one day remember thy bower,
  One day when all days are one day to me?—
Thinking, "I stirred not, and yet had the power!"—
  Yearning, "Ah God, if again it might be!"
Peace, peace! such a small lamp illumes, on this highway,
  So dimly so few steps in front of my feet,—
Yet shows me that her way is parted from my way....
  Out of sight, beyond light, at what goal may we meet?

DAWN ON THE NIGHT-JOURNEY.

TILL dawn the wind drove round me. It is past
  And still, and leaves the air to lisp of bird,
  And to the quiet that is almost heard
Of the new-risen day, as yet bound fast
In the first warmth of sunrise. When the last
  Of the sun's hours to-day shall be fulfilled,
  There shall another breath of time be stilled
For me, which now is to my senses cast
As much beyond me as eternity,
  Unknown, kept secret. On the newborn air
The moth quivers in silence. It is vast,
Yea, even beyond the hills upon the sea,
  The day whose end shall give this hour as sheer
As chaos to the irrevocable Past.

A LITTLE WHILE.

A little while a little love
   The hour yet bears for thee and me
   Who have not drawn the veil to see
If still our heaven be lit above.
Thou merely, at the day's last sigh,
   Hast felt thy soul prolong the tone;
And I have heard the night-wind cry
     And deemed its speech mine own.

A little while a little love
   The scattering autumn hoards for us
   Whose bower is not yet ruinous
Nor quite unleaved our songless grove.
Only across the shaken boughs
   We hear the flood-tides seek the sea,
And deep in both our hearts they rouse
     One wail for thee and me.

A little while a little love
   May yet be ours who have not said
   The word it makes our eyes afraid
To know that each is thinking of.
Not yet the end: be our lips dumb
   In smiles a little season yet:
I'll tell thee, when the end is come,
     How we may best forget.

TROY TOWN.

HEAVENBORN HELEN, Sparta's queen,
　　(O Troy Town!)
Had two breasts of heavenly sheen,
The sun and moon of the heart's desire:
All Love's lordship lay between.
　　(O Troy's down,
　　　Tall Troy's on fire!)

Helen knelt at Venus' shrine,
　　(O Troy Town!)
Saying, "A little gift is mine,
A little gift for a heart's desire.
Hear me speak and make me a sign!
　　(O Troy's down,
　　　Tall Troy's on fire!)

"Look, I bring thee a carven cup;
　　(O Troy Town!)
See it here as I hold it up,—
Shaped it is to the heart's desire,
Fit to fill when the gods would sup.
　　(O Troy's down,
　　　Tall Troy's on fire!)

"It was moulded like my breast;
　　(O Troy Town!)
He that sees it may not rest,
Rest at all for his heart's desire.
O give ear to my heart's behest!
　　(O Troy's down,
　　　Tall Troy's on fire!)

"See my breast, how like it is;
    (O Troy Town!)
See it bare for the air to kiss!
Is the cup to thy heart's desire?
O for the breast, O make it his!
    (O Troy's down,
      Tall Troy's on fire!)

"Yea, for my bosom here I sue;
    (O Troy Town!)
Thou must give it where 'tis due,
Give it there to the heart's desire.
Whom do I give my bosom to?
    (O Troy's down,
      Tall Troy's on fire!)

"Each twin breast is an apple sweet.
    (O Troy Town!)
Once an apple stirred the beat
Of thy heart with the heart's desire :—
Say, who brought it then to thy feet?
    (O Troy's down,
      Tall Troy's on fire!)

"They that claimed it then were three:
    (O Troy Town!)
For thy sake two hearts did he
Make forlorn of the heart's desire.
Do for him as he did for thee!
    (O Troy's down,
      Tall Troy's on fire!)

"Mine are apples grown to the south,
    (O Troy Town!)
Grown to taste in the days of drouth,
Taste and waste to the heart's desire:
Mine are apples meet for his mouth."
    (O Troy's down,
      Tall Troy's on fire!)

Venus looked on Helen's gift,
    (O Troy Town!)
Looked and smiled with subtle drift,
Saw the work of her heart's desire:—
"There thou kneel'st for Love to lift!"
    (O Troy's down,
    Tall Troy's on fire!)

Venus looked in Helen's face,
    (O Troy Town!)
Knew far off an hour and place,
And fire lit from the heart's desire;
Laughed and said, "Thy gift hath grace!"
    (O Troy's down,
    Tall Troy's on fire!)

Cupid looked on Helen's breast,
    (O Troy Town!)
Saw the heart within its nest,
Saw the flame of the heart's desire,—
Marked his arrow's burning crest.
    (O Troy's down,
    Tall Troy's on fire!)

Cupid took another dart,
    (O Troy Town!)
Fledged it for another heart,
Winged the shaft with the heart's desire,
Drew the string and said, "Depart!"
    (O Troy's down,
    Tall Troy's on fire!)

Paris turned upon his bed,
    (O Troy Town!)
Turned upon his bed and said,
Dead at heart with the heart's desire —
"Oh to clasp her golden head!"
    (O Troy's down,
    Tall Troy's on fire!)

EDEN BOWER.

It was Lilith the wife of Adam:
   (*Sing Eden Bower!*)
Not a drop of her blood was human,
But she was made like a soft sweet woman.

Lilith stood on the skirts of Eden;
   (*Alas the hour!*)
She was the first that thence was driven;
With her was hell and with Eve was heaven.

In the ear of the Snake said Lilith :—
   (*Sing Eden Bower!*)
"To thee I come when the rest is over;
A snake was I when thou wast my lover.

"I was the fairest snake in Eden.
   (*Alas the hour!*)
By the earth's will, new form and feature
Made me a wife for the earth's new creature.

"Take me thou as I come from Adam:
   (*Sing Eden Bower!*)
Once again shall my love subdue thee;
The past is past and I am come to thee.

"O but Adam was thrall to Lilith!
   (*Alas the hour!*)
All the threads of my hair are golden,
And there in a net his heart was holden.

"O and Lilith was queen of Adam!
        (*Sing Eden Bower!*)
All the day and the night together
My breath could shake his soul like a feather.

"What great joys had Adam and Lilith!—
        (*Alas the hour!*)
Sweet close rings of the serpent's twining,
As heart in heart lay sighing and pining.

"What bright babes had Lilith and Adam!—
        (*Sing Eden Bower!*)
Shapes that coiled in the woods and waters,
Glittering sons and radiant daughters.

"O thou God, the Lord God of Eden!
        (*Alas the hour!*)
Say, was this fair body for no man,
That of Adam's flesh thou mak'st him a woman?

"O thou Snake, the King-snake of Eden!
        (*Sing Eden Bower!*)
God's strong will our necks are under,
But thou and I may cleave it in sunder.

"Help, sweet Snake, sweet lover of Lilith!
        (*Alas the hour!*)
And let God learn how I loved and hated
Man in the image of God created.

'Help me once against Eve and Adam!
        (*Sing Eden Bower!*)
Help me once for this one endeavour,
And then my love shall be thine for ever!

"Strong is God, the fell foe of Lilith:
        (*Alas the hour!*)
Nought in heaven or earth may affright Him;
But join thou with me and we will smite Him.

"Strong is God, the great God of Eden:
   (*Sing Eden Bower!*)
Over all He made He hath power;
But lend me thou thy shape for an hour!

"Lend thy shape for the love of Lilith!
   (*Alas the hour!*)
Look, my mouth and my cheek are ruddy,
And thou art cold, and fire is my body.

"Lend thy shape for the hate of Adam!
   (*Sing Eden Bower!*)
That he may wail my joy that forsook him,
And curse the day when the bride-sleep took him.

"Lend thy shape for the shame of Eden!
   (*Alas the hour!*)
Is not the foe-God weak as the foeman
When love grows hate in the heart of a woman?

"Wouldst thou know the heart's hope of Lilith?
   (*Sing Eden Bower!*)
Then bring thou close thine head till it glisten
Along my breast, and lip me and listen.

"Am I sweet, O sweet Snake of Eden?
   (*Alas the hour!*)
Then ope thine ear to my warm mouth's cooing
And learn what deed remains for our doing.

"Thou didst hear when God said to Adam:—
   (*Sing Eden Bower!*)
'Of all this wealth I have made thee warden;
Thou'rt free to eat of the trees of the garden:

"'Only of one tree eat not in Eden;
   (*Alas the hour!*)
All save one I give to thy freewill,—
The Tree of the Knowledge of Good and Evil.'

"O my love, come nearer to Lilith!
            (*Sing Eden Bower!*)
In thy sweet folds bind me and bend me,
And let me feel the shape thou shalt lend me

"In thy shape I'll go back to Eden;
            (*Alas the hour!*)
In these coils that Tree will I grapple,
And stretch this crowned head forth by the apple.

"Lo, Eve bends to the breath of Lilith!
            (*Sing Eden Bower!*)
O how then shall my heart desire
All her blood as food to its fire!

"Lo, Eve bends to the words of Lilith!—
            (*Alas the hour!*)
'Nay, this Tree's fruit,—why should ye hate it,
Or Death be born the day that ye ate it?

"'Nay, but on that great day in Eden,
            (*Sing Eden Bower!*)
By the help that in this wise Tree is,
God knows well ye shall be as He is.'

"Then Eve shall eat and give unto Adam;
            (*Alas the hour!*)
And then they both shall know they are naked,
And their hearts ache as my heart hath achèd.

"Ay, let them hide 'mid the trees of Eden,
            (*Sing Eden Bower!*)
As in the cool of the day in the garden
God shall walk without pity or pardon.

"Hear, thou Eve, the man's heart in Adam!
            (*Alas the hour!*)
Of his brave words hark to the bravest:—
'This the woman gave that thou gavest.'

"Hear Eve speak, yea list to her, Lilith!
   (*Sing Eden Bower!*)
Feast thine heart with words that shall sate it—
'This the serpent gave and I ate it.'

"O proud Eve, cling close to thine Adam,
   (*Alas the hour!*)
Driven forth as the beasts of his naming
By the sword that for ever is flaming.

"Know, thy path is known unto Lilith!
   (*Sing Eden Bower!*)
While the blithe birds sang at thy wedding,
There her tears grew thorns for thy treading.

"O my love, thou Love-snake of Eden!
   (*Alas the hour!*)
O to-day and the day to come after!
Loose me, love,—give breath to my laughter.

"O bright Snake, the Death-worm of Adam!
   (*Sing Eden Bower!*)
Wreathe thy neck with my hair's bright tether,
And wear my gold and thy gold together!

"On that day on the skirts of Eden,
   (*Alas the hour!*)
In thy shape shall I glide back to thee,
And in my shape for an instant view thee.

"But when thou'rt thou and Lilith is Lilith,
   (*Sing Eden Bower!*)
In what bliss past hearing or seeing
Shall each one drink of the other's being!

"With cries of 'Eve!' and 'Eden!' and 'Adam!'
   (*Alas the hour!*)
How shall we mingle our love's caresses,
I in thy coils, and thou in my tresses!

"With those names, ye echoes of Eden,
            (*Sing Eden Bower!*)
Fire shall cry from my heart that burneth,—
'Dust he is and to dust returneth!'

"Yet to-day, thou master of Lilith,—
            (*Alas the hour!*)
Wrap me round in the form I'll borrow
And let me tell thee of sweet to-morrow.

"In the planted garden eastward in Eden,
            (*Sing Eden Bower!*)
Where the river goes forth to water the garden,
The springs shall dry and the soil shall harden.

"Yea, where the bride-sleep fell upon Adam,
            (*Alas the hour!*)
None shall hear when the storm-wind whistles
Through roses choked among thorns and thistles.

"Yea, beside the east-gate of Eden,
            (*Sing Eden Bower!*)
Where God joined them and none might sever,
The sword turns this way and that for ever.

"What of Adam cast out of Eden?
            (*Alas the hour!*)
Lo! with care like a shadow shaken,
He tills the hard earth whence he was taken.

"What of Eve too, cast out of Eden?
            (*Sing Eden Bower!*)
Nay, but she, the bride of God's giving,
Must yet be mother of all men living.

"Lo, God's grace, by the grace of Lilith!
            (*Alas the hour!*)
To Eve's womb, from our sweet to-morrow,
God shall greatly multiply sorrow.

"Fold me fast, O God-snake of Eden!
                (*Sing Eden Bower!*)
What more prize than love to impel thee?
Grip and lip my limbs as I tell thee!

"Lo! two babes for Eve and for Adam!
                (*Alas the hour!*)
Lo! sweet Snake, the travail and treasure,—
Two men-children born for their pleasure!

"The first is Cain and the second Abel:
                (*Sing Eden Bower!*)
The soul of one shall be made thy brother,
And thy tongue shall lap the blood of the other."
                (*Alas the hour!*)

LOVE-LILY.

Between the hands, between the brows,
  Between the lips of Love-Lily,
A spirit is born whose birth endows
  My blood with fire to burn through me;
Who breathes upon my gazing eyes,
  Who laughs and murmurs in mine ear,
At whose least touch my colour flies,
  And whom my life grows faint to hear.

Within the voice, within the heart,
  Within the mind of Love-Lily,
A spirit is born who lifts apart
  His tremulous wings and looks at me;
Who on my mouth his finger lays,
  And shows, while whispering lutes confer,
That Eden of Love's watered ways
  Whose winds and spirits worship her.

Brows, hands, and lips, heart, mind, and voice,
  Kisses and words of Love-Lily,—
Oh! bid me with your joy rejoice
  Till riotous longing rest in me!
Ah! let not hope be still distraught,
  But find in her its gracious goal,
Whose speech Truth knows not from her thought
  Nor Love her body from her soul.

SUNSET WINGS.

To-night this sunset spreads two golden wings
    Cleaving the western sky;
Winged too with wind it is, and winnowings
Of birds; as if the day's last hour in rings
    Of strenuous flight must die.

Sun-steeped in fire, the homeward pinions sway
    Above the dovecote-tops;
And clouds of starlings, ere they rest with day,
Sink, clamorous like mill-waters, at wild play,
    By turns in every copse:

Each tree heart-deep the wrangling rout receives,—
    Save for the whirr within,
You could not tell the starlings from the leaves;
Then one great puff of wings, and the swarm heaves
    Away with all its din.

Even thus Hope's hours, in ever-eddying flight,
    To many a refuge tend;
With the first light she laughed, and the last light
Glows round her still; who natheless in the night
    At length must make an end.

And now the mustering rooks innumerable
    Together sail and soar,
While for the day's death, like a tolling knell,
Unto the heart they seem to cry, Farewell,
    No more, farewell, no more!

  Hope not plumed, as 'twere a fiery dart?
    And oh! thou dying day,
Even as thou goest must she too depart,
And Sorrow fold such pinions on the heart
    As will not fly away?

THE CLOUD CONFINES.

The day is dark and the night
  To him that would search their heart;
  No lips of cloud that will part
Nor morning song in the light:
    Only, gazing alone,
    To him wild shadows are shown,
    Deep under deep unknown
And height above unknown height.
        Still we say as we go,—
          "Strange to think by the way,
        Whatever there is to know,
          That shall we know one day."

The Past is over and fled;
  Named new, we name it the old;
  Thereof some tale hath been told,
But no word comes from the dead;
    Whether at all they be,
    Or whether as bond or free,
    Or whether they too were we,
Or by what spell they have sped.
        Still we say as we go,—
          "Strange to think by the way,
        Whatever there is to know,
          That shall we know one day."

What of the heart of hate
  That beats in thy breast, O Time?—
  Red strife from the furthest prime,
And anguish of fierce debate;

War that shatters her slain,
And peace that grinds them as grain,
And eyes fixed ever in vain
On the pitiless eyes of Fate.
  Still we say as we go,—
   "Strange to think by the way,
  Whatever there is to know,
   That shall we know one day."

What of the heart of love
 That bleeds in thy breast, O Man?—
 Thy kisses snatched 'neath the ban
Of fangs that mock them above;
 Thy bells prolonged unto knells,
 Thy hope that a breath dispels,
 Thy bitter forlorn farewells
And the empty echoes thereof?
  Still we say as we go,—
   "Strange to think by the way,
  Whatever there is to know,
   That shall we know one day."

The sky leans dumb on the sea,
 Aweary with all its wings;
 And oh! the song the sea sings
Is dark everlastingly.
 Our past is clean forgot,
 Our present is and is not,
 Our future's a sealed seedplot,
And what betwixt them are we?—
  We who say as we go,—
   "Strange to think by the way,
  Whatever there is to know,
   That shall we know one day."

DOWN STREAM.

Between Holmscote and Hurstcote
   The river-reaches wind,
The whispering trees accept the breeze,
   The ripple's cool and kind:
With love low-whispered 'twixt the shores,
   With rippling laughters gay,
With white arms bared to ply the oars,
   On last year's first of May.

Between Holmscote and Hurstcote
   The river's brimmed with rain,
Through close-met banks and parted banks
   Now near, now far again:
With parting tears caressed to smiles,
   With meeting promised soon,
With every sweet vow that beguiles,
   On last year's first of June.

Between Holmscote and Hurstcote
   The river's flecked with foam,
'Neath shuddering clouds that hang in shrouds
   And lost winds wild for home:
With infant wailings at the breast,
   With homeless steps astray,
With wanderings shuddering tow'rds one rest
   On this year's first of May.

Between Holmscote and Hurstcote
   The summer river flows
With doubled flight of moons by night
   And lilies' deep repose:

With lo! beneath the moon's white stare
  A white face not the moon,
With lilies meshed in tangled hair,
  On this year's first of June.

Between Holmscote and Hurstcote
  A troth was given and riven,
From heart's trust grew one life to two,
  Two lost lives cry to Heaven:
With banks spread calm to meet the sky,
  With meadows newly mowed,
The harvest-paths of glad July,
  The sweet school-children's road.

THREE SHADOWS.

I LOOKED and saw your eyes
   In the shadow of your hair
As a traveller sees the stream
   In the shadow of the wood;
And I said, "My faint heart sighs
   Ah me! to linger there,
To drink deep and to dream
   In that sweet solitude."

I looked and saw your heart
   In the shadow of your eyes,
As a seeker sees the gold
   In the shadow of the stream;
And I said, "Ah me! what art
   Should win the immortal prize,
Whose want must make life cold
   And Heaven a hollow dream?"

I looked and saw your love
   In the shadow of your heart,
As a diver sees the pearl
   In the shadow of the sea;
And I murmured, not above
   My breath, but all apart,—
"Ah! you can love, true girl,
   And is your love for me?"

A DEATH-PARTING.

Leaves and rain and the days of the year,
   (*Water-willow and wellaway,*)
All these fall, and my soul gives ear,
And she is hence who once was here.
   (*With a wind blown night and day.*)

Ah! but now, for a secret sign,
   (*The willow's wan and the water white,*)
In the held breath of the day's decline
Her very face seemed pressed to mine.
   With a wind blown day and night.)

O love, of my death my life is fain;
   (*The willows wave on the water-way,*)
Your cheek and mine are cold in the rain,
But warm they'll be when we meet again.
   (*With a wind blown night and day.*)

Mists are heaved and cover the sky;
   (*The willows wail in the waning light,*)
O loose your lips, leave space for a sigh,—
They seal my soul, I cannot die.
   (*With a wind blown day and night.*)

Leaves and rain and the days of the year,
   (*Water-willow and wellaway,*)
All still fall, and I still give ear,
And she is hence, and I am here.
   (*With a wind blown night and day.*)

SPRING.

SOFT-LITTERED is the new-year's lambing-fold,
   And in the hollowed haystack at its side
   The shepherd lies o' nights now, wakeful-eyed
At the ewes' travailing call through the dark cold.
The young rooks cheep 'mid the thick caw o' the old:
   And near unpeopled stream-sides, on the ground,
   By her Spring cry the moorhen's nest is found,
Where the drained flood-lands flaunt their marigold.

Chill are the gusts to which the pastures cower,
   And chill the current where the young reeds stand
   As green and close as the young wheat on land:
Yet here the cuckoo and the cuckoo-flower
Plight to the heart Spring's perfect imminent hour
   Whose breath shall soothe you like your dear one's hand

UNTIMELY LOST.

OLIVER MADOX BROWN. BORN 1855; DIED 1874.

UPON the landscape of his coming life
   A youth high-gifted gazed, and found it fair:
   The heights of work, the floods of praise, were there.
What friendships, what desires, what love, what wife?—
All things to come. The fanned springtide was rife
   With imminent solstice; and the ardent air
   Had summer sweets and autumn fires to bear;—
Heart's ease full-pulsed with perfect strength for strife.

A mist has risen: we see the youth no more:
   Does he see on and strive on? And may we
   Late-tottering world-worn hence, find *his* to be
The young strong hand which helps us up that shore?
Or, echoing the No More with Nevermore,
Must Night be ours and his? We hope: and he?

PARTED PRESENCE.

Love, I speak to your heart,
  Your heart that is always here.
  Oh draw me deep to its sphere,
Though you and I are apart;
And yield, by the spirit's art,
  Each distant gift that is dear.
  O love, my love, you are here!

Your eyes are afar to-day,
  Yet, love, look now in mine eyes.
  Two hearts sent forth may despise
All dead things by the way.
All between is decay,
  Dead hours and this hour that dies
  O love, look deep in mine eyes!

Your hands to-day are not here,
  Yet lay them, love, in my hands.
  The hourglass sheds its sands
All day for the dead hours' bier;
But now, as two hearts draw near,
  This hour like a flower expands.
  O love, your hands in my hands!

Your voice is not on the air,
  Yet, love, I can hear your voice:
  It bids my heart to rejoice
As knowing your heart is there,—
A music sweet to declare
  The truth of your steadfast choice.
  O love, how sweet is your voice!

PARTED PRESENCE.

To-day your lips are afar,
   Yet draw my lips to them, love.
   Around, beneath, and above,
Is frost to bind and to bar;
But where I am and you are,
   Desire and the fire thereof.
   O kiss me, kiss me, my love!

Your heart is never away,
   But ever with mine, for ever,
   For ever without endeavour,
To-morrow, love, as to-day;
Two blent hearts never astray,
   Two souls no power may sever,
   Together, O my love, for ever!

SPHERAL CHANGE.

In this new shade of Death, the show
   Passes me still of form and face;
Some bent, some gazing as they go,
   Some swiftly, some at a dull pace,
   Not one that speaks in any case.

If only one might speak!—the one
   Who never waits till I come near;
But always seated all alone
   As listening to the sunken air,
   Is gone before I come to her.

O dearest! while we lived and died
   A living death in every day,
Some hours we still were side by side,
   When where I was you too might stay
   And rest and need not go away.

O nearest, furthest! Can there be
   At length some hard-earned heart-won home,
Where,—exile changed for sanctuary,—
   Our lot may fill indeed its sum,
   And you may wait and I may come?

ALAS, SO LONG!

Ah! dear one, we were young so long,
　It seemed that youth would never go,
For skies and trees were ever in song
　And water in singing flow
In the days we never again shall know.
　　　Alas, so long!
　　Ah! then was it all Spring weather?
　　Nay, but we were young and together.

Ah! dear one, I've been old so long,
　It seems that age is loth to part,
Though days and years have never a song,
　And oh! have they still the art
That warmed the pulses of heart to heart?
　　　Alas, so long!
　　Ah! then was it all Spring weather?
　　Nay, but we were young and together.

Ah! dear one, you've been dead so long,—
　How long until we meet again,
Where hours may never lose their song
　Nor flowers forget the rain
In glad noonlight that never shall wane?
　　　Alas, so long!
　　Ah! shall it be then Spring weather,
　　And ah! shall we be young together?

INSOMNIA.

Thin are the night-skirts left behind
　　By daybreak hours that onward creep,
　　And thin, alas! the shred of sleep
That wavers with the spirit's wind:
But in half-dreams that shift and roll
　　And still remember and forget,
My soul this hour has drawn your soul
　　　　A little nearer yet.

Our lives, most dear, are never near,
　　Our thoughts are never far apart,
　　Though all that draws us heart to heart
Seems fainter now and now more clear.
To-night Love claims his full control,
　　And with desire and with regret
My soul this hour has drawn your soul
　　　　A little nearer yet.

Is there a home where heavy earth
　　Melts to bright air that breathes no pain,
　　Where water leaves no thirst again
And springing fire is Love's new birth?
If faith long bound to one true goal
　　May there at length its hope beget,
My soul that hour shall draw your soul
　　　　For ever nearer yet.

POSSESSION.

There is a cloud above the sunset hill,
   That wends and makes no stay,
For its goal lies beyond the fiery west;
A lingering breath no calm can chase away,
The onward labour of the wind's last will;
A flying foam that overleaps the crest
Of the top wave: and in possession still
A further reach of longing; though at rest
   From all the yearning years,
Together in the bosom of that day
Ye cling, and with your kisses drink your tears.

CHIMES.

I.

Honey-flowers to the honey-comb
And the honey-bee's from home.

A honey-comb and a honey-flower,
And the bee shall have his hour.

A honeyed heart for the honey-comb,
And the humming bee flies home.

A heavy heart in the honey-flower,
And the bee has had his hour.

II.

A honey cell's in the honeysuckle,
And the honey-bee knows it well.

The honey-comb has a heart of honey
And the humming bee's so bonny.

A honey-flower's the honeysuckle,
And the bee's in the honey-bell.

The honeysuckle is sucked of honey,
And the bee is heavy and bonny.

III.

Brown shell first for the butterfly
And a bright wing by and by.

Butterfly, good-bye to your shell,
And, bright wings, speed you well.

Bright lamplight for the butterfly
And a burnt wing by and by.

Butterfly, alas for your shell,
And, bright wings, fare you well.

IV.

Lost love-labour and lullaby,
And lowly let love lie.

Lost love-morrow and love-fellow
And love's life lying low.

Lovelor labour and life laid by
And lowly let love lie.

Late love-longing and life-sorrow
And love's life lying low.

V.

Beauty's body and benison
With a bosom-flower new blown.

Bitter beauty and blessing bann'd
With a breast to burn and brand.

Beauty's bower in the dust o'erblown
With a bare white breast of bone.

Barren beauty and bower of sand
With a blast on either hand.

VI.

Buried bars in the breakwater
And bubble of the brimming weir.

Body's blood in the breakwater
And a buried body's bier.

Buried bones in the breakwater
And bubble of the brawling weir.

Bitter tears in the breakwater
And a breaking heart to bear.

VII.

Hollow heaven and the hurricane
And hurry of the heavy rain.

Hurried clouds in the hollow heaven
And a heavy rain hard-driven.

The heavy rain it hurries amain
And heaven and the hurricane.

Hurrying wind o'er the heaven's hollow
And the heavy rain to follow.

ADIEU.

Waving whispering trees,
What do you say to the breeze
   And what says the breeze to you?
'Mid passing souls ill at ease,
Moving murmuring trees,
   Would ye ever wave an Adieu?

Tossing turbulent seas,
Winds that wrestle with these,
   Echo heard in the shell,—
'Mid fleeting life ill at ease,
Restless ravening seas,—
   Would the echo sigh Farewell?

Surging sumptuous skies,
For ever a new surprise,
   Clouds eternally new,—
Is every flake that flies,
Widening wandering skies,
   For a sign—Farewell, Adieu?

Sinking suffering heart
That know'st how weary thou art,—
   Soul so fain for a flight,—
Aye, spread your wings to depart,
Sad soul and sorrowing heart,—
   Adieu, Farewell, Good-night.

SOOTHSAY.

Let no man ask thee of anything
Not yearborn between Spring and Spring.
More of all worlds than he can know,
Each day the single sun doth show.
A trustier gloss than thou canst give
From all wise scrolls demonstrative,
The sea doth sigh and the wind sing.

Let no man awe thee on any height
Of earthly kingship's mouldering might.
The dust his heel holds meet for thy brow
Hath all of it been what both are now;
And thou and he may plague together
A beggar's eyes in some dusty weather
When none that is now knows sound or sight,

Crave thou no dower of earthly things
Unworthy Hope's imaginings.
To have brought true birth of Song to be
And to have won hearts to Poesy,
Or anywhere in the sun or rain
To have loved and been beloved again,
Is loftiest reach of Hope's bright wings.

The wild waifs cast up by the sea
Are diverse ever seasonably.
Even so the soul-tides still may land
A different drift upon the sand.
But one the sea is evermore :
And one be still, 'twixt shore and shore,
As the sea's life, thy soul in thee.

Say, hast thou pride? How then may fit
Thy mood with flatterers' silk-spun wit?
Haply the sweet voice lifts thy crest,
A breeze of fame made manifest.
Nay, but then chaf'st at flattery? Pause:
Be sure thy wrath is not because
It makes thee feel thou lovest it.

Let thy soul strive that still the same
Be early friendship's sacred flame.
The affinities have strongest part
In youth, and draw men heart to heart:
As life wears on and finds no rest,
The individual in each breast
Is tyrannous to sunder them.

In the life-drama's stern cue-call,
A friend's a part well-prized by all:
And if thou meet an enemy,
What art thou that none such should be?
Even so: but if the two parts run
Into each other and grow one,
Then comes the curtain's cue to fall.

Whate'er by other's need is claimed
More than by thine,—to him unblamed
Resign it: and if he should hold
What more than he thou lack'st, bread, gold,
Or any good whereby we live,—
To thee such substance let him give
Freely: nor he nor thou be shamed.

Strive that thy works prove equal: lest
That work which thou hast done the best
Should come to be to thee at length
(Even as to envy seems the strength
Of others) hateful and abhorr'd,—
Thine own above thyself made lord,—
Of self-rebuke the bitterest.

SOOTHSAY.

Unto the man of yearning thought
And aspiration, to do nought
Is in itself almost an act,—
Being chasm-fire and cataract
Of the soul's utter depths unseal'd,
Yet woe to thee if once thou yield
Unto the act of doing nought!

How callous seems beyond revoke
The clock with its last listless stroke!
How much too late at length!—to trace
The hour on its forewarning face,
The thing thou hast not dared to do! . .
Behold, this *may* be thus! Ere true
It prove, arise and bear thy yoke.

Let lore of all Theology
Be to thy soul what it *can* be:
But know,—the Power that fashions man
Measured not out thy little span
For thee to take the meting-rod
In turn, and so approve on God
Thy science of Theometry.

To God at best, to Chance at worst,
Give thanks for good things, last as first.
But windstrown blossom is that good
Whose apple is not gratitude.
Even if no prayer uplift thy face,
Let the sweet right to render grace
As thy soul's cherished child be nurs'd.

Didst ever say, "Lo, I forget"?
Such thought was to remember yet.
As in a gravegarth, count to see
The monuments of memory.
Be this thy soul's appointed scope:—
Gaze onward without claim to hope,
Nor, gazing backward, court regret.

FIVE ENGLISH POETS.

I. THOMAS CHATTERTON.

WITH Shakspeare's manhood at a boy's wild heart,—
   Through Hamlet's doubt to Shakspeare near allied,
   And kin to Milton through his Satan's pride,—
At Death's sole door he stooped, and craved a dart;
And to the dear new bower of England's art,—
   Even to that shrine Time else had deified,
   The unuttered heart that soared against his side,—
Drove the fell point, and smote life's seals apart.

Thy nested home-loves, noble Chatterton;
   The angel-trodden stair thy soul could trace
   Up Redcliffe's spire; and in the world's armed space
Thy gallant sword-play:—these to many an one
Are sweet for ever; as thy grave unknown
   And love-dream of thine unrecorded face.

II. WILLIAM BLAKE.

(TO FREDERICK SHIELDS, ON HIS SKETCH OF BLAKE'S
WORK-ROOM AND DEATH-ROOM, 3 FOUNTAIN COURT, STRAND.)

This is the place. Even here the dauntless soul,
    The unflinching hand, wrought on; till in that nook,
    As on that very bed, his life partook
New birth, and passed. Yon river's dusky shoal,
Whereto the close-built coiling lanes unroll,
    Faced his work-window, whence his eyes would stare,
    Thought-wandering, unto nought that met them there,
But to the unfettered irreversible goal.

This cupboard, Holy of Holies, held the cloud
    Of his soul writ and limned; this other one,
His true wife's charge, full oft to their abode
    Yielded for daily bread the martyr's stone,
    Ere yet their food might be that Bread alone,
The words now home-speech of the mouth of God.

III. SAMUEL TAYLOR COLERIDGE.

His Soul fared forth (as from the deep home-grove
    The father-songster plies the hour-long quest),
    To feed his soul-brood hungering in the nest;
But his warm Heart, the mother-bird, above
Their callow fledgling progeny still hove
    With tented roof of wings and fostering breast
    Till the Soul fed the soul-brood. Richly blest
From Heaven their growth, whose food was Human Love.

Yet ah! Like desert pools that show the stars
    Once in long leagues,—even such the scarce-snatched hours
    Which deepening pain left to his lordliest powers:—
Heaven lost through spider-trammelled prison-bars.
Six years, from sixty saved! Yet kindling skies
Own them, a beacon to our centuries.

IV. JOHN KEATS.

THE weltering London ways where children weep
   And girls whom none call maidens laugh,—strange road
   Miring his outward steps, who inly trode
The bright Castalian brink and Latmos' steep :—
Even such his life's cross-paths ; till deathly deep
   He toiled through sands of Lethe ; and long pain,
   Weary with labour spurned and love found vain,
In dead Rome's sheltering shadow wrapped his sleep.

O pang-dowered Poet, whose reverberant lips
And heart-strung lyre awoke the Moon's eclipse,—
   Thou whom the daisies glory in growing o'er,—
Their fragrance clings around thy name, not writ
But rumour'd in water, while the fame of it
   Along Time's flood goes echoing evermore.

V. PERCY BYSSHE SHELLEY.

(INSCRIPTION FOR THE COUCH, STILL PRESERVED, ON WHICH HE PASSED THE LAST NIGHT OF HIS LIFE.)

'TWIXT those twin worlds,—the world of Sleep, which gave
   No dream to warn,—the tidal world of Death,
   Which the earth's sea, as the earth, replenisheth,—
Shelley, Song's orient sun, to breast the wave,
Rose from this couch that morn. Ah ! did he brave
   Only the sea ?—or did man's deed of hell
   Engulph his bark 'mid mists impenetrable ? . . .
No eye discerned, nor any power might save.

When that mist cleared, O Shelley ! what dread veil
   Was rent for thee, to whom far-darkling Truth
   Reigned sovereign guide through thy brief ageless youth ?
Was the Truth *thy* Truth, Shelley ?—Hush ! All-Hail,
Past doubt, thou gav'st it ; and in Truth's bright sphere
Art first of praisers, being most praisèd here.

TO PHILIP BOURKE MARSTON, INCITING ME TO POETIC WORK.

Sweet Poet, thou of whom these years that roll
   Must one day yet the burdened birthright learn,
   And by the darkness of thine eyes discern
How piercing was the sight within thy soul;—
Gifted apart, thou goest to the great goal,
   A cloud-bound radiant spirit, strong to earn,
   Light-reft, that prize for which fond myriads yearn
Vainly light-blest,—the Seër's aureole.

And doth thine ear, divinely dowered to catch
   All spheral sounds in thy song blent so well,
   Still hearken for my voice's slumbering spell
With wistful love? Ah! let the Muse now snatch
My wreath for thy young brows, and bend to watch
   Thy veiled transfiguring sense's miracle.

TIBER, NILE, AND THAMES.

The head and hands of murdered Cicero,
   Above his seat high in the Forum hung,
   Drew jeers and burning tears. When on the rung
Of a swift-mounted ladder, all aglow,
Fulvia, Mark Antony's shameless wife, with show
   Of foot firm-poised and gleaming arm upflung,
   Bade her sharp needle pierce that god-like tongue
Whose speech fed Rome even as the Tiber's flow.

And thou, Cleopatra's Needle, that hadst thrid
Great skirts of Time ere she and Antony hid
   Dead hope!—hast thou too reached, surviving death,
A city of sweet speech scorned,—on whose chill stone
Keats withered, Coleridge pined, and Chatterton,
   Breadless, with poison froze the God-fired breath?

RALEIGH'S CELL IN THE TOWER.

Here writ was the World's History by his hand
    Whose steps knew all the earth; albeit his world
    In these few piteous paces then was furl'd.
Here daily, hourly, have his proud feet spann'd
This smaller speck than the receding land
    Had ever shown his ships; what time he hurl'd
    Abroad o'er new-found regions spiced and pearl'd
His country's high dominion and command.

Here dwelt two spheres. The vast terrestrial zone
    His spirit traversed; and that spirit was
    Itself the zone celestial, round whose birth
    The planets played within the zodiac's girth;
    Till hence, through unjust death unfeared, did pass
His spirit to the only land unknown.

WINTER.

How large that thrush looks on the bare thorn-tree!
    A swarm of such, three little months ago,
    Had hidden in the leaves and let none know
Save by the outburst of their minstrelsy.
A white flake here and there—a snow-lily
    Of last night's frost—our naked flower-beds hold;
    And for a rose-flower on the darkling mould
The hungry redbreast gleams. No bloom, no bee.

The current shudders to its ice-bound sedge:
    Nipped in their bath, the stark reeds one by one
    Flash each its clinging diamond in the sun:
'Neath winds which for this winter's sovereign pledge
Shall curb great king-masts to the ocean's edge
    And leave memorial forest-kings o'erthrown.

THE LAST THREE FROM TRAFALGAR

AT THE ANNIVERSARY BANQUET, 21ST OCTOBER 187*.

In grappled ships around The Victory,
   Three boys did England's Duty with stout cheer,
   While one dread truth was kept from every ear,
More dire than deafening fire that churned the sea:
For in the flag-ship's weltering cockpit, he
   Who was the Battle's Heart without a peer,
   He who had seen all fearful sights save Fear,
Was passing from all life save Victory.

And round the old memorial board to-day,
   Three greybeards—each a warworn British Tar—
   View through the mist of years that hour afar:
Who soon shall greet, 'mid memories of fierce fray,
The impassioned soul which on its radiant way
   Soared through the fiery cloud of Trafalgar.

CZAR ALEXANDER THE SECOND.

(13TH MARCH 1881.)

From him did forty million serfs, endow'd
   Each with six feet of death-due soil, receive
   Rich freeborn lifelong land, whereon to sheave
Their country's harvest. These to-day aloud
Demand of Heaven a Father's blood,—sore bow'd
   With tears and thrilled with wrath; who, while they grieve,
   On every guilty head would fain achieve
All torment by his edicts disallow'd.

He stayed the knout's red-ravening fangs; and first
   Of Russian traitors, his own murderers go
   White to the tomb. While he,—laid foully low
With limbs red-rent, with festering brain which erst
Willed kingly freedom,—'gainst the deed accurst
   To God bears witness of his people's woe.

III.—SONNETS ON PICTURES.

FOR

AN ANNUNCIATION,

EARLY GERMAN.

The lilies stand before her like a screen
  Through which, upon this warm and solemn day,
  God surely hears. For there she kneels to pray
Who wafts our prayers to God—Mary the Queen.
She was Faith's Present, parting what had been
  From what began with her, and is for aye.
  On either hand, God's twofold system lay:
With meek bowed face a Virgin prayed between.

So prays she, and the Dove flies in to her,
  And she has turned. At the low porch is one
  Who looks as though deep awe made him to smile.
Heavy with heat, the plants yield shadow there;
  The loud flies cross each other in the sun;
  And the aisled pillars meet the poplar-aisle.

FOR

OUR LADY OF THE ROCKS

BY LEONARDO DA VINCI.

MOTHER, is this the darkness of the end,
   The Shadow of Death? and is that outer sea
   Infinite imminent Eternity?
And does the death-pang by man's seed sustained
In Time's each instant cause thy face to bend
   Its silent prayer upon the Son, while He
   Blesses the dead with His hand silently
To His long day which hours no more offend?

Mother of grace, the pass is difficult,
   Keen as these rocks, and the bewildered souls
     Throng it like echoes, blindly shuddering through.
   Thy name, O Lord, each spirit's voice extols,
     Whose peace abides in the dark avenue
Amid the bitterness of things occult.

FOR

A VENETIAN PASTORAL

BY GIORGIONE.

(In the Louvre.)

WATER, for anguish of the solstice:—nay,
  But dip the vessel slowly,—nay, but lean
  And hark how at its verge the wave sighs in
Reluctant. Hush! beyond all depth away
The heat lies silent at the brink of day:
  Now the hand trails upon the viol-string
  That sobs, and the brown faces cease to sing,
Sad with the whole of pleasure. Whither stray
Her eyes now, from whose mouth the slim pipes creep
  And leave it pouting, while the shadowed grass
    Is cool against her naked side? Let be:—
Say nothing now unto her lest she weep,
  Nor name this ever. Be it as it was,—
    Life touching lips with Immortality.

FOR

AN ALLEGORICAL DANCE OF WOMEN

BY ANDREA MANTEGNA.

(*In the Louvre.*)

SCARCELY, I think; yet it indeed *may* be
   The meaning reached him, when this music rang
   Clear through his frame, a sweet possessive pang,
And he beheld these rocks and that ridged sea.
But I believe that, leaning tow'rds them, he
   Just felt their hair carried across his face
   As each girl passed him; nor gave ear to trace
How many feet; nor bent assuredly
His eyes from the blind fixedness of thought
   To know the dancers. It is bitter glad
     Even unto tears. Its meaning filleth it,
     A secret of the wells of Life: to wit:—
   The heart's each pulse shall keep the sense it had
With all, though the mind's labour run to nought.

FOR

RUGGIERO AND ANGELICA

BY INGRES.

I.

A REMOTE sky, prolonged to the sea's brim:
   One rock-point standing buffeted alone,
   Vexed at its base with a foul beast unknown,
Hell-birth of geomaunt and teraphim:
A knight, and a winged creature bearing him,
   Reared at the rock: a woman fettered there,
   Leaning into the hollow with loose hair
And throat let back and heartsick trail of limb.

The sky is harsh, and the sea shrewd and salt:
   Under his lord the griffin-horse ramps blind
     With rigid wings and tail. The spear's lithe stem
   Thrills in the roaring of those jaws: behind,
That evil length of body chafes at fault.
     She does not hear nor see—she knows of them.

II.

CLENCH thine eyes now,—'tis the last instant, girl:
   Draw in thy senses, set thy knees, and take
   One breath for all: thy life is keen awake,—
Thou mayst not swoon. Was that the scattered whirl
Of its foam drenched thee?—or the waves that curl
   And split, bleak spray wherein thy temples ache?
   Or was it his the champion's blood to flake
Thy flesh?—or thine own blood's anointing, girl?

Now, silence: for the sea's is such a sound
   As irks not silence; and except the sea,
     All now is still. Now the dead thing doth cease
   To writhe, and drifts. He turns to her: and she,
Cast from the jaws of Death, remains there, bound,
     Again a woman in her nakedness.

FOR

A VIRGIN AND CHILD

BY HANS MEMMELINCK.

(In the Academy of Bruges.)

MYSTERY: God, man's life, born into man
    Of woman. There abideth on her brow
      The ended pang of knowledge, the which now
Is calm assured. Since first her task began
She hath known all. What more of anguish than
    Endurance oft hath lived through, the whole space
      Through night till day, passed weak upon her face
While the heard lapse of darkness slowly ran?

All hath been told her touching her dear Son,
    And all shall be accomplished. Where He sits
      Even now, a babe, He holds the symbol fruit
Perfect and chosen. Until God permits,
    His soul's elect still have the absolute
Harsh nether darkness, and make painful moan.

FOR

A MARRIAGE OF ST. CATHERINE

BY THE SAME.

(In the Hospital of St. John at Bruges.)

MYSTERY: Catherine the bride of Christ.
  She kneels, and on her hand the holy Child
  Now sets the ring. Her life is hushed and mild,
Laid in God's knowledge—ever unenticed
From God, and in the end thus fitly priced.
  Awe, and the music that is near her, wrought
  Of angels, have possessed her eyes in thought:
Her utter joy is hers, and hath sufficed.

There is a pause while Mary Virgin turns
  The leaf, and reads. With eyes on the spread book,
    That damsel at her knees reads after her.
    John whom He loved, and John His harbinger,
  Listen and watch. Whereon soe'er thou look,
The light is starred in gems and the gold burns.

FOR

THE WINE OF CIRCE

BY EDWARD BURNE JONES.

Dusk-haired and gold-robed o'er the golden wine
  She stoops, wherein, distilled of death and shame,
  Sink the black drops; while, lit with fragrant flame,
Round her spread board the golden sunflowers shine.
Doth Helios here with Hecatè combine
  (O Circe, thou their votaress?) to proclaim
  For these thy guests all rapture in Love's name,
Till pitiless Night give Day the countersign?

Lords of their hour, they come. And by her knee
  Those cowering beasts, their equals heretofore,
Wait; who with them in new equality
  To-night shall echo back the sea's dull roar
  With a vain wail from passion's tide-strown shore
Where the dishevelled seaweed hates the sea,

FOR

THE HOLY FAMILY

BY MICHELANGELO.

(*In the National Gallery.**)

TURN not the prophet's page, O Son ! He knew
   All that Thou hast to suffer, and hath writ.
   Not yet Thine hour of knowledge.   Infinite
The sorrows that Thy manhood's lot must rue
And dire acquaintance of Thy grief.   That clue
   The spirits of Thy mournful ministerings
   Seek through yon scroll in silence.   For these things
The angels have desired to look into.

Still before Eden waves the fiery sword,—
   Her Tree of Life unransomed : whose sad Tree
   Of Knowledge yet to growth of Calvary
   Must yield its Tempter,—Hell the earliest dead
Of Earth resign,—and yet, O Son and Lord,
   The seed o' the woman bruise the serpent's head.

---

* In this picture the Virgin Mother is seen withholding from the Child Saviour the prophetic writings in which His sufferings are foretold. Angelic figures beside them examine a scroll.

FOR

SPRING

BY SANDRO BOTTICELLI.

(In the Accademia of Florence.)

WHAT masque of what old wind-withered New-Year
   Honours this Lady?* Flora, wanton-eyed
    For birth, and with all flowrets prankt and pied:
Aurora, Zephyrus, with mutual cheer
Of clasp and kiss: the Graces circling near,
   'Neath bower-linked arch of white arms glorified:
    And with those feathered feet which hovering glide
O'er Spring's brief bloom, Hermes the harbinger.

Birth-bare, not death-bare yet, the young stems stand
   This Lady's temple-columns: o'er her head
    Love wings his shaft. What mystery here is read
Of homage or of hope? But how command
Dead Springs to answer? And how question here
These mummers of that wind-withered New-Year?

  * The same lady, here surrounded by the masque of Spring, is evidently the subject of a portrait by Botticelli formerly in the Pourtalès collection in Paris. This portrait is inscribed "Smeralda Bandinelli."

IV.—SONNETS AND VERSES

FOR ROSSETTI'S OWN WORKS OF ART.

MARY'S GIRLHOOD.

(*For a Picture.*)

I.

This is that blessed Mary, pre-elect
   God's Virgin. Gone is a great while, and she
   Dwelt young in Nazareth of Galilee.
Unto God's will she brought devout respect,
Profound simplicity of intellect,
   And supreme patience. From her mother's knee
   Faithful and hopeful; wise in charity;
Strong in grave peace; in pity circumspect.

So held she through her girlhood; as it were
   An angel-watered lily, that near God
     Grows and is quiet. Till, one dawn at home
She woke in her white bed, and had no fear
   At all,—yet wept till sunshine, and felt awed:
     Because the fulness of the time was come.

II.

THESE are the symbols. On that cloth of red
   I' the centre is the Tripoint: perfect each,
   Except the second of its points, to teach
That Christ is not yet born. The books—whose head
Is golden Charity, as Paul hath said—
   Those virtues are wherein the soul is rich:
   Therefore on them the lily standeth, which
Is Innocence, being interpreted.

The seven-thorn'd briar and the palm seven-leaved
   Are her great sorrow and her great reward.
      Until the end be full, the Holy One
Abides without. She soon shall have achieved
   Her perfect purity: yea, God the Lord
      Shall soon vouchsafe His Son to be her Son.

THE PASSOVER IN THE HOLY FAMILY.

(For a Drawing.*)

Here meet together the prefiguring day
   And day prefigured. "Eating, thou shalt stand,
   Feet shod, loins girt, thy road-staff in thine hand,
With blood-stained door and lintel,"—did God say
By Moses' mouth in ages passed away.
   And now, where this poor household doth comprise
   At Paschal-Feast two kindred families,—
Lo! the slain lamb confronts the Lamb to slay.

The pyre is piled. What agony's crown attained,
   What shadow of Death the Boy's fair brow subdues
Who holds that blood wherewith the porch is stained
   By Zachary the priest? John binds the shoes
   He deemed himself not worthy to unloose;
And Mary culls the bitter herbs ordained.

---

* The scene is in the house-porch, where Christ holds a bowl of blood from which Zacharias is sprinkling the posts and lintel. Joseph has brought the lamb and Elizabeth lights the pyre. The shoes which John fastens and the bitter herbs which Mary is gathering form part of the ritual.

MARY MAGDALENE

AT THE DOOR OF SIMON THE PHARISEE.

(*For a Drawing.**)

"Why wilt thou cast the roses from thine hair?
   Nay, be thou all a rose,—wreath, lips, and cheek.
   Nay, not this house,—that banquet-house we seek;
See how they kiss and enter; come thou there.
This delicate day of love we two will share
   Till at our ear love's whispering night shall speak.
   What, sweet one,—hold'st thou still the foolish freak?
Nay, when I kiss thy feet they'll leave the stair."

"Oh loose me! Seest thou not my Bridegroom's face
   That draws me to Him? For His feet my kiss,
   My hair, my tears He craves to-day:—and oh!
What words can tell what other day and place
   Shall see me clasp those blood-stained feet of His?
   He needs me, calls me, loves me: let me go!"

---

* In the drawing Mary has left a procession of revellers, and is ascending by a sudden impulse the steps of the house where she sees Christ. Her lover has followed her, and is trying to turn her back.

MICHAEL SCOTT'S WOOING.

(For a Drawing.)

Rose-sheathed beside the rosebud tongue
   Lurks the young adder's tooth;
   Milk-mild from new-born hemlock-bluth
The earliest drops are wrung:
   And sweet the flower of his first youth
When Michael Scott was young.

ASPECTA MEDUSA.

(For a Drawing.)

Andromeda, by Perseus saved and wed,
Hankered each day to see the Gorgon's head:
Till o'er a fount he held it, bade her lean,
And mirrored in the wave was safely seen
That death she lived by.

           Let not thine eyes know
Any forbidden thing itself, although
It once should save as well as kill: but be
Its shadow upon life enough for thee.

CASSANDRA.

(*For a Drawing.**)

I.

Rend, rend thine hair, Cassandra: he will go.
  Yea, rend thy garments, wring thine hands, and cry
  From Troy still towered to the unreddened sky.
See, all but she that bore thee mock thy woe :—
He most whom that fair woman arms, with show
  Of wrath on her bent brows; for in this place
  This hour thou bad'st all men in Helen's face
The ravished ravishing prize of Death to know.

What eyes, what ears hath sweet Andromache,
  Save for her Hector's form and step; as tear
    On tear make salt the warm last kiss he gave?
He goes. Cassandra's words beat heavily
  Like crows above his crest, and at his ear
    Ring hollow in the shield that shall not save.

---

* The subject shows Cassandra prophesying among her kindred, as Hector leaves them for his last battle. They are on the platform of a fortress, from which the Trojan troops are marching out. Helen is arming Paris; Priam soothes Hecuba; and Andromache holds the child to her bosom.

II.

"O Hector, gone, gone, gone! O Hector, thee
    Two chariots wait, in Troy long bless'd and curs'd;
    And Grecian spear and Phrygian sand athirst
Crave from thy veins the blood of victory.
Lo! long upon our hearth the brand had we,
    Lit for the roof-tree's ruin: and to-day
    The ground-stone quits the wall,—the wind hath way,—
And higher and higher the wings of fire are free.

O Paris, Paris! O thou burning brand,
    Thou beacon of the sea whence Venus rose,
Lighting thy race to shipwreck! Even that hand
    Wherewith she took thine apple let her close
    Within thy curls at last, and while Troy glows
Lift thee her trophy to the sea and land."

VENUS VERTICORDIA.

(For a Picture.)

She hath the apple in her hand for thee,
   Yet almost in her heart would hold it back;
  She muses, with her eyes upon the track
Of that which in thy spirit they can see.
Haply, "Behold, he is at peace," saith she;
   "Alas! the apple for his lips,—the dart
   That follows its brief sweetness to his heart,—
The wandering of his feet perpetually!"

A little space her glance is still and coy;
   But if she give the fruit that works her spell,
Those eyes shall flame as for her Phrygian boy.
    Then shall her bird's strained throat the woe foretell,
   And her far seas moan as a single shell,
And through her dark grove strike the light of Troy.

PANDORA.

(For a Picture.)

What of the end, Pandora? Was it thine,
   The deed that set these fiery pinions free?
   Ah! wherefore did the Olympian consistory
In its own likeness make thee half divine?
Was it that Juno's brow might stand a sign
   For ever? and the mien of Pallas be
   A deadly thing? and that all men might see
In Venus' eyes the gaze of Proserpine?

What of the end? These beat their wings at will,
The ill-born things, the good things turned to ill,—
   Powers of the impassioned hours prohibited.
Aye, clench the casket now! Whither they go
Thou mayst not dare to think: nor canst thou know
   If Hope still pent there be alive or dead.

A SEA-SPELL.

(For a Picture.)

Her lute hangs shadowed in the apple-tree,
   While flashing fingers weave the sweet-strung spell
   Between its chords; and as the wild notes swell,
The sea-bird for those branches leaves the sea.
But to what sound her listening ear stoops she?
   What netherworld gulf-whispers doth she hear,
   In answering echoes from what planisphere,
Along the wind, along the estuary?

She sinks into her spell: and when full soon
   Her lips move and she soars into her song,
   What creatures of the midmost main shall throng
In furrowed surf-clouds to the summoning rune:
Till he, the fated mariner, hears her cry,
And up her rock, bare-breasted, comes to die?

ASTARTE SYRIACA.

(For a Picture.)

Mystery: lo! betwixt the sun and moon
   Astarte of the Syrians: Venus Queen
   Ere Aphrodite was. In silver sheen
Her twofold girdle clasps the infinite boon
Of bliss whereof the heaven and earth commune:
   And from her neck's inclining flower-stem lean
   Love-freighted lips and absolute eyes that wean
The pulse of hearts to the spheres' dominant tune.

Torch-bearing, her sweet ministers compel
   All thrones of light beyond the sky and sea
   The witnesses of Beauty's face to be:
That face, of Love's all-penetrative spell
Amulet, talisman, and oracle,—
   Betwixt the sun and moon a mystery.

MNEMOSYNE

(For a Picture.)

Thou fill'st from the winged chalice of the soul
Thy lamp, O Memory, fire-winged to its goal.

FIAMMETTA.

(For a Picture.)

Behold Fiammetta, shown in Vision here.
   Gloom-girt 'mid Spring-flushed apple-growth she stands;
   And as she sways the branches with her hands,
Along her arm the sundered bloom falls sheer,
In separate petals shed, each like a tear;
   While from the quivering bough the bird expands
   His wings. And lo! thy spirit understands
Life shaken and shower'd and flown, and Death drawn
     near.

All stirs with change. Her garments beat the air:
   The angel circling round her aureole
   Shimmers in flight against the tree's grey bole:
While she, with reassuring eyes most fair,
A presage and a promise stands; as 'twere
   On Death's dark storm the rainbow of the Soul.

"FOUND."

(*For a Picture.*)

"THERE is a budding morrow in midnight:"—
  So sang our Keats, our English nightingale.
  And here, as lamps across the bridge turn pale
In London's smokeless resurrection-light,
Dark breaks to dawn. But o'er the deadly blight
  Of Love deflowered and sorrow of none avail,
  Which makes this man gasp and this woman quail,
Can day from darkness ever again take flight?

Ah! gave not these two hearts their mutual pledge,
Under one mantle sheltered 'neath the hedge
  In gloaming courtship? And, O God! to-day
He only knows he holds her;—but what part
Can life now take? She cries in her locked heart,—
  "Leave me—I do not know you—go away!"

THE DAY-DREAM.

(*For a Picture.*)

THE thronged boughs of the shadowy sycamore
   Still bear young leaflets half the summer through;
   From when the robin 'gainst the unhidden blue
Perched dark, till now, deep in the leafy core,
The embowered throstle's urgent wood-notes soar
   Through summer silence. Still the leaves come new;
   Yet never rosy-sheathed as those which drew
Their spiral tongues from spring-buds heretofore.

Within the branching shade of Reverie
Dreams even may spring till autumn; yet none be
   Like woman's budding day-dream spirit-fann'd.
Lo! tow'rd deep skies, not deeper than her look,
She dreams; till now on her forgotten book
   Drops the forgotten blossom from her hand.

# V.—POEMS IN ITALIAN
(OR ITALIAN AND ENGLISH),
FRENCH AND LATIN.

GIOVENTÙ E SIGNORÌA.

È GIOVINE il signore,
   Ed ama molte cose,—
   I canti, le rose,
La forza e l'amore.

Quel che più vuole
   Ancor non osa:
Ahi più che il sole,
   Più ch' ogni rosa,
   La cara cosa,
Donna a gioire.

È giovine il signore,
   Ed ama quelle cose
   Che ardor dispose
In cuore all' amore.

Bella fanciulla,
   Guardalo in viso;
Non mancar nulla,
   Motto o sorriso;
   Ma viso a viso
Guarda a gradire.

È giovine il signore,
   Ed ama tutte cose,
   Vezzose, giojose,
Tenenti all' amore.

YOUTH AND LORDSHIP.

(Italian Street-Song.)

My young lord's the lover
   Of earth and sky above,
Of youth's sway and youth's play,
   Of songs and flowers and love.

Yet for love's desire
   Green youth lacks the daring;
Though one dream of fire,
   All his hours ensnaring,
   Burns the boy past bearing—
The dream that girls inspire.

My young lord's the lover
   Of every burning thought
That Love's will, that Love's skill
   Within his breast has wrought.

Lovely girl, look on him
   Soft as music's measure;
Yield him, when you've won him,
   Joys and toys at pleasure;
   But to win your treasure,
Softly look upon him.

My young lord's the lover
   Of every tender grace
That woman, to woo man,
   Can wear in form or face.

Prendilo in braccio
  Adesso o mai;
Per più mi taccio,
  Chè tu lo sai;
Bacialo e l'avrai,
  Ma non lo dire.

È giovine il signore,
  Ed ama ben le cose
  Che Amor nascose,
Che mostragli Amore.

Deh trionfando
  Non farne pruova;
Ahimè! che quando
  Gioja più giova,
  Allor si trova
Presso al finire.

È giovine il signore,
  Ed ama tante cose,
  Le rose, le spose,
Quante gli dona Amore.

YOUTH AND LORDSHIP.

Take him to your bosom
  Now, girl, or never;
Let not your new blossom
  Of sweet kisses sever;
  Only guard for ever
Your boast within your bosom.

My young lord's the lover
  Of every secret thing,
Love-hidden, love-bidden
  This day to banqueting.

Lovely girl, with vaunting
  Never tempt to-morrow:
From all shapes enchanting
  Any joy can borrow,
  Still the spectre Sorrow
Rises up for haunting.

And now my lord's the lover
  Of ah! so many a sweet,—
Of roses, of spouses,
  As many as love may greet.

PROSERPINA.

(PER UN QUADRO.)

Lungi è la luce che in sù questo muro
   Rifrange appena, un breve istante scorta
   Del rio palazzo alla soprana porta.
Lungi quei fiori d'Enna, O lido oscuro,
Dal frutto tuo fatal che omai m'è duro.
   Lungi quel cielo dal tartareo manto
   Che quì mi cuopre: e lungi ahi lungi ahi quanto
Le notti che saran dai dì che furo.

Lungi da me mi sento; e ognor sognando
   Cerco e ricerco, e resto ascoltatrice;
   E qualche cuore a qualche anima dice,
(Di cui mi giunge il suon da quando in quando,
Continuamente insieme sospirando,)—
   "Oimè per te, Proserpina infelice!"

LA RICORDANZA.

Maggior dolore è ben la Ricordanza,
O nell' amaro inferno amena stanza?

PROSERPINA.

(For a Picture.)

AFAR away the light that brings cold cheer
   Unto this wall,—one instant and no more
   Admitted at my distant palace-door.
Afar the flowers of Enna from this drear
Dire fruit, which, tasted once, must thrall me here.
   Afar those skies from this Tartarean grey
   That chills me: and afar, how far away,
The nights that shall be from the days that were.

Afar from mine own self I seem, and wing
   Strange ways in thought, and listen for a sign:
   And still some heart unto some soul doth pine,
(Whose sounds mine inner sense is fain to bring,
Continually together murmuring,)—
   "Woe's me for thee, unhappy Proserpine!"

MEMORY.

Is Memory most of miseries miserable,
Or the one flower of ease in bitterest hell?

LA BELLA MANO.

(PER UN QUADRO.)

O BELLA Mano, che ti lavi e piaci
  In quel medesmo tuo puro elemento
  Donde la Dea dell' amoroso avvento
Nacque, (e dall' onda s'infuocar le faci
Di mille inispegnibili fornaci):—
  Come a Venere a te l'oro e l'argento
  Offron gli Amori; e ognun riguarda attento
La bocca che sorride e te che taci.

In dolce modo dove onor t' invii
  Vattene adorna, e porta insiem fra tante
  Di Venere e di vergine sembiante;
Umilemente in luoghi onesti e pii
Bianca e soave ognora; infin che sii,
  O Mano, mansueta in man d'amante.

CON manto d'oro, collana, ed anelli,
  Le piace aver con quelli
Non altro che una rosa ai suoi capelli.

ROBE d'or, mais rien ne veut
Qu' une rose à ses cheveux.

LA BELLA MANO.

(*For a Picture.*)

O LOVELY hand, that thy sweet self dost lave
   In that thy pure and proper element,
   Whence erst the Lady of Love's high advènt
Was born, and endless fires sprang from the wave :—
Even as her Loves to her their offerings gave,
   For thee the jewelled gifts they bear; while each
   Looks to those lips, of music-measured speech
The fount, and of more bliss than man may crave.

In royal wise ring-girt and bracelet-spann'd,
   A flower of Venus' own virginity,
Go shine among thy sisterly sweet band;
   In maiden-minded converse delicately
   Evermore white and soft; until thou be,
O hand! heart-handsel'd in a lover's hand.

WITH golden mantle, rings, and necklace fair,
   It likes her best to wear
Only a rose within her golden hair.

A GOLDEN robe, yet will she wear
Only a rose in her golden hair.

BARCAROLA.

Per carità,
  Mostrami amore:
  Mi punge il cuore,
Ma non si sa
  Dove è amore.
Che mi fa
La bella età,
Sè non si sa
Come amerà?
  Ahi me solingo!
  Il cuor mi stringo!
  Non più ramingo,
Per carità!

Per carità,
  Mostrami il cielo:
  Tutto è un velo,
E non si sa
  Dove è il cielo.
Se si sta
Così colà,
Non si sa
Se non si va.
  Ahi me lontano!
  Tutto è in vano!
  Prendimi in mano,
Per carità!

BARCAROLA.

Oltre tomba
Qualche cosa?
E che ne dici?
Saremo felici?
Terra mai posa,
E mar rimbomba.

BAMBINO FACIATO.

A Pippo Pipistrello
  Farfalla la fanciulla:
"O vedi quanto è bello
  Ridendo in questa culla!
E noi l'abbiamo fatto,
Noi due insiem d'un tratto,
  E senza noi fia nulla."

THOMÆ FIDES.

"Digitum tuum, Thoma,
Infer, et vide manûs!
Manum tuam, Thoma,
Affer, et mitte in latus."
 "Dominus et Deus,
  Deus," dixit,
 "Et Dominus meus.

"Quia me vidisti,
Thoma, credidisti.
Beati qui non viderunt,
Thoma, et crediderunt.'
 "Dominus et Deus,
  Deus," dixit,
 "Et Dominus meus."

VI.—VERSICLES AND FRAGMENTS.

THE ORCHARD-PIT.

Piled deep below the screening apple-branch
   They lie with bitter apples in their hands:
And some are only ancient bones that blanch,
And some had ships that last year's wind did launch,
   And some were yesterday the lords of lands.

In the soft dell, among the apple-trees,
   High up above the hidden pit she stands,
And there for ever sings, who gave to these,
That lie below, her magic hour of ease,
   And those her apples holden in their hands.

This in my dreams is shown me; and her hair
   Crosses my lips and draws my burning breath;
Her song spreads golden wings upon the air,
Life's eyes are gleaming from her forehead fair,
   And from her breasts the ravishing eyes of Death.

Men say to me that sleep hath many dreams,
   Yet I knew never but this dream alone:
There, from a dried-up channel, once the stream's,
The glen slopes up; even such in sleep it seems
   As to my waking sight the place well known.
   *   *   *   *   *

My love I call her, and she loves me well:
   But I love her as in the maelstrom's cup
The whirled stone loves the leaf inseparable
That clings to it round all the circling swell,
   And that the same last eddy swallows up.

TO ART.

I LOVED thee ere I loved a woman, Love

ON BURNS.

IN whomsoe'er, since Poesy began,
A Poet most of all men we may scan,
Burns of all poets is the most a Man.

FIN DI MAGGIO.

OH! May sits crowned with hawthorn-flower,
   And is Love's month, they say;
And Love's the fruit that is ripened best
   By ladies' eyes in May.

And the Sibyl, you know. I saw her with my own eyes at Cumæ, hanging in a jar; and, when the boys asked her, "What would you, Sibyl?" she answered, "I would die."—PETRONIUS.

"I SAW the Sibyl at Cumæ"
   (One said) "with mine own eye.
She hung in a cage, and read her rune
   To all the passers-by.
Said the boys, 'What wouldst thou, Sibyl?'
   She answered, 'I would die.'"

As balmy as the breath of her you love
When deep between her breasts it comes to you.

"Was it a friend or foe that spread these lies?"
"Nay, who but infants question in such wise?
'Twas one of my most intimate enemies."

At her step the water-hen
Springs from her nook, and skimming the clear stream,
Ripples its waters in a sinuous curve,
And dives again in safety.

Would God I knew there were a God to thank
When thanks rise in me!

I shut myself in with my soul,
And the shapes come eddying forth.

If I could die like the British Queen
  Who faced the Roman war,
Or hang in a cage for my country's sake
  Like Black Bess of Dunbar!

She bound her green sleeve on my helm,
  Sweet pledge of love's sweet meed:
Warm was her bared arm round my neck
  As well she bade me speed;
And her kiss clings still between my lips,
  Heart's beat and strength at need.

WHERE is the man whose soul has never waked
To sudden pity of the poor torn past?

As much as in a hundred years, she's dead:
Yet is to-day the day on which she died.

WHO shall say what is said in me,
With all that I might have been dead in me?

ELLIS & ELVEY'S PUBLICATIONS.

London: 29, New Bond Street, W.

Two Vols., crown 8vo, cloth gilt, bound from the Author's own design, **18s.**

The Collected Works of Dante Gabriel Rossetti.

CONTENTS.

VOL. I. POEMS, PROSE TALES, AND LITERARY PAPERS.
VOL. II. TRANSLATIONS (including DANTE'S "VITA NUOVA" AND THE EARLY ITALIAN POETS), PROSE NOTICES OF FINE ARTS.

Copies can be had in morocco extra, bound from the Author's own design.

Crown 8vo, with Portrait, cloth gilt, price **6s.**

The Poetical Works of Dante Gabriel Rossetti.

EDITED, WITH PREFACE, BY W. M. ROSSETTI.

A NEW EDITION IN ONE VOLUME.

This volume contains all the Original Poems of D. G. Rossetti, as printed in the Collected Works.

The Portrait, which is issued as a Frontispiece, is an engraving by Mr. C. W. SHERBORN, from a Photograph of the Poet taken at Cheyne Walk, Chelsea, in 1864, never before published.

Copies can be had in the best Levant morocco, or calf, in a variety of styles and colours.

The Siddal Edition of Rossetti's Works.

Small 8vo, with Photogravure Frontispiece, cloth extra, gilt edges, price **2s. 6d.** *per volume net.*

List of Volumes.

THE HOUSE OF LIFE: A Sonnet Sequence.

BALLADS: Rose Mary—The White Ship—The King's Tragedy.

THE NEW LIFE ("La Vita Nuova") of Dante Alighieri. Translated by D. G. ROSSETTI.

POEMS: Part I. Sister Helen—The Blessed Damozel—Stratton Water, etc., etc.

POEMS: Part II. A Last Confession—The Staff and Scrip, etc., etc.

POEMS: Part III. The Stream's Secret—Jenny—Eden Bower, etc., etc.

POEMS: Part IV. The Bride's Prelude—Love's Nocturn, etc., etc.

ELLIS & ELVEY'S PUBLICATIONS.

Crown 4to, printed on Hand-made Paper, bound in Art Canvas, price **5s.** *net.*

LENORE.

By GOTTFRIED AUGUST BURGER.

TRANSLATED FROM THE GERMAN BY

DANTE GABRIEL ROSSETTI.

This Poem was translated into English Verse by D. G. ROSSETTI at the age of 16, and is now printed for the first time from his Original Manuscript, with a Prefatory Note by his brother, W. M. ROSSETTI.

Small 8vo, with specially designed covers, sewed, **6d.**

THE WHITE SHIP:
A Ballad.

BY

DANTE GABRIEL ROSSETTI.

A clearly printed edition of this favourite Ballad, intended for the use of Schools, to which copies are supplied in packets of 13 for 4s. 3d. net.

Crown 8vo, cloth gilt, price **6s.**

(UNIFORM WITH THE CHEAP EDITION OF ROSSETTI'S POETICAL WORKS.)

DANTE AND HIS CIRCLE:
With the Italian Poets Preceding him

(1100—1200—1300).

A Collection of Lyrics,

EDITED AND TRANSLATED IN THE ORIGINAL METRES BY

DANTE GABRIEL ROSSETTI.

PART I.—DANTE'S VITA NUOVA, ETC.—POETS OF DANTE'S CIRCLE.
PART II.—POETS CHIEFLY BEFORE DANTE.

A NEW EDITION, WITH A NEW PREFACE,
By W. M. ROSSETTI.

Two vols., demy 8vo, cloth gilt, with 10 portraits in Collotype, **24s.**

DANTE GABRIEL ROSSETTI:
His Family-Letters.

With a MEMOIR by W. M. ROSSETTI.

Also a limited number of Large-Paper copies, printed on hand-made paper, bound in half-vellum extra, gilt tops, price £3 3s.

ELLIS & ELVEY'S PUBLICATIONS.

AN IMPORTANT REMAINDER.

*Royal 8vo, 350 pp., with Facsimiles, published at £1 5s.;
Reduced to 7s. 6d. net.*

The POETICAL WORKS of WILLIAM BASSE
(1602-1653).

Now for the first time collected and edited, with Introduction and Notes.

By R. WARWICK BOND, M.A. OXON.

William Basse is probably best known as the author of the "Angler's Song," which he wrote for Izaak Walton, who printed it in the "Compleat Angler." Besides this, however, Basse wrote a large amount of poetry, much of which has never been printed: and during his life, which covers roughly the period from 1583 to 1653, he was connected and associated with many of the poets and chief personages of the day.

Crown 8vo, cloth, price 5s.

LECTURES on the HISTORY of LITERATURE
DELIVERED BY THOMAS CARLYLE, APRIL TO JULY, 1838.

Now printed for the first time.

WITH PREFACE AND NOTES BY PROFESSOR J. R. GREENE.

OPINIONS OF THE PRESS.

"In what he says about Dante and his age, about Luther and the Reformation, about Cervantes and chivalry, about Swift, Johnson, Hume, and Gibbon, and finally about Goethe and his influence, we seem once more to catch vivid glimpses of the Carlyle whom we know and admire."—*The Times.*

"Students of Carlyle will be glad to have brought within their reach these notes of lectures delivered by him more than half a century ago, . . . they serve to give us much insight into Carlyle's own culture, and his wide acquaintance with literature."—*The Athenæum.*

"In the lectures before us are to be found all the wonted characteristics of Carlyle. . . . there is the same nervous strength, the occasional uncouthness of expression, the poetic power of imagery with which we are familiar in the 'French Revolution.'"—*The Daily Telegraph.*

"A very interesting and valuable volume."—*The Court Circular.*

Crown 8vo, cloth gilt, price 6s.

SOME FRENCH & SPANISH MEN of GENIUS
SKETCHES OF

MARIVAUX, VOLTAIRE, ROUSSEAU, DIDEROT, BEAUMARCHAIS, MIRABEAU, DANTON AND ROBESPIERRE, BERANGER, VICTOR HUGO, EUGENE SUE AND ZOLA, CERVANTES AND LOPE DE VEGA, CALDERON.

By JOSEPH FORSTER,

AUTHOR OF "FOUR GREAT TEACHERS," ETC.

OPINIONS OF THE PRESS.

"Mr. Forster is a sensible and agreeable writer, who is not content with giving his opinion, but who fortifies himself with characteristic extracts from the authors about whom he writes."—*Daily News.*

"Pleasantly written—interesting and characteristic."—*Globe.*

"Some agreeable and not unprofitable half-hours may be spent in company with this book."—*Graphic.*

"Pleasantly and intelligently written, and will prove profitable reading."—*Scotsman.*

"Sincère, vibrant, de lecture amusante et très suffisamment exact."—*Le Livre Moderne.*

ELLIS & ELVEY'S PUBLICATIONS.

Crown 8vo, vellum cloth, price **6s.**

MIRABILIA VRBIS ROMÆ.
THE MARVELS OF ROME; or, A PICTURE OF THE GOLDEN CITY.

An English Version of the Mediæval Guide-book,
with a Supplement of Illustrative Matter and Notes.

By FRANCIS MORGAN NICHOLS.

"Mr. Nichols has produced a work which must, as we think, fascinate all who are interested in the classical and mediæval antiquities of Rome."—*Guardian.*

"Many people will be grateful to Mr. Nichols for his very careful English rendering of this curious and interesting little work. The translator's copious notes give the book a strong additional interest, and even an original value of its own."—*Scots Observer.*

"Admirably printed, and bears every mark of competent scholarship"—*The Nation (New York).*

Crown 4to, on hand-made paper, cloth, price **£2 2s.**

Impression of 128 Copies only.

THE HALL OF LAWFORD HALL.

Records of an Essex House and of its Proprietors from the Saxon Times to the Reign of Henry VIII.

AN HISTORICAL AND TOPOGRAPHICAL WORK,

By Francis Morgan Nichols, F.S.A.

OPINIONS OF THE PRESS.

"An excellent book. . . . It contains a most valuable contribution to the history of England from Henry VI. to Henry VIII., and what is practically a very able life, and exhaustive account of the tragical death, of Humphrey, Duke of Gloucester, from original sources. . . . As a contribution to local history it also deserves the highest praise."—*Athenæum.*

"To trace the fortunes of an actual house from Saxon times to the reign of Henry VIII. has all the attraction of a novel, especially as it continually brings us into touch with such well-known historical characters as Duke Humphrey and Erasmus, Lord Mountjoy, and others."—*Globe.*

"The local and county history that are found in these pages make it a volume much to be desired by Essex collectors. . . . It throws real light on the by-paths of our national history."—*Antiquary.*

"Mr. Nichols has woven in with the history of Lawford Hall so many valuable and interesting points connected with the history of the country, and he treats his subject in so readable and pleasant a style, that we are inclined to wish either that he had set himself the task of surveying some larger field of history, or that this local work, which possesses so much of general interest, could find its way into the hands of more readers."—*Essex Standard.*

Eighth Edition, small 8vo, half-bound, price **5s.**

HUNTING SONGS.

By the late R. E. EGERTON-WARBURTON,

OF ARLEY HALL, CHESHIRE.

29, NEW BOND STREET, LONDON, W.